C000244676

COOKING FROM CHINA'S FUJIAN PROVINCE

HIPPOCRENE COOKBOOK LIBRARY

Afghan Food & Cookery
Alps, Cuisines of the
Aprovecho: A Mexican-American Border Cookbook
Argentina Cooks!, Exp. Ed.
Austrian Cuisine, Best of, Exp. Ed.
Bolivian Kitchen, My Mother's
Brazil: A Culinary Journey
Burma, Flavors of
Cajun Cuisine, Stir the Pot: The History of
Cajun Women, Cooking with
Calabria, Cucina di
Caucasus Mountains, Cuisines of the
Chile, Tasting
China's Fujian Province, Cooking from
Colombian Cooking, Secrets of
Croatian Cooking, Best of, Exp. Ed.
Czech Cooking, Best of, Exp. Ed.
Danube, All Along The, Exp. Ed.
Egyptian Cooking
English Country Kitchen, The
Estonian Tastes and Traditions
Filipino Food, Fine
Finnish Cooking, Best of
French Fashion, Cooking in the (Bilingual)
Germany, Spoonfuls of
Greek Cooking, Regional
Greek Cuisine, The Best of, Exp. Ed.
Gypsy Feast
Haiti, Taste of
Havana Cookbook, Old (Bilingual)
Hungarian Cookbook, Exp. Ed.
Icelandic Food & Cookery
India, Flavorful
Indian Spice Kitchen, The, Exp. Ed.
International Dictionary of Gastronomy
Irish-Style, Feasting Galore
Jewish-Iraqi Cuisine, Mama Nazima's
Korean Cuisine, Best of
Laotian Cooking, Simple
Latvia, Taste of
Lebanese Cookbook, The
Ligurian Kitchen, A
Macau, Taste of
Malta, Taste of, Exp. Ed.
Mexican Culinary Treasures
Middle Eastern Kitchen, The
Naples, My Love for
Nepal, Taste of
New Hampshire: from Farm to Kitchen
New Jersey Cookbook, Farms and Foods of the Garden State:
Norway, Tastes and Tales of
Ohio, Farms and Foods of
Persian Cooking, Art of
Pied Noir Cookbook: French Sephardic Cuisine
Piemontese, Cucina: Cooking from Italy's Piedmont
Poland's Gourmet Cuisine
Polish Cooking, Best of, Exp. Ed.
Polish Country Kitchen Cookbook
Polish Cuisine, Treasury of (Bilingual)
Polish Heritage Cookery, Ill. Ed.
Polish Holiday Cookery
Polish Traditions, Old
Portuguese Encounters, Cuisines of
Pyrenees, Tastes of
Quebec, Taste of
Rhine, All Along The
Romania, Taste of, Exp. Ed.
Russian Cooking, Best of, Exp. Ed.
Scotland, Traditional Food From
Scottish-Irish Pub and Hearth Cookbook
Sephardic Israeli Cuisine
Sicilian Feasts
Slovenia, Flavors of
Smorgasbord Cooking, Best of
South Indian Cooking, Healthy
Spanish Family Cookbook, Rev. Ed.
Sri Lanka, Exotic Tastes of
Swedish Kitchen, A
Taiwanese Cuisine, Best of
Thai Cuisine, Best of, Regional
Trinidad and Tobago, Sweet Hands: Island Cooking from
Turkish Cuisine, Taste of
Tuscan Kitchen, Tastes from a
Ukrainian Cuisine, Best of, Exp. Ed.
Uzbek Cooking, Art of
Wales, Good Food from
Warsaw Cookbook, Old
Vietnamese Kitchen, A

COOKING FROM CHINA'S FUJIAN PROVINCE

ONE OF CHINA'S EIGHT GREAT CUISINES

JACQUELINE M. NEWMAN

HIPPOCRENE BOOKS, INC.
NEW YORK

The following recipes are used with permission:
Fish Slices with Sweet and Sour Wine Sauce, page 91, from Pei Mei Fu
Fried Squid in Shrimp Paste, page 94, from Liang Quongbai
Chicken Cubes in Three Sauces, page 116, from the Amoy Food Company

For information, address:
Hippocrene Books, Inc.
171 Madison Avenue
New York, NY 10016
www.hippocrenebooks.com

Library of Congress Cataloging-in-Publication Data

Newman, Jacqueline M., 1932-
Cooking from China's Fujian Province : one of China's eight great cuisines / Jacqueline M. Newman.
p. cm.
Includes index.
ISBN-13: 978-0-7818-1183-5
ISBN-10: 0-7818-1183-X
1. Cookery, Chinese--Fujian style. 2. Cookery--China--Fujian Sheng.
I. Title.
TX724.5.C5N44 2008
641.5951--dc22

2007044332

Printed in the United States of America.

DEDICATION

This book is dedicated to Leonard:
May we cook and consume Chinese delights for many years to come;
and to Beverly and Leo, Michael and Polly,
Justin, Ryan, Devin, Emily, Brett, and Ben—
You are great, and a great culinary audience.

ACKNOWLEDGMENTS

Thanks to Angela Cheng, Hsi-ming Lee, Lena Yang,
the Amoy Company of Fujian,
and the many others not mentioned who tested and tasted,
and offered invaluable research and recipes;
and to all others whose input helped to make this volume
a reliable resource.

TABLE OF CONTENTS

Acknowledgments v

Introduction 3

Appetizers 7

Soups and Congees 45

Fish and Seafood 77

Poultry and Game 111

Meats 139

Starches 163

Vegetables 175

Sweet Dishes 191

Beverages 203

Miscellaneous Recipes 213

Glossary 221

Resources 239

Index 241

INTRODUCTION

The foods of China provide daily sustenance to more than one-quarter of the world's population—almost a billion and a half people. More people in the entire world are eating Chinese foods than the foods of any other single culture. In all, the Chinese cuisine has more than ten thousand different kinds of dishes. Many dishes have regional cooking styles, use regional ingredients, and conform to regional tastes. Most originated in China, which is approximately the physical size of the United States. There is no better way to understand this cuisine than to examine it geographically.

Some view Chinese food simplistically, that is, by the compass points of north, south, east, and west. Others more knowledgeably speak of eight outstanding Chinese culinary styles linked to particular regions. Alphabetically, they are: Anhui, Fujian, Guangdong, Hunan, Jiangsu, Shandong, Sichuan, and Zhejiang; however, there are far more regions in China than just these eight.

The People's Republic of China is a country with sixty-one regions, politically speaking. They include twenty-two provinces, five autonomous regions, thirty-one autonomous prefectures, and three major municipalities. Does each of these divisions have a distinctive cuisine? Most culinary aficionados would say no, but they do give credence to twenty-seven major regional culinary influences, and they include those eight mentioned above. Some of the twenty-seven are better known than others, some hardly known at all outside of their own country. All together, and again alphabetically, but not in any order of importance, they are: Anhui, Beijing, Fujian, Gansu, Guangdong, Guangzi, Guizhou, Hainan, Henan, Hong Kong, Hubei, Hunan, Inner Mongolia, Jiangsu, Jiangxi, Liaoning, Qinghai, Shaanxi, Shandong, Shanghai, Shanxi, Sichuan, Tianjin, Xinjiang, Xizang (Tibet), Yunnan, and Zhejiang.

One of these culinary influences, from an important coastal cuisine hardly known outside of China, is the food of the Fujian province. The Fujianese people and their food have descended from an ancient Min culture reputed to be thousands of years old. Certainly, their foods have more than a thousand years of recorded history.

THE FUJIANESE PEOPLE

The Fujian province is as linguistically mixed as its foods. Most people speak Fujianese, also known as Min, along with several other dialects. In the middle of the province, they speak Henghua, dialectically related to Taiwanese; in the north and east they speak the Fuzhou dialect; while in the south, the dialect is Xiamenese. In one southeastern corner, the dialect is Hakka; and in the very far west it is Gan.

The *Book of Rites*, known to the Chinese as the *Zhou Li*, says there were seven Min tribes. Their numbers have grown to more than 30 million descendants who still live in this province, and boast a ten-thousand-year history. With easy access to the sea, many Fujianese people were and still are travelers. The mountains hem them in on three sides, so getting out is easiest using sea routes. Despite pleasant and comfortable winters and falls, many Fujianese have left the country, never to return. Perhaps very hot and sticky summers, lack of jobs, and inadequate incomes contributed to their decisions. There are now Fujianese living everywhere in Southeast Asia and in virtually every other nation in the world. An estimated one-third of the roughly 20 million overseas Chinese have Fujianese heritage.

THE FOODS OF FUJIAN

About 300,000-plus people from Fujian have migrated to and now live in the United States. Most arrived in the past twenty years or so and live in New York City where many own or work in Chinese restaurants. Restaurants specializing in Fujianese foods are frequented by immigrants from this province who long for a taste of home, and by others who know and enjoy their foods.

Fujian is an eastern province south of Shanghai. Despite its unfamiliarity to most Westerners, Fujian's distinctive cuisine has spread its wings to neighboring islands within Asia, including Taiwan and Hainan, and beyond.

In Fujian there is an emphasis upon how ingredients are cut, cooked, and uniquely seasoned. Dishes often include different kinds of mushrooms and other foods of the land mixed with those of the sea. More than two hundred different kinds of fish, shellfish, turtles, and frogs are commonly prepared—stewed, braised, quick- or slow-cooked, steamed, and/or stir-fried. Minute amounts of sugar season their savory dishes; coriander and sesame oil flavor many others; and garnishes are often featured in their presentations. Soups and stews predominate, but whatever the dish, its final flavors really are uniquely Fujianese. Other foods important to this cuisine include ground dry pork, other dried and powdered meats, five-spice powder, and their very special red rice and white rice wine lees (sediment). These are used in many local dishes and dipping sauces; the latter are served to further enhance the many fine foods served in the region's Ningda administrative prefecture and in its eight municipalities known as Fuzhou, Longyuan, Nanping, Putian, Quanzhou, Sanming, Xiamen, and Zhangzhou.

One particular dish is known all over China and by Chinese all over the world as being classically Fujianese. In English, it is known as "Buddha Jumps Over The Wall." The name, capitalized for emphasis, implies that the dish has such deliciousness that a Buddha getting the slightest whiff of it would jump over the monastery wall for a taste. Often served in a rice-wine jar, it comprises many colors, shapes, aromas, flavors, and foods. It can and often does include shark's fin, abalone, fresh and dried scallops, ham, chicken, mushrooms, yams, a berry known as *medlar* or wolfberry, herbs, scallions and garlic shoots, white and black pepper, sugar, salt, soy sauce, wine and wine lees.

Another dish recognizable to all Chinese is Fujian's fish balls. They are called *yue wan*. Still another is *banmien bianrou*, the noodles or dumplings of this province. All three of these dishes are examples of meat and fish served together in one dish. These and other Fujianese dishes use a plethora of ingredients, with as many variations as there are chefs. They may be thick and stew-like, or thin and served as a soup, again depending upon the tastes of the person preparing them.

FUJIAN'S CULINARY RESOURCES

The Fujian province is about the size of England. It includes about forty-five thousand square miles with very diverse topography. The northern, southern, and western borders are mountainous with an elevated, rugged terrain. The eastern edge is ragged and stretches to the sea with almost two thousand miles of coastline. Between the mountains and sea are acres and acres of fertile farmland. In addition to its main land, Fujian includes nearly one thousand islands close to its provincial shores.

Great cuisines need great food resources. Fujian has them and takes advantage of what is produced in its mountains, rich agricultural lowland areas, extensive coastline, and easily accessed sea. Fishing is a major industry. Historically, fishermen did, and still do, bring back tastes and ingredients from afar. The Fujianese mix what is brought from beyond the region with what is available at home. Likewise, outside influences and traditional practices combine to create a mix of the best of everything from everywhere. Locals say this is why their cuisine occupies an important place in the Chinese culinary culture.

Indeed, within Asia, Fujian cooking is recognized as one of the best cuisines in China. This is because its great food resources are coupled with a considerable respect for knowledge about foods developed and supported since the earliest of times. Here, the local food has been and is written about and discussed at all levels of society.

In Fujian, 35 percent of the land is forested. Its timber makes great cooking equipment, fine homes, and valuable industrial products. Many minerals, including copper and tungsten, fuel the economy, as do all the local agricultural and aquacultural products. Fujian has almost twice the amount of arable land devoted to agriculture than does any other province in China: 20 versus 11 percent. This province's subtropical climate is drenched with sixty or more inches of rainfall a year, and its mountains leach nutrients to lower lands. These conditions yield a fertile and very productive soil.

FUJIAN'S SUBREGIONS

There are three culinary subregions within Fujian. One is called Fuzhou-style. This is popular in eastern and northern parts of the province, and uses foods primarily from its capital city of Fuzhou. It also includes foods from some municipalities, such as Mintung, Minchung, and Minbei. Its foods are lightly seasoned, less salty, and less sweet than others in the province. Fuzhou cooking features delicious and elegant soups and stews, often with sweet-and-sour flavors. Many dishes include red rice or white rice wine lees as a seasoning. Red rice wine lees is most popular. Red rice is injected with the *Monascus purpureus* fungi, which the Chinese call *hung chiu*. Wine lees is popular in all of Fujian's northern regions. Also popular are dumplings, fish balls, and lots of fresh seafood.

A second form of Fujian cuisine, popular in Xiamen and Quanzhou, is southern- or Minnan-style. Here, Fujianese foods predominate, with additional ingredients from Xiamen, Quanzhou, Jiangzhou, and Taiwan. These dishes are aromatic, light, tender, somewhat sweet, and many contain chili peppers. They often feature custards, hot sauces, or citrus flavorings as well.

The third Fujianese culinary style is western, and is called Minxi. This style features more salty and piquant foods. Many of them are thicker, more strongly flavored, and heavier than the other two subregional styles. Minxi foods have more *Hakka* flavors, and they incorporate many local herbs.

HOME-GROWN SPECIALTIES

The staple grains in Fujian cuisine are wheat and rice. In some years, weather depleted them, as was the case about four hundred years ago during a major famine. At that time, provincial leaders sent abroad, primarily to the Philippines, for sweet potatoes. They knew the nutritious vegetable could stem starvation. This ingredient added another staple food to the Fujianese mix, one now popular throughout the province. There are also many litchi gardens and farms for other fruits and vegetables. Mushrooms and other foraged foods are still collected in the wild but many of them are now cultivated.

Fujian is home to many large tea plantations. Local people prefer theirs fully fermented—that is, the tea fully oxidized into a red tea. The color red denotes its brew; Westerners call it black tea for the color of its leaf. Years ago *pu-er* teas from the Wu-i Mountains made their way to England, where they are popularly known as Keemun tea. This tea is unique. It is made with large leaves and is oxided twice. Lots of it grows and is processed in northeastern areas of the province.

Tea is one major food export; another is filament noodles made by pulling the dough. These noodles and the technology to make them are now popular and found all over Southeast Asia. At home and abroad, Fujianese soy sauce is famous, too. The best is made in a town east of Fuzhou. It is unique because no flour is used in its first fermentation. Another exported specialty are Fujianese fish sauces. They are popular at most meals, and served with minced garlic.

The recipes that follow are but a small percentage of popular Fujianese dishes. In Fujian, local cooks customarily make these classic dishes with many variations. Therefore, feel free to be inventive as you prepare and enjoy them.

NOTE: The generic term "bean curd" has been used in place of the Chinese *doufu* and the Japanese *tofu* for soy based ingredients. We have indicated that the Chinese black mushrooms are the same as shiitake mushrooms throughout and that wolfberries are also called goji berries. Please be sure to check the Glossary starting on page 221 for explanations of other lesser-known Fujian ingredients. Most are available in Asian food markets or on the Internet and will give you new and delicious ways to enhance your culinary journey through the Fujian province.

APPETIZERS

FIRST COURSES AT REGULAR MEALS can be small plates of specific dishes, or they can be omitted entirely. Not so at banquets or special family meals. Then, special foods are in order such as jellyfish, bird's nest, shark's fin, and other less common foods, the more expensive the more appropriate. There can be many special dishes to begin a special meal. Sometimes they are on a large platter at the table's center, with smaller plates of food around the platter. Sometimes they stand alone. This dish might be nameless, but more likely it will have a fancy title such as "Stars around the Moon." These first-course banquet dishes are arranged artistically to invite admiration and appreciation. At very special or fancy occasions, there can be a large platter with cold appetizers followed by a platter or plates of hot ones coming one by one, as do main dishes. Correct serving protocol deems one portion appropriate for each individual, so diners will not overindulge. These early cold and hot plates are to whet appetites and leave adequate space for the remaining dishes. At special Chinese meals, another purpose for these cold and hot dishes is to inspire conversation, hence the importance of their novelty, contrast, and presentation.

At banquets and formal meals in the Fujian province, first-course items can be made with an additional half teaspoon or more of sugar. On special occasions, the Fujianese like their first courses to be a mite sweeter than usual. At family meals, however, these same dishes are made without this additional sweetness. The recipes in this chapter do not include the extra sugar.

At home, a family might have but one or two small dishes as a first course, cold or hot. Usually these are presented with minimal if any garnish or fancy arrangement, and are simply served in small portions.

Informally, all of these appetizers can be enjoyed as snacks or hors d'oeuvres, they can be served first, or used as a side dish, or used in some cases as the component of another dish at any time during the meal. Banquets demand more protocol and standardization of their use; not so family meals. So, enjoy these appetizers however and whenever you please.

BEAN CURD DUMPLINGS

This and most dishes in this chapter can be an appetizer or snack, main course, lunch, or dinner dish. At main meals, the dumplings might be made larger; for children or elders, made smaller. For large parties, larger bean curd circles are used; these are cut into triangles after they are completely cooked. **SERVES 8**

- 1 large rectangular dried or soft bean curd sheet (approximately 10 by 20 inches)
- 1 egg, beaten
- ¼ pound chopped or ground roast pork
- 4 large shrimp, peeled, deveined, and minced
- 3 tablespoons chopped Chinese chives
- 2 tablespoons sweet-potato flour
- ½ teaspoon salt
- ⅛ teaspoon coarsely ground black pepper
- 1 teaspoon sugar
- ½ teaspoon sesame oil
- ¼ cup vegetable oil

1. Cut the bean curd sheet into eight equal pieces, and brush top of each piece with the beaten egg. Reserve any leftover beaten egg for the next step.

2. Stir together the pork, shrimp, chives, sweet-potato flour, salt, pepper, sugar, and sesame oil. Divide the meat mixture into eight cigar-shaped pieces and put one portion on the longer end of each bean curd sheet, leaving a slight margin along the edge and sides. Fold in the side edges and roll up the sheet, completely enclosing the filling. Press down gently to make a flat package. Using the leftover beaten egg alone or mixed with a tablespoon or two of water to extend it, seal each packet. Put the packets, seam side down, on a plate.

3. Heat the vegetable oil in a wok or skillet, and pan-fry the packets, seam side down, until lightly browned and crisp. Turn and fry the other side, then drain on paper towels. Serve warm.

BEAN CURD-WRAPPED BEEF

People in Fujian like wraps and use many different casings. Bean curd, seaweed, lotus and other leaves, and thin omelets are but a few examples. Both the exteriors and the contents vary, and may be vegetable, animal, or any combination thereof. **SERVES 8**

- 2 rectangular bean curd sheets (approximately 10 by 20 inches), each cut into 4 pieces
- 1 tablespoon sesame oil
- 1 pound beef, hand-minced or ground
- 1 onion, minced
- 4 scallions, white and green parts minced separately
- 10 water chestnuts, minced
- 1 (3-inch) square firm bean curd, mashed
- 1 egg, beaten
- 3 cloves garlic, peeled and minced
- ¼ cup tapioca, water-chestnut, or lotus-root flour
- 2 tablespoons black soy sauce
- 1 tablespoon five-spice powder
- 1 tablespoon sugar
- 1 tablespoon Chinese red or black rice vinegar
- 1 tablespoon peeled, minced fresh ginger
- ½ cup vegetable oil

1. Brush each bean curd sheet on one side with the sesame oil.

2. Mix together the beef, onion, white part of the scallions, water chestnuts, and mashed bean curd. (The Chinese like to stir in only one direction while doing so.)

3. Add the egg, then the garlic and tapioca flour, and stir gently.

4. Mix in the black soy sauce, five-spice powder, sugar, vinegar, and fresh ginger, stirring gently.

5. Divide the mixture into eight cigar-shaped pieces. Put one portion on the shorter side of each bean curd piece and roll, though not tightly.

6. Heat the oil in a deep skillet or wok, and fry the rolls, two at a time, turning often, until lightly browned. Drain on paper towels.

7. When all are fried, put the rolls in a bamboo or regular steamer, or use a heatproof ceramic plate propped on empty tuna cans in a pot. Steam over boiling water for 20 minutes. Remove from the steamer and cut each packet in half on an angle, then place them standing on end on a platter, sprinkle the green part of the scallions on their tops, and serve.

BEEF ROLLS

Beef rolls are popular in many regions of southern China, Fujian included. This particular recipe is unusual for two reasons—its main ingredient, minced beef, is rolled in a sheet of seaweed and there is the surprise within. **SERVES 6**

½ pound ground beef
¼ pound ground pork
1 carrot, half minced finely, the other half sliced on an angle and boiled for 30 seconds
2 teaspoons thin soy sauce
2 teaspoons Chinese rice wine
1 teaspoon sesame oil
1 teaspoon sugar
¼ teaspoon mixed ground star anise, ground white pepper, ground cloves, and salt
3 teaspoons cornstarch
1 egg white, very lightly beaten
2 sheets dried seaweed
10 quail eggs, cooked for 5 minutes, then peeled
½ cup corn oil

1. Mix together the beef, pork, minced carrot, soy sauce, rice wine, sesame oil, sugar, seasoning mixture, and 2 teaspoons of the cornstarch.

2. Brush egg white on one side of each seaweed sheet and spread half the meat mixture evenly on half of each sheet. Brush the rest of the egg white over the meat and line up five quail eggs evenly spaced in the middle of each batch of meat mixture.

3. Roll up the meat and seaweed, starting from the meat end so the eggs are covered and in the center of the rolled meat, and the uncovered seaweed is around the meat. Dust each roll with the remaining cornstarch, and tuck in the ends of each roll, covering the meat completely.

4. Pour half the corn oil into a wok or skillet, and heat until about 300°F. Gently put one roll into the oil and fry for about 2 minutes, rolling it over periodically until browned on all sides, about 2 minutes, then drain on paper towels. Fry the second roll in the same manner using the rest of the oil.

5. Cut each roll into pieces, through the middle of each quail egg, making six sections per roll. Put them on a flat plate, half-egg side up. Scatter the boiled carrots around the plate to surround the meat rolls and serve.

BOBIN SCALLION PANCAKES

Bobin pancakes, their local name, are thin and somewhat transparent. They can be deep-fried, steamed, or pan-fried alone, or used as a wrapping for any number of cooked fillings. The filled pancakes are fried after rolling. Some families wrap their filling for this in thin sheets of fried egg instead. Either way, they are dipped in a thin batter before frying. SERVES 10

PANCAKES:
2 cups all-purpose flour
1 teaspoon coarse salt
1 cup boiling water
1 tablespoon sesame oil
1 cup coarsely chopped scallion greens

FILLING:
¼ pound soft bean curd, mashed
¼ pound pork belly (raw fresh bacon), diced finely, boiled for 10 minutes, then drained well
¼ pound bamboo shoots, finely minced
¼ pound peeled carrots, finely minced
2 ounces skinless, boneless fresh white fish, minced
1 teaspoon salt
2 teaspoons sugar
¼ teaspoon ground white pepper
2 tablespoons chopped peanuts or pine nuts
¼ cup coarsely chopped fresh coriander (cilantro) leaves

TO FRY:
3 tablespoons flour or cornstarch
3 tablespoons cool water
3 cups vegetable oil

DIPPING SAUCE:
1 teaspoon chili paste with garlic
2 tablespoons hoisin sauce
1 teaspoon plum sauce

1. For the pancakes, stir the flour and salt in a bowl, and make a well in the center. Pour in 1 cup of boiling water and stir rapidly until the dough makes a ball. Remove dough from the bowl, brush with the sesame oil, cover, and let rest for 10 minutes. Then knead the dough until smooth, incorporating the scallions. Cover and set aside for an hour. Divide the dough into twenty parts and roll each into a 6-inch thin circle.

2. For the filling, mix the bean curd, pork belly, bamboo shoots, carrots, fish, salt, sugar, pepper, nuts, and coriander leaves. Divide into twenty portions. Put a filling portion along one edge of each pancake, fold in the sides, and roll until closed.

CONTINUED

Wet a finger with a little water and wet the end of the dough and press gently to seal it. Let rest on the seam until all are made.

3. To fry, mix the flour and water into a batter. Heat the vegetable oil in a wok. Dip two filled pancakes at a time into the batter, seam side down, and deep-fry in the oil until golden and crisp on all sides. Drain on paper towels and continue until all are fried.

4. Make the dipping sauce by combining the chili paste, hoisin sauce, and plum sauce. Serve on the side.

DEEP-FRIED HARD-COOKED EGGS

This unusual recipe is popular with some living in Fujianese seaports. One sailor told us his granny said she learned it from Malaysian neighbors. Another fellow listening in disagreed; he called it a typical winter dish in his seaport village and said people of all ages adore it. SERVES 10

1 cup vegetable oil	2 tablespoons sugar or maltose
1 cup shallots, skins removed and sliced, or use a thinly sliced onion	1 tablespoon lemon juice
10 hard-cooked eggs, peeled	½ teaspoon salt
	1 tablespoon oyster sauce

1. Heat the oil in a wok or medium-size pot. Add the shallot slices and deep-fry them until crisp, about 1 minute, then remove and drain on paper towels.

2. Add the eggs to the wok and deep-fry for 2 to 3 minutes until lightly browned, then remove and drain.

3. Discard all but 1 tablespoon of the oil. Cut the eggs into quarters. Put half the shallots on a serving plate, top with the eggs, and then top with the remaining shallots.

4. Reheat the reserved oil, add the sugar, lemon juice, salt, and oyster sauce, and bring this mixture to a boil. Pour over the eggs and shallots and serve.

DOUBLE-COOKED EGGS

This recipe can also be a garnish, cut in small pieces to circle the edge of a meat, seafood, or vegetarian dish. Those who refrain from eating meat enjoy its complimentary looks, taste, and nutrition. **SERVES 5 TO 10**

5 large eggs, their large ends pierced with a pin
¼ teaspoon salt
1 tablespoon vegetable oil
2 red chili peppers, seeded and diced
2 scallions, minced
1 tablespoon dark soy sauce
1 teaspoon sugar
2 teaspoons Chinese white rice vinegar

1. Put the eggs in a small pot with 3 cups of cold water and the salt. Bring to just below a boil, lower the heat, and simmer for 10 minutes, stirring every 2 minutes to keep the yolks centered. Transfer the eggs to cool in cold water and then carefully peel them. Cut each egg in half.

2. Heat a wok, pour in the oil, then add the chili peppers and scallion pieces. After 30 seconds, put the cut edge of each egg face down into the oil and fry for 1 minute, then carefully turn the eggs over and fry for an additional 1 minute. Remove the eggs and drain them on a paper towel. Return to the pan.

3. In a bowl, stir together the soy sauce, sugar, and rice vinegar, and pour over the eggs in the pan. Stir gently to coat the eggs with the sauce. Serve as its own dish, or use as described above to decorate another dish.

DUCK TONGUES

This appetizer is loved for both its texture and its taste. Some restaurants don't remove either the cartilage or bone or both. Fancy eateries and home cooks remove both of these when the tongues are half cooked, and then they complete the cooking process. **SERVES 10**

30 duck tongues
3 slices peeled fresh ginger
2 scallions, trimmed, left whole, and tied in a knot
1 tablespoon Chinese red or black rice wine
1 teaspoon sesame oil
1 tablespoon thin soy sauce
1 teaspoon sugar
1 teaspoon water-chestnut flour or cornstarch
½ carrot, shredded
1 scallion, shredded

1. Simmer the duck tongues, ginger, and knotted scallions in 2 cups of water for 20 minutes. Drain and allow to cool for another 20 minutes.

2. If desired, bend each tongue in such a way as to be able to pull out the thin cartilage from the center to the tip, then remove the larger bone in the back half of each tongue.

3. Mix the rice wine, sesame oil, soy sauce, sugar, and water-chestnut flour in a shallow bowl that will fit in a steamer. Add the duck tongues, mix well, and allow to marinate for 20 minutes.

4. Place the bowl in a steamer and steam the tongues over boiling water for 20 minutes. Drain and discard the liquid, and put the tongues in a serving bowl. Scatter carrot and scallion shreds over the tongues and serve.

EGG WHITE SPRING ROLLS

Egg yolks are a wonderful way to seal wontons, dumplings, and similar items. Not wanting to waste anything, this recipe allows use of the large number of egg whites usually left over from making dumplings. The egg whites can be frozen and saved for this use. SERVES 10

¼ pound fresh shrimp, shelled, deveined, and coarsely diced
1 bunch Chinese chives (about a dozen), thinly sliced
¼ pound lean pork, chopped fine or ground
2 dried Chinese black mushrooms (shiitake), soaked for 20 minutes, stems removed, cut in half, then slivered
¼ teaspoon salt
Pinch of ground white pepper
¼ teaspoon five-spice powder
2 cups mung bean sprouts, heads and tails removed
1 teaspoon sesame oil
1 tablespoon corn oil
12 egg whites
1 tablespoon baking powder
3 tablespoons vegetable oil

1. Mix together the shrimp, chives, pork, and mushrooms, then add the salt and pepper, five-spice powder, mung bean sprouts, and sesame oil.

2. Heat the corn oil in a pan, add the shrimp mixture and stir-fry for 2 minutes, then remove from the heat.

3. In a bowl, mix the egg whites and baking powder with 2 tablespoons of cool water. Beat gently.

4. Heat the vegetable oil in a 6- or 7-inch skillet, and pour in a few tablespoons of the egg-white mixture. Cook on both sides, just until set, and place on a plate. Repeat with the remaining egg mixture. Do not stack the pancakes—place each on an individual plate. This should make ten egg-white pancakes.

5. Divide the shrimp filling mixture into ten parts. Put one portion on each egg-white pancake, and roll up egg roll-style, folding in the ends. Place on a serving platter and serve warm.

FISH-STUFFED BEAN CURD

Any fish or seafood—or any food, for that matter—can be used when stuffing bean curd, also known as doufu or tofu. These can be used in any number of casserole and claypot dishes, and also as the only or one of many ingredients in a soup. **SERVES 5 TO 10**

- ¼ pound skinless and boneless fish, minced
- ¼ cup minced or ground pork
- ¼ cup shrimp, peeled, deveined, and minced
- 1 tablespoon dried shrimp, soaked for 30 minutes, then minced
- 1 egg white, lightly beaten
- 5 pieces (about 1 pound) firm bean curd
- 1 tablespoon cornstarch
- 1 tablespoon corn oil

1. Mix together the fish, pork, fresh and dried shrimp, and half of the egg white.

2. Cut each bean curd piece in half diagonally to make 10 triangles. Remove 1 teaspoon of bean curd from the long edge of each triangle making a small pocket. Mash the removed part and mix it with the fish mixture.

3. Dust the pocket in each bean curd triangle with cornstarch and stuff each with one-tenth of the fish mixture, mounding slightly.

4. Heat the oil in a wok or pan and put the bean curd in, stuffed side down. Add ½ cup of water to the pan, cover, and simmer for 10 minutes. Remove and place stuffed side up on a platter, then serve.

FLUFFY EGGS WITH PORK FLOSS

Pork floss looks like brown hair. See page 217 to make your own and be one of the rare people who do. Years back, with no car, we made our own. Now, busier than ever, we purchase it made with pork or sometimes made with beef.
SERVES 3 TO 6

6 eggs	½ teaspoon salt
3 cups oil	3 tablespoons pork floss (page 217)

1. Beat the eggs until light in color and beginning to thicken. Then add the salt and beat for another minute.

2. Heat a wok, pour in the oil and heat. Slowly pour in the eggs, stirring constantly, until they coagulate into thin, threadlike pieces. When they rise to the top, remove and drain them on paper towels. Immediately strain the oil and reserve it in the refrigerator for another use.

3. Put the eggs into a preheated bowl, top with the pork floss, and serve.

HAIR SEAWEED ROLLS

A misnomer, the moss-like wrapping in this recipe is neither hair nor seaweed. Called *facai* in Chinese, it is a seaweed-like vegetable, the *cai* meaning "vegetable." Used in this and many other ways, *facai* symbolizes good luck. It is very popular in dishes during the Chinese New Year. SERVES 5 TO 10

- ¼ cup hair vegetable, soaked in warm water for 30 minutes, then drained well and cut with scissors into 1- to 2-inch lengths
- ½ cup peeled water chestnuts, minced
- 2 dried Chinese black mushrooms (shiitake), soaked, stems removed, and minced
- 1 teaspoon sesame oil
- 1 tablespoon cornstarch or water-chestnut flour
- Pinch of salt
- Pinch of ground white pepper
- 1 cup all-purpose flour
- ½ cup rice flour
- 1 egg white
- 3 large round (each about 8 or 9 inches in diameter) spring roll wrappers
- 5 tablespoons vegetable oil

1. Mix together the hair vegetable, water chestnuts, mushrooms, sesame oil, cornstarch, salt, and pepper, and divide into three parts.

2. Make a batter with both flours and the egg white. Set aside.

3. Put a spring roll wrapper on a dry counter top and put one part of the hair vegetable mixture at one edge of the dough. Roll up, folding in the ends. Seal the edge with a wet finger. Repeat until all wrappers and filling are used.

5. Heat a flat-bottomed skillet or a wok, and pour in and heat the vegetable oil. Dip a roll into the egg-white batter, coating all sides, then put the battered vegetable roll, seam side down, into the hot oil. Quickly repeat with the other rolls, and reduce the heat to low. Fry the rolls turning frequently, until lightly browned on all sides. Remove and drain on paper towels. Cut each roll into three or four pieces, and set them on one edge on a platter to serve.

LONG BEAN CUPS

Cups in name only, these twisted circles of long beans make round holders for the shrimp and pork mixture. Each is topped with half a quail egg making them beautiful presentations. **SERVES 10**

- 20 long beans, 12 to 15 inches in length, ends removed
- 2 tablespoons cornstarch
- ½ pound shrimp, peeled, deveined, and minced
- ¼ cup plus 1 tablespoon ground pork
- 3 whole water chestnuts, minced
- 1 egg white
- ¼ teaspoon ground white pepper
- 1 tablespoon thin soy sauce
- 5 quail eggs, cooked for 5 minutes, then peeled, and cut in half
- 1 teaspoon sesame oil

1. Simmer the long beans for 4 minutes, and remove from the water. Twist two long beans around each other making them into a circle and tucking in their ends so they do not unravel. Repeat with the remaining beans. Dust each circle with cornstarch, reserving any unused cornstarch. Place the beans on a flat surface.

2. Gently mix together the shrimp, pork, water chestnuts, egg white, pepper, and soy sauce.

3. Take one-tenth of the shrimp mixture, and mound it in a long bean circle. Use a thumb to make an indentation in the shrimp mixture, and then lightly dust it with some of the remaining cornstarch. Put half a quail egg, yolk side up, into the indentation. Gently push it in so that it adheres, then pour a few drops of sesame oil on the quail egg. Repeat until you have 10 cups.

4. Spread the remaining sesame oil on the surface of a small, heatproof serving plate that fits into a steamer. Put the long bean rings around its outside and put one in the center. Steam for 6 minutes over boiling water, then remove the plate and serve the bean circles.

LOTUS BALLS

Lotus is an elegant plant that grows in many places. This dish uses the oval-shaped seeds of the root three ways: chopped, as a sweetened paste, and dried and ground as flour. These balls are popular during the Moon Festival, but many Fujianese and bakeries make them year-round. **SERVES 12**

2 cups glutinous rice flour
¼ cup brown rock sugar, crushed
¼ cup canned or boiled lotus seeds, chopped coarsely
½ cup sweetened lotus-seed paste
2 tablespoons lotus-seed flour
½ cup sesame seeds
1 cup plus 1 tablespoon vegetable oil
1 egg white, lightly beaten

1. Mix together the rice flour, sugar, and 10 tablespoons of cold water, and form a ball of dough. Knead the dough until it feels smooth, then roll it into a 12-inch long, fat, cigar-shaped piece of dough. Cut it into twelve pieces and roll out each piece until about 3 inches in diameter.

2. Combine the chopped lotus seeds and the lotus-seed paste. Divide the mixture into twelve parts, and put one part on the center of each circle of dough. Seal the dough around the filling, pinching it together with your fingers. Make each into a ball.

3. Mix the lotus-seed flour and sesame seeds in a deep saucer.

4. Oil a large platter with the tablespoon of vegetable oil. Dip each ball into the egg white, then roll into the sesame-seed mixture and set on the oiled platter.

5. Heat the cup of oil, and fry six balls at a time until they puff slightly and turn golden brown. Remove with a slotted spoon and drain on paper towels. Repeat until all are fried. Serve the balls warm, not chilled, as they toughen when cool.

MIXED SEAFOOD PANCAKES

Oyster pancakes are loved by the Fujianese, and every Fujianese restaurant serves them. Any seafood can be used in place of the oysters, with or instead of the foods of the sea already in this recipe. Locals use what is fresh, handy, and bountiful. **SERVES 6**

- ½ cup all-purpose flour
- 3 cups rice flour
- 3 eggs, beaten until light in color
- ½ cup fish or chicken broth
- ½ teaspoon coarse salt
- 1 scallion, minced
- 2 shrimp, peeled, deveined, and coarsely chopped
- 2 clams, coarsely chopped
- 2 oysters, coarsely chopped
- 1 scallop, coarsely chopped
- 3 tablespoons skinless and boneless fish, coarsely chopped
- ½ teaspoon black sesame seeds
- 3 tablespoons vegetable oil
- 2 cloves garlic, finely minced

1. Mix both flours, the eggs, broth, ½ cup of water, and salt until well blended.

2. Add the minced scallion, seafood and fish, and sesame seeds.

3. Heat a wok or skillet, pour in and heat 1 tablespoon of the oil, then add one-third of the minced garlic. Stir for 30 seconds, then add one-third of the seafood mixture. Lower the heat and cook until browned on the underside, 3 to 4 minutes. Turn the pancake over and cook for another 3 minutes. Transfer to a warm plate, and repeat until all ingredients are used. Cut each pancake in half and serve immediately.

SHRIMP CHIPS

Though available dry, packaged and ready to be fried, these chips are so much better homemade. Ground scallops, abalone, and other seafood can also be used to make the chips. They need two days to dry, so planning ahead is a must. **SERVES 10 AS A SNACK, OR USE HALF THE RECIPE UNDER OR IN A MAIN DISH**

½ cup shrimp, peeled, deveined, and minced into a paste
4 cups mung-bean flour
½ teaspoon salt
Pinch of ground white pepper
4 teaspoons baking powder
2 egg whites
2 cups vegetable oil

1. Mix the shrimp paste with 3 cups of the mung-bean flour. Add the salt, pepper, and baking powder.

2. In a medium pot bring 1 cup of water to a boil and add the shrimp mixture. Remove the contents from the pot and allow it to cool for 20 minutes, then knead the dough for 2 minutes. Mix the rest of the mung-bean flour with the egg whites, and stir this into the shrimp mixture making a paste. Oil a steamer basket. Make two snakelike rolls of the shrimp paste. Place the rolls in the basket and steam them over rapidly boiling water for 30 minutes.

3. Cover the steamer basket and refrigerate overnight. In the morning, cut each piece of snakelike dough into very thin slices. Spread the slices on a cookie sheet, and let rest an hour or so before baking.

4. Preheat an oven to 200°F. Bake the chips for 20 minutes. Cool completely. Then rebake them at 200°F twice more each day for two days, until they are dry and hard.

5. Heat the oil and deep-fry a half dozen of these disks. In a few seconds, they will expand twenty-fold. Drain them on paper towels, and repeat until all are fried. Cool and use immediately, or store in a covered tin for a few days until used.

SOY SAUCE EGGS

These eggs, related to tea eggs, are darker outside and their color is more uniform. They taste saltier than tea eggs and have a licorice flavor. They are often made using pigeon eggs, then placed whole or halved as a garnish around a dish. **SERVES 10**

- 10 chicken eggs or 20 pigeon eggs, at room temperature
- 10 tablespoons dark or mushroom soy sauce
- 1 tablespoon thick soy sauce
- ¼ cup Chinese rice wine
- 5 whole star anise
- 1 teaspoon Sichuan peppers
- 2 tablespoons brown sugar
- 1 stick cinnamon
- 1 tablespoon fennel seeds
- 1 teaspoon cloves

1. Put the eggs into a pot and cover them with cold water. Slowly bring to just below a boil, and simmer for 12 minutes for chicken eggs or 8 minutes for pigeon eggs. Remove the eggs from the heat and shell them, discarding the cooking water.

2. Put the peeled eggs back in the pot, add all the other ingredients, and bring to just below a boil. Simmer for 15 minutes, remove the eggs and cool under cold-running water. Serve.

Steamed Sea Cucumber Pockets

Somewhat akin to dumplings, these pockets of dough are popular filled with minced pork or fish paste and chopped sea cucumber. No matter what food partners with this gelatinous sea creature, be sure to use all the ginger recommended for a great taste. **SERVES 10**

- 1 large or two small presoaked sea cucumbers, insides removed, chopped
- 1 scallion, tied in a knot
- 2 slices peeled fresh ginger, plus 2 tablespoons minced
- ¼ pound chopped or ground pork, or raw fish paste
- 2 tablespoons sesame oil
- 1 tablespoon Chinese rice wine
- ¼ teaspoon ground white pepper
- ¼ teaspoon five-spice powder
- 1 teaspoon salt
- 1 cup all-purpose flour
- 1 tablespoon cornstarch
- ½ teaspoon vegetable oil

1. Bring 2 cups of water to a boil and add the sea cucumber, scallion knot, and ginger slices. Lower the heat and simmer for 20 minutes, drain, and discard the water, scallion, and sliced ginger.

2. Mix together the cooked sea cucumber, minced ginger, pork, sesame oil, rice wine, pepper, five-spice powder, and salt. Stir for 2 minutes, then refrigerate for 1 hour.

3. Mix together the flour, cornstarch, and ½ cup of warm water, and knead until smooth. Set aside in a closed plastic bag or in a bowl with a tight-fitting lid for 1 hour. Then remove and roll into a single 1-inch-thick cigar-shaped roll. Cut the roll into 1-inch pieces, and roll out each piece into a 3-inch circle.

4. Put a teaspoon of the sea-cucumber mixture in the center of each rolled piece of dough, wet one-half of the circle's edge, and fold the dough in half. Pinch dough together, making a sealed, stuffed pocket. Flatten each one slightly.

5. Oil a steamer rack and put the dough pockets on it. Do not let them touch each other. Cover and steam over boiling water for 12 minutes if pork, 10 minutes if fish. Remove to a minimally oiled serving platter.

STEAMED SEAFOOD ROLLS

This mixture can be made into rolls or seafood balls, then used in soups or other dishes. It can also be used as the exterior portion of fish balls. If the latter, wrap the fish mixture around chopped or ground pork, and roll in sweet-potato flour before steaming them. **SERVES 10**

- ½ pound any white fish, skinned, boned, and minced
- ½ pound shrimp, peeled, deveined, and minced
- 4 teaspoons minced, peeled fresh ginger
- ½ cup minced fresh coriander (cilantro) with stems
- 8 canned or cooked water chestnuts, minced
- 4 scallions, minced
- 1 small chili pepper, cut in half, seeded, and minced
- 1 tablespoon sesame oil
- 1 tablespoon Fujianese white rice wine
- 1 teaspoon thin soy sauce
- 1 teaspoon sugar
- 1 teaspoon coarse salt
- 30 round (3- to 4-inch) dumpling wrappers
- ¼ cup cornstarch, for dusting hands
- 1 egg, beaten
- 1 tablespoon vegetable oil

1. Mix together the minced fish, shrimp, ginger, coriander, water chestnuts, scallions, and chili pepper until the mixture feels sticky. Then add the sesame oil, rice wine, soy sauce, sugar, and salt.

2. Put 1 tablespoon of the filling on one edge of a wrapper. Dust your hands with cornstarch and fold in the sides and wet them slightly with egg, then roll up completely, sealing the edge with additional egg. Put seam side down on a heatproof plate oiled with the vegetable oil. Repeat with remaining wrappers, making sure no two rolls touch each other; use two or more oiled plates, as necessary.

3. Put the plates with the rolls in a steamer over boiling water, and steam for 10 minutes. Serve hot.

STUFFED LOTUS DISKS

Best fried just before serving, this appetizer is so popular that doubling the recipe, party or not, is a good idea. The disks can also be used as a garnish for stir-fried main dishes and in soups for a textural contrast when added just before serving them. SERVES 10

2 lotus roots, peeled, cut 30 thin slices, mince the rest
½ pound hand-chopped or ground fatty pork loin
½ teaspoon sugar
½ teaspoon salt
1½ teaspoons chicken or pork bouillon powder
2 teaspoons cornstarch
½ cup all-purpose flour
½ teaspoon baking powder
1 cup vegetable oil

1. Mix together the minced lotus root, pork, sugar, salt, and bouillon powder.

2. Take two slices of lotus root, and coat one side of each with cornstarch. Put 2 teaspoons of the meat mixture between the lotus root disks, with the cornstarch sides facing the meat. Close like a sandwich. Repeat until all the disks are used. Reserve any leftover filling for another use.

3. Stir together the flour and baking powder, and mix in 3 cups of water to make a batter.

4. Heat the oil, dip a lotus sandwich into the batter, allow the excess batter to drip off, and put the sandwich into the hot oil. Fry four or five at a time until crisp and golden. Drain on paper towels, and repeat until all have been fried. Serve immediately.

STUFFED MEAT AND RADISH BUNS

Also known by their colloquial name of "Pig Pine Logs," these buns are long and narrow, shaped like thin pine tree branches used to pen in animals. Popular steamed, extras can be reheated by first frying them in hot oil for 3 minutes, then steaming them. **SERVES 8**

- 1½ cups regular rice flour
- 1½ cups glutinous rice flour
- 2 tablespoons vegetable oil
- ½ pound ground pork
- ½ cup shredded white radish, half fresh and half dried, or all of one kind
- 3 shallots, peeled and minced
- 1 tablespoon Fujianese or other Chinese rice wine
- 1 tablespoon white or red rice wine lees
- Pinch of ground white pepper
- 2 tablespoons cornstarch mixed with 1 tablespoon cold water
- 8 pieces parchment paper about 3 x 4 inches each

1. Mix both rice flours with 4 to 5 tablespoons of cold water, knead until smooth, then shape into a ball. Bring 4 cups water to a boil and boil the dough until it floats to the surface, then remove and cool. Divide the dough into eight pieces and roll each into an oval.

2. Heat the oil in a wok and stir-fry the pork until it is no longer pink. Add the shredded radish and minced shallots, and stir-fry for 1 minute more. Strain this meat mixture, return it to the hot wok, and allow it to cool about 5 minutes. Add the rice wine, wine lees, pepper, and cornstarch mixture. Let this mixture rest for 10 minutes.

3. Divide the pork filling into eight parts, placing each on a piece of dough. Fold over the dough and crimp to seal so each bun is longer than it is wide. Stretch them about ½-inch to 1-inch lengthwise, then place each on a piece of parchment paper.

4. Bring 2 or more quarts of water to a boil in the bottom pan of a steamer. Place the buns with their paper on a bamboo steamer rack over the boiling water, and cover with a steamer cover. Steam for 20 minutes, and then transfer the buns to a serving platter.

SOUPS AND CONGEES

THROUGHOUT CHINA, SOUPS come in many varieties. However, nowhere is this truer than in the Fujian province, where they can be thin or thick; simple or complex; sweet, sour, or piquant. Some soups are cooked quickly, a few are slow-cooked. Some are virtual broths, and almost every one of them is loaded with multiple ingredients. In Fujian, it is customary that every meal include two or more soups, and that every banquet serve more than two.

Throughout southern China, soups based upon rice are called *congees*. In the north, these same soups are called *juk*. Congees are cooked for a long time, until the rice is very soft, to the point where the grains start to fall apart. They are popular for breakfast and often eaten at lunch. They are adored by the young and the elderly. Frequently, congees include the leftovers of previous meals as some or all of their ingredients.

Some regular soups are actually cooked as stews, then additional broth or water is added to be able to serve them as soups. Many main-dish stews in this book can be prepared and served as soups instead, or stew leftovers can be thinned into soups. All the chapters in this book include recipes for other dishes that, with the addition of broth, can be served as a soup.

In the Fujian province and throughout China, it is common to have thinner soups early in the meal; thicker ones are served in the middle and at the end of some meals. Specific to this province, sweeter soups are popular close to the end of a meal, if not the very last dish served.

BEEF WITH MUSHROOMS IN SOUP

Soups and many other dishes usually take their names from the largest or most important ingredient. With a name and ingredient change, this soup can use pork ribs, pork shoulder, or any other meat—chef's choice. It can be served with or without bones, and with any one or more vegetable, such as chayote, pumpkin, or spinach. **SERVES 10**

1 pound beef ribs, chopped into 1-inch pieces
5 large dried Chinese black mushrooms (shiitake), soaked in warm water for 20 minutes, stems removed, then diced
2 dried scallops, soaked for 1 hour, drained, and hand shredded
4 slices peeled fresh ginger
2 cloves garlic, peeled and sliced
1 chayote, peeled and diced (if using an older or larger one, remove the seed)
¼ pound Chinese pumpkin, peeled and diced
8 dried Chinese red or brown dates, pitted and quartered
6 cups boiling water
1 tomato, blanched and skin removed, seeded, and diced coarsely
1 teaspoon salt
1 teaspoon sugar
¼ cup coarsely chopped fresh coriander (cilantro) leaves

1. In a pot, bring 6 cups of water to a boil. Add the meat and simmer for 1 hour. Remove the meat and discard the bones, reserving the broth. Cut the meat into 1-inch cubes, trim and discard any fat.

2. Strain the broth into a larger pot, add the meat, mushrooms, scallops, ginger, garlic, chayote, pumpkin, dates, and 6 cups of boiling water. Lower the heat and simmer for another hour and a half.

3. Add the tomato, salt, and sugar, and simmer for 10 more minutes. Remove the soup from the heat and add the coriander before putting into a tureen to serve.

CHICKEN SOUP IN COCONUT

Sometimes called "Twice-Cooked Coconut," this recipe can be steamed once, but for a longer period of time. I think the result is much better with this recipe, which calls for the coconut meat to be cooked twice. **SERVES 6 TO 8**

- ¼ pound boneless, skinless chicken breast, diced
- ¼ pound hand-minced pork
- 20 canned gingko nuts, gently mashed
- 1 large whole coconut, 1 inch of the top sawed off, the coconut water and top set aside
- 1 teaspoon Chinese white rice vinegar
- 1 large carrot, peeled and finely diced
- 1 tablespoon chicken bouillon powder
- 1 teaspoon thin soy sauce
- 1 egg white
- 2 teaspoons fermented white rice
- 1 teaspoon cornstarch mixed with 1 tablespoon cold water
- 1 teaspoon sesame oil

1. Mix together the chicken breast, pork, and mashed gingko nuts. Form into ten meatballs. Chill them in the refrigerator for 1 hour.

2. Strain the coconut water and set it aside. Rinse the coconut, and then brush the inside with the rice vinegar. Put 2 tablespoons of the coconut water into the coconut and set in a steamer, keeping it upright by placing crunched foil around it. Fill the pot halfway up with water.

3. Put the carrot pieces, bouillon powder, soy sauce, egg white, fermented rice, 2 cups of water, and the cornstarch mixture into the coconut and stir. Cover the coconut with its lid and steam over boiling water for 30 minutes.

4. Remove the top from the coconut, put in the meatballs, fill the coconut to the rim with boiling water, replace the top, and steam for 2 more hours. Remove coconut lid, add the sesame oil to the mixture, and place the coconut in a serving bowl.

CHICKEN SOUP WITH PEAR

The chicken in this recipe can also be simmered for 30 minutes, and its bones and skin discarded. Then cook the meat another hour with the other ingredients. The Chinese eat their soup with a large porcelain soup spoon and chopsticks, so they prefer their meat left on the bone. They claim it tastes sweeter that way. **SERVES 10**

½ chicken or 4 chicken thighs, cut into 2-inch pieces
3 almost-ripe Seckel or other firm pears, quartered and cored
½ teaspoon sugar
⅛ teaspoon salt
2 tablespoons dried Chinese wolfberries (goji berries)

1. Bring 2 cups of water to a boil. Blanch the chicken pieces for 1 minute in the boiling water, then drain and discard the water.

2. Bring 3 quarts of cold water to a boil, add the chicken, lower the heat, and simmer for 30 minutes. Add the pear pieces, sugar, salt, and wolfberries, and simmer for 20 minutes, then transfer to a tureen or serving bowl. Serve hot.

YAM CONGEE

People from Fujian have been called "Yams" because they eat lots of these tubers. This congee can be consumed as the only staple starch at breakfast and/or at lunch. One Fujianese chap told me that years ago his family ate this particular dish for breakfast and lunch, sometimes at dinner, as well. It was all they could afford. **SERVES 6**

½ cup short-grain rice	1 yam, peeled and diced into ½- to 1-inch cubes
½ teaspoon salt	

1. Soak the rice in 4 cups of warm water for 1 hour. Then place the rice and water in a heatproof bowl that will fit in a steamer.

2. Add the salt and yam. Put the bowl in a steamer over boiling water and steam for 2 hours. For those who like their rice very soft, add ½ cup more water to the rice mixture before steaming it.

CORN SOUP WITH SHRIMP

Popularly prepared with many different additions such as scallops, chicken, abalone, squid, even beef and pork, this easy-to-make soup graces many a Fujianese lunch or dinner table several times a week. **SERVES 10**

- ¼ cup fresh shrimp, peeled, deveined, and minced coarsely
- 2 egg whites, beaten until frothy
- 2 tablespoons cornstarch
- 1 tablespoon thin soy sauce, or 1 teaspoon coarse salt
- 8 cups chicken stock
- 2 teaspoons minced Yunnan or Smithfield ham
- 1 (12-ounce) can creamed-style corn

1. Mix together the shrimp, egg whites, cornstarch, and soy sauce or salt.

2. Bring the chicken stock to a simmer, add the shrimp mixture and simmer for 10 minutes, then add the ham and corn. Simmer for another 2 minutes, until heated almost to the boiling point. Transfer to a tureen or bowl to serve.

EIGHT TREASURE SOUP

To the Chinese, eight is a lucky number, so this soup is popular on auspicious occasions such as important birthdays, an engagement, the return of a married couple to the bride's parents' home, and so on. It brings luck. The ingredients are left to each chef's choice; and many of them include more than eight items in their soup. SERVES 10 TO 12

- 5 dried Chinese black mushrooms (shiitake), soaked in 1 cup of warm water for 20 minutes, stems discarded, and each cut into quarters; soaking liquid reserved
- 1 large white tree ear fungus, soaked for 20 minutes in warm water, then torn into ½-inch pieces
- ½ cup bamboo pith mushrooms, tough ends discarded, each cut in half across the width
- ¼ cup whole cashew nuts, fresh roasted or deep-fried for 1 minute
- 1 tablespoon almonds, boiled for 1 minute, skins removed
- 1 teaspoon bitter almonds, skins removed
- 5 candied Chinese brown dates, quartered
- 1 cup cooked whole chestnuts
- 1 cup water chestnuts
- 1 carrot, peeled and diced
- 1 cup watercress, rinsed and cut into 2-inch lengths
- 1 teaspoon salt

1. In a large pot, heat 10 cups water or chicken broth almost to the boiling point. Add all ingredients except the watercress and salt. Cover, and simmer for 2 hours.

2. Remove the cover, add two more cups of boiling water, stir well, and then add the watercress and salt. Serve hot.

FISH BALL SOUP

Fragrant and flavorful, fish balls can be purchased frozen. Young folk now use them to prepare this soup more often. Their parents made the fish balls from scratch and did so immediately before serving; that was why, in earlier days, this soup was reserved for special occasions. Here is how to prepare it the old-fashioned way. **SERVES 10**

- 4 teaspoons small dried shrimp, soaked in warm water for 1 hour, then minced
- ½ pound of one or more skinless and boneless fish, such as dace, sea bass, or red snapper, minced
- 1 scallion, green part only, minced
- 1 (2-inch) piece of dried tangerine peel, soaked until soft, then minced
- 2 slices peeled fresh ginger, minced
- ½ teaspoon ground white pepper
- 1 tablespoon water-chestnut flour
- 1 tablespoon sesame oil
- 2 quarts chicken or fish stock, warmed slightly
- 1 teaspoon salt
- 1 tablespoon cornstarch mixed with 1 tablespoon cold water

1. Mix together the shrimp, fish, scallion, tangerine peel, ginger, and pepper. Stir in one direction for about 5 minutes until the mixture gets sticky, and then form into 1-inch balls. Dust the fish balls with the water-chestnut flour.

2. Heat the sesame oil in a pot or a heatproof casserole, and fry the fish balls for 1 minute. Slowly add the stock and salt, and bring to just below the boiling point. Lower the heat and simmer for 2 minutes. Then increase the temperature, add the cornstarch mixture, and stir for 1 minute. Serve hot.

JELLYFISH SOUP

There may be no visible jellyfish when eating this soup. Prized for their texture, much of the jellyfish in this recipe melts into the broth. Visible or not, the Chinese believe the jellyfish's contribution to this soup's health value is important. This imperial food, they say, energizes everyone's *qi*. SERVES 10

¼ pound pork loin, slivered
1 whole jellyfish, rinsed, then soaked for an hour and drained
½ cup peeled and slivered fresh or canned water chestnuts
¼ carrot, slivered
½ teaspoon coarse salt
8 cups superior chicken stock (see page 234)
1 Chinese black mushroom (shiitake), soaked, stem removed

1. Blanch the pork for 2 minutes in 2 cups of boiling water, then drain. Discard the water.

2. Sliver the jellyfish and cut into 2-inch lengths.

3. Put all ingredients into a pot and bring almost to the boiling point, lower the heat and simmer for 2 hours. Transfer to a tureen or bowl to serve.

MIXED-MEAT DUMPLING SOUP

The dumplings and their fillings add wonderful flavor to this soup as do a number of other ingredients. While the meat used is usually added raw, cooked meats (but not fish or other seafood) are also popular. Cooked vegetables are rarely included. **SERVES 10**

- 2 tablespoons minced crabmeat
- ¼ cup finely minced or ground pork
- ¼ cup coarsely minced beef
- 2 slices peeled fresh ginger, finely minced; plus 2 slices, slivered
- 2 large cloves garlic, minced finely; plus 1 clove, slivered
- 2 tablespoons Chinese chives, minced finely
- 1 teaspoon sesame oil
- 1 egg yolk
- 1 tablespoon cornstarch
- 30 thin 2-inch dumpling wrappers
- 2 teaspoons Chinese rice wine
- 2 quarts superior chicken stock (see page 234) or chicken broth
- 2 tablespoons coarsely minced coriander (cilantro) leaves
- 1 (½-ounce) package thin Fujianese wheat noodles

1. Mix together the crabmeat, pork, beef, minced ginger, and minced garlic. Stir until well combined. Add the chives, sesame oil, egg yolk, and cornstarch, and mix until the cornstarch is moistened.

2. Put one dumpling wrapper on a dry, flat surface. Place ½ teaspoon of the filling mixture in the center, and wet one corner of the wrapper before folding in half, slightly askew, and seal. Repeat until all wrappers are filled, sealed, and set aside. Should any of the mixture be left over, make ½ teaspoon meatballs and set them aside as well.

3. In a large pot mix together the slivered ginger, slivered garlic, rice wine, and chicken stock and heat to just below the boiling point. Then add the dumplings and any leftover meatballs, and simmer for 8 minutes. Add the coriander and noodles, and simmer for 1 more minute. Transfer to a tureen or bowl to serve.

MUNG BEAN SOUP

Seamen probably brought this soup back from India, Macau, or places in between, and added sweet potatoes to it for a taste of home. Some make this soup with one or more other varieties of legumes. The seeds that grow into long beans which are related to cow peas are popular. **SERVES 10**

- 2 cups dried mung and/or other beans, soaked for 3 hours in cold water
- 1 cup peeled and diced (1½-inch pieces) sweet potatoes
- 1 teaspoon vegetable oil
- 1 small hot red chili pepper, seeded and minced
- 3 tablespoons peeled, minced fresh ginger
- 1 teaspoon curry powder or paste
- 2 teaspoons thin soy sauce
- 4 dried Chinese black mushrooms (shiitake), soaked for 30 minutes in 1 cup warm water
- ½ teaspoon sugar
- ¼ teaspoon coarse salt
- ⅛ teaspoon ground white pepper
- 8 cups superior stock (see page 234)
- ⅛ cup coarsely minced fresh coriander (cilantro) leaves

1. Drain the beans and discard any broken ones. Put them in a large stockpot and add the sweet potatoes.

2. In a medium skillet or wok, combine the oil, chili pepper, ginger, and curry, and stir-fry for 1 minute. Then add the soy sauce and mix well. Add this mixture to the stockpot.

3. Remove and discard the mushroom stems. Squeeze the water from the mushrooms into the stockpot, dice them, and add the mushrooms to the stockpot along with the remaining ingredients except the coriander.

4. Bring to a boil, lower the heat, and simmer for 1 hour. Add the coriander and transfer to a tureen or bowl to serve.

PAPAYA SOUP

This soup can also be served cold as a beverage. Summer or winter, it is sold hot or cold, sometimes with fewer ingredients, on the streets of larger Fujianese cities. It is refreshing either way. **SERVES 4 TO 6**

1 2-inch piece dried tangerine peel, soaked for 30 minutes, then minced
1 ripe papaya, peeled, seeds removed and discarded, minced
10 dried Chinese red dates, pitted and minced
4 dried figs, soaked for 30 minutes in warm water, then minced
6 pieces dried lily bulbs, boiled for 30 minutes
¼ cup pine nuts

1. Mix all the ingredients, then puree in a blender with 2 cups of water until no solid pieces remain.

2. Bring 10 cups of water to a boil, add all of the puree, and simmer for 3 hours. Serve hot, warm, or cold.

PEANUT AND SESAME SEED SOUP

This soup can also be served as a beverage between meals, in which case the all-purpose flour is often replaced with peanut flour. When served cold, the addition of more sugar is a popular variation, sometimes as much as twice the amount given below. **SERVES 8**

- 1 cup all-purpose or peanut flour, or a combination of both
- ¼ cup sesame seeds, toasted and cooled
- ¼ cup peanut oil
- 1 tablespoon lard
- 3 scallions, minced
- ½ cup sugar
- 3 tablespoons cornstarch mixed with 1 teaspoon sesame oil
- 6 cups boiling water

1. Put the flour in a heatproof soup bowl, loosely cover it with foil, and steam for 30 minutes over rapidly boiling water. Allow to cool.

2. Grind half the sesame seeds with a mortar and pestle.

3. Heat a wok or skillet, and add and heat the peanut oil and lard. Carefully add the scallions and stir-fry for 1 minute. Add the flour, sugar, both batches of sesame seeds, and the cornstarch mixture. Mix well, then add 6 cups of boiling water and boil for 1 minute. Serve hot or cold.

PICKLED PIG'S FEET SOUP

Popular for nursing mothers, this soup is served during the first thirty days after childbirth. Black vinegar is said to cleanse body channels. It also dissolves calcium from the pig bones, replenishing it in the mother's milk. Peanuts, the Chinese believe, increase breast milk production, so mother and baby benefit as she recuperates from childbirth. MAKES 12 ONE-CUP SERVINGS

- 12 pounds pig's feet, cut into 2- to 3-inch pieces, any hair removed with tweezers
- 1 tablespoon vegetable oil
- ¼ pound fresh ginger, peeled and chopped
- 2 cups Chinese black rice vinegar
- 1 tablespoon salt
- 3 tablespoons rock sugar
- 1 cup shelled peanuts, skins removed and discarded

1. Put the pig's feet pieces in a 10- or 12-quart stockpot, cover with water, and bring to a boil. Boil for 3 minutes and then discard the water. Add the same amount of water and bring it to just below the boiling point, lower the heat, and simmer for 1 hour.

2. Heat the oil in a small pan, then fry the ginger for 2 minutes, being careful not to allow it to burn. Add to the pot along with the black rice vinegar, salt, and sugar, and simmer for 5 hours. Add the peanuts and simmer for an additional hour. Serve hot.

NOTE: After childbirth, new mothers are served some bones and a cup of boiling soup once or twice a day for thirty days.

PORK AND SEA CUCUMBER SOUP

Smooth sea cucumber is preferred, and it and the pork can be used in any amount. Starchy vegetables such as gingko, sweet potatoes, bamboo shoots, and water chestnuts, in amounts equal to the seafood and land meats, are often additions. With less stock, this dish is a popular main dish. **SERVES 10**

½ pound pork, cut into 1-inch cubes, and blanched for 1 minute
½ pound presoaked sea cucumber, cut into ½-inch cubes
16 water chestnuts, quartered
½ cup (1-inch squares) winter bamboo shoots
10 dried Chinese black mushrooms (shiitake), soaked, stems discarded, quartered
1 tablespoon vegetable oil
1 tablespoon sesame oil
1 tablespoon Chinese rice wine
1 tablespoon Chinese black rice vinegar
½ tablespoon salt
½ tablespoon sugar
1 tablespoon thin soy sauce
1 teaspoon chili oil
1 slice peeled fresh ginger, minced
⅛ teaspoon ground white pepper
⅛ teaspoon ground black pepper
2 tablespoons sweet-potato flour or cornstarch
2 quarts chicken, fish, or beef broth
2 eggs, beaten
1 scallion, minced

1. Mix together the pork, sea cucumber, water chestnuts, bamboo shoots, and mushroom pieces.

2. In a large pot, heat the vegetable and sesame oils, and stir-fry the pork mixture in them for 2 minutes. Add the rice wine, vinegar, salt, sugar, soy sauce, chili oil, ginger, white and black pepper, sweet-potato flour, and broth, and bring to a boil. Lower the heat and simmer for 1 hour.

3. When ready to serve, stir in the eggs and sprinkle in the minced scallion before pouring into a large soup tureen or bowl.

PORK SOUP WITH LOTUS SEEDS

This soup is believed to invigorate one's *qi*, or vital energy, and to improve circulation. It is popular in wintertime, and whenever someone has a bad cold and/or pneumonia, or when a person feels general malaise. **SERVES 10**

- 1 pound boneless pork, sliced and cut into thin strips
- 3 (2-inch) pieces dried tangerine peel, soaked in ¼ cup warm water, drained and then slivered
- 5 tablespoons canned lotus seeds, or dried lotus seeds simmered in water for 2 hours
- 2 tablespoons dried Chinese wolfberries (goji berries)
- 1 tablespoon Job's tears or barley
- 1 teaspoon salt
- 2 tablespoons white rice wine lees

1. Blanch the pork strips in a pot of boiling water. Rinse in cold water and drain.

2. Put all the ingredients in a large pot, add 4 quarts of water, and bring to just below the boiling point. Lower the heat and simmer for 2 hours. If the pork is not soft enough, simmer for an additional 30 minutes and taste again. Cook until it is soft. Serve hot.

PORK, VEGETABLE, AND FISH SOUP

Mixing meat, fish, and vegetables in soups and stews is common in Fujian, and using red or white rice wine lees makes this dish and others like it distinctively Fujianese. Meats, fish, and vegetables can vary, but the rice wine lees gives this a special taste. SERVES 10

¼ pound pork, hand chopped
10 cups chicken stock or water
1 large carrot, peeled, diced
½ cup peeled and diced white or green radishes
2 slices peeled fresh ginger, diced
½ clove garlic, peeled and chopped
1 1-inch piece dried tangerine peel, soaked until soft, then chopped
1 to 3 teaspoons minced Yunnan or Smithfield ham
2 tablespoons white rice wine lees
1 teaspoon red rice wine lees
¼ pound skinless and boneless fresh fish
2 sprigs fresh coriander (cilantro), stems removed

1. Blanch the pork for 2 minutes in 2 cups of boiling water. Drain, and discard the water.

2. Bring the chicken stock to a boil, lower the heat, and then add the pork, carrot, radishes, ginger, garlic, and tangerine peel. Simmer for 1 hour.

3. Add the ham and both wine lees, and simmer for another 30 minutes. Add the fish, simmer for 10 more minutes, then add the coriander. Pour into a tureen or bowl to serve.

PUMPKIN, CORN, AND FISH SOUP

Considered warming, this winter soup is of value year round for those with weak stomachs and/or weak kidneys. Its multi-ingredient mix also is thought to bring health to all. Packaged cooked chestnuts and canned corn are timesavers if substituted for fresh. **SERVES 10**

- 1 cup fresh chestnuts, boiled for 30 minutes, shells and skins removed and discarded
- 1 pound Chinese pumpkin, peeled and seeded, cut into 1-inch pieces
- 1 ear fresh corn, kernels removed from the cob
- ¼ teaspoon dried tangerine peel, soaked and slivered
- 1 white tree ear fungus, soaked for 20 minutes, then cut into 1-inch pieces
- 1 pound carp, skin and bones discarded, the flesh cut into 2-inch pieces
- ¼ teaspoon salt
- 1 scallion, green part only, minced

1. Mash half the chestnuts, and cut the rest in half.

2. Bring 10 cups water to a boil, and add the chestnuts, pumpkin, corn, and tangerine peel. Simmer for 1 hour.

3. Add the fungus, carp, and salt, and simmer for 20 more minutes, then pour into a tureen or bowl and sprinkle with scallions. Serve hot.

QUAIL EGG SWEET SOUP

This soup is popular at dim sum meals and snack times. It rarely begins a meal, but can be served at other times and at banquets. At a wedding banquet, two quail eggs per person would be appropriate, as they signify and honor the wedded couple. SERVES 10

- ½ cup bitter almonds, blanched and peeled
- 1½ cups regular almonds, blanched and peeled
- 3 tablespoons hard large white sugar crystals
- 1 tablespoon hard large brown sugar crystals
- 3 egg whites
- 10 fresh raw quail eggs

1. Soak the two kinds of almonds separately overnight. Then drain and process each kind separately with 1 cup of water in a blender or food processor. Strain each batch and put their liquid into a large pot. Reprocess each batch of ground nuts with one more cup of water, strain, and put the liquid in the same pot.

2. Mix both sets of almond solids and the liquid in the pot, and add both kinds of sugar and 8 cups of additional water. Slowly bring to just below the boiling point and simmer for 30 minutes, stirring frequently.

3. Raise the heat and bring the soup to a very gentle boil. Add the egg whites while stirring well. Remove from the heat, and pour into individual preheated soup bowls.

4. Immediately break a raw quail egg into the center of each bowl, wait one minute and then serve.

Rice Noodles, Chicken, and Jellyfish Soup

This soup, omitting the stock, can be served as a cold dish, if the carrots and celery are cooked for 2 minutes. The entire dish should be enhanced with a tablespoon or two of Chinese rice vinegar. SERVES 12 OR MORE

- 1 whole skinless, boneless chicken breast
- 2 dried jellyfish, rinsed well
- 2 (10- to 12-inch) steamed rice noodle sheets
- 1 carrot, cut into 2-inch-long slivers
- 2 stalks celery, strings removed, cut into 2-inch-long slivers
- ½ teaspoon salt
- 1 teaspoon sesame oil
- 2 tablespoons thin soy sauce
- 1 tablespoon lightly toasted sesame seeds
- 16 cups chicken stock

1. Simmer the chicken breast in water for 10 minutes. When cool enough to handle, hand-shred the breast meat into very thin slivers about 2 inches long.

2. Bring a pot of water to a boil. Put the jellyfish in a strainer basket, lower them into the boiling water for 15 seconds, remove, and plunge into ice water. Drain well, then roll up and cut the jellyfish into the thinnest slivers possible. Cut the jellyfish strips into 2-inch lengths.

3. Shred the rice noodle sheets and cut into 2-inch lengths.

4. Combine all the ingredients and simmer for 30 minutes, then pour into a bowl or soup tureen to serve.

SEA CUCUMBER SOUP

Made and served with red rice wine lees, this traditional soup has many names. Basically the same soup with a different name appeared in *Flavor and Fortune*, in an issue that included an article about foods of Fujian. **SERVES 10**

½ pound soaked sea cucumber, cut into ½-inch cubes
½ cup corn oil
3 ounces pork loin, cut into ½-inch cubes
3 tablespoons cubed bamboo shoots
4 dried Chinese black mushrooms (shiitake), soaked, stems removed and discarded, cut into ½-inch cubes
8 cups chicken stock
1 tablespoon red rice wine lees
½ teaspoon sugar
½ teaspoon salt
½ teaspoon thin soy sauce
¼ teaspoon chili oil
¼ teaspoon sesame oil
1 chicken egg
1 tablespoon cornstarch
½ teaspoon Chinese black rice vinegar
½ teaspoon Chinese white rice vinegar
1 scallion, very thinly sliced
5 hard-cooked pigeon eggs, cut in half with a zigzag edge, the bottom of each half sliced off so the halves can stand upright

1. Simmer the sea cucumber in 2 cups of water for 1 hour, or until tender. Drain.

2. Heat a wok or deep pot, add the corn oil, deep-fry the pork cubes for 1 minute. Drain them on paper towels. Remove all but 1 tablespoon of the oil from the wok or pot.

3. Reheat the reserved oil and stir-fry the sea cucumber, pork, bamboo shoots, and mushrooms for 1 minute. Then add the stock, red rice wine lees, sugar, salt, soy sauce, and chili and sesame oils. Simmer uncovered for 30 minutes.

4. Beat the chicken egg with the cornstarch and 1 tablespoon of cold water, and stir into the soup in a thin stream; then add the vinegars and scallion. Put a pigeon egg half in each individual soup bowl, and gently pour hot soup over the eggs.

SLEEP-WELL SOUP

This unusual name comes from the presence in the soup of ginseng, said to enhance one's *qi*, or vital energy. With the chicken, it helps those who need more sleep, and relaxes them enough to doze off easily after enjoying its fine taste. **SERVES 8 TO 10**

1 (2- to 3-pound) chicken, quartered, skin removed
¼ cup fresh ginseng, scrubbed and sliced
1 carrot, peeled, quartered lengthwise, and angle cut into ½-inch lengths
4 candied Chinese brown dates, each cut into 4 to 6 pieces
20 dried Chinese wolfberries (goji berries)
¼ teaspoon salt

1. Bring 4 cups of water to a boil, blanch the chicken for 1 minute, drain, and discard the water.

2. Bring 3 quarts of water to a boil, add the chicken pieces, ginseng, carrot, and dates, lower the heat, and simmer for 1 hour.

3. Add the wolfberries and salt, and simmer for another 20 minutes. Pour into individual soup bowls to serve.

SPICY BEEF NOODLE SOUP

This soup can also be served as a main course. To do so, remove 4 cups of liquid near the end of the cooking time and reduce. Then, at the very end of the cooking process, thicken the broth with 2 tablespoons cornstarch mixed with an equal amount of cold water. **SERVES 10 TO 12**

1 cup white rice wine lees or Chinese white rice wine
2 (2-inch square) pieces of tangerine peel, soaked for 20 minutes, drained, then minced
1 bunch fresh coriander (cilantro), washed, leaves and stems minced separately
¾ cup thin soy sauce
1 (2-inch by 1-inch) piece Chinese brick sugar
6 scallions, white and green parts minced separately
6 slices peeled fresh ginger, minced
6 cloves garlic, peeled and minced
6 star anise
6 whole dried red chili peppers
2 pounds short ribs
2 quarts chicken or beef broth
6 tablespoons minced pickled mustard greens
½ pound very thin dried Fujianese noodles
1 cup mung beans, tails removed
3 tablespoons cornstarch mixed with 3 tablespoons cold water (optional)

1. Using a large soup pot or Dutch oven, bring 2 quarts of water to a boil. Add the wine lees, tangerine peel, coriander stems, soy sauce, sugar, white scallion parts, ginger, garlic, star anise, and chili peppers. Lower the heat and simmer, covered, for 1 hour.

2. Add the short ribs and simmer for another 2 hours. Remove the meat and discard the bones. Cut the meat into small pieces and place back into the pot. Add the broth, mustard greens, and dried noodles, and bring to a boil, stirring continuously for 1 minute. (If serving as a main dish, remove 4 cups of liquid at this time, and reduce it in a separate pan to 1 cup, and then return that 1 cup to the main pot. Add the cornstarch mixture and simmer until slightly thickened.)

3. Add the mung beans to the soup and simmer for 1 minute, then pour into a tureen to serve.

SQUID SOUP WITH VEGETABLES

This soup needs careful attention so that you do not overcook the squid. Locals use whatever vegetables are in season, mostly firm ones. A few leafy vegetables can go into the pot at the same time as the squid as they, too, should not be overcooked. SERVES 8

- 2 tablespoons vegetable oil
- ½ pound squid, cleaned of any cartilage, and cut into 1-inch lengths
- 2 tablespoons Chinese white rice vinegar
- 1 small onion, thinly sliced
- ½ cup bamboo shoots or water chestnuts, or both, sliced into matchsticks
- 1 cup snow peas, strings removed, each cut in half across the width and on an angle
- 6 cups chicken broth
- 3 teaspoons salt
- 1 teaspoon sugar

1. Heat the oil in a wok or deep pot and stir-fry the squid for 30 seconds; remove the squid and mix with the rice vinegar. Set aside.

2. Reheat the wok and oil, and stir-fry the onion slices until soft, then add the bamboo shoots and snow peas and stir-fry another minute. Add the broth, salt, and sugar. Bring slowly to a boil, and return the squid to the soup and just heat through. Pour into individual bowls to serve.

STEWED MUTTON SOUP

This recipe can be made with red or white rice wine lees; red is the preferred choice. To make this particular dish into a stew, double the mutton and half the liquid. SERVES 10

- 1 pound mutton, cut into 2-inch cubes
- 1 tablespoon vegetable oil
- 4 slices peeled fresh ginger, each quartered
- 4 large scallions, cut on an angle into 1-inch pieces
- 1 teaspoon sugar
- 2 tablespoons red or white rice wine lees
- 8 cups water or superior beef stock (see page 234)

1. Blanch the mutton in 2 cups of boiling water for 2 minutes, drain, and discard the water.

2. In a wok or large pot, heat the oil and stir-fry the meat for 2 minutes. Add the ginger and scallion pieces and stir-fry for another minute.

3. Add the sugar and wine lees, and stir-fry for 1 more minute, then add the water, lower the heat, and simmer for 1 hour, or until meat is very tender. Pour into a tureen and serve.

TANGERINE AND DOUBLE LOTUS SOUP

This soup can double as a sweet dish if you add white tree ear fungus with the red dates. Tangerines are grown and adored in Fujian and lotus is also a locally grown favorite. When serving this as a sweet dish, also try adding litchi, longans, and other fruits. **SERVES 6 TO 8**

4 tangerines, peeled, seeded and sectioned, all strings removed
¼ cup brown rock sugar, crushed
2 tablespoons white rice wine lees
¼ cup dried lotus seeds, soaked overnight in 4 cups water in the refrigerator
¼ pound or 2 sections lotus root, peeled and sliced thin across the holes
4 pitted dried Chinese red dates, quartered

1. Mix the tangerine sections, rock sugar, and wine lees and marinate for 3 to 4 hours. Remove the citrus slices and set them aside. Reserve the marinade.

2. Bring the soaked lotus seeds and 3 cups of water to a boil, lower the heat, and simmer until tender, about an hour. Drain and set aside.

3. Heat the reserved marinade, and add the lotus root slices, dates, and 1 cup of water. Simmer for 30 minutes or until tender, add the reserved lotus seeds, and simmer for another 5 minutes. Add the tangerine slices and simmer for another 10 minutes. Pour into individual bowls and serve hot or warm.

TARO ROOT, PORK BELLY, AND RED BEAN CURD SOUP

As with many other dishes in this regional cuisine, this popular recipe is sometimes first prepared with less water and served as a casserole and the next day, with added stock, presented anew as a soup. **SERVES 8**

- 1 pound pork belly (raw unsmoked bacon), diced into ½-inch cubes and boiled for 10 minutes, meat drained and liquid discarded
- 1 tablespoon thin soy sauce
- 2 tablespoons vegetable oil
- 2 teaspoons sugar
- 2 squares fermented red bean curd, mashed
- 1 star anise
- 2 cloves garlic, peeled and sliced
- 2 scallions, cut into 1-inch pieces, white and green parts kept separate
- 1 pound taro root, peeled, cut into 1-inch cubes and simmered for 30 minutes, then set aside
- 1½ tablespoons sweet-potato flour
- 1½ tablespoons cornstarch
- ¼ cup cold water
- 4 to 6 cups boiling water

1. Mix the cooked pork belly with the soy sauce, and let rest for 20 minutes.

2. Heat the vegetable oil and fry the meat for 2 minutes or until lightly browned, then add the sugar and stir well. Remove from the heat.

3. Bring 1 cup of water to a boil, add the pork and fermented bean curd, lower the heat and simmer for 10 minutes. Add the star anise, garlic, and white scallion pieces and simmer for another 10 minutes.

4. Put the green scallion pieces in the bottom of a heatproof bowl that will fit in a steamer, add the pork mixture, then the taro cubes. Mix the flour, cornstarch, and ¼ cup cold water and add this starch mixture to the bowl along with the 4 to 6 cups of boiling water. Cover and steam over boiling water for 30 minutes. Pour into a soup tureen to serve.

TARO SOUP

This favorite young folk's soup can be made with taro root, sweet potato, or both; some families, young and old, also add tapioca. Adding fruit is another preferred variation, as is adding coconut milk made by grating fresh coconut and mixing it with hot water. (Note: the liquid inside a coconut is coconut water, not coconut milk.) **SERVES 8 TO 10**

2 cups grated fresh coconut
½ pound taro root, peeled and cut into 1-inch squares
¼ pound sugar cubes
1 ripe peach, 2 plums, 1 nectarine, or 1 mango, peeled, pitted, minced, then mashed
1 ounce very thin dried Fuijianese noodles

1. Mix the grated coconut with 2 cups of warm water and let stand for 30 minutes. Pour the mixture through a cheesecloth placed over a large bowl. Twist the cloth tightly to extract as much liquid as possible. Repeat process twice more using new water each time; then discard the coconut meat and put the liquids in a large pot.

2. In another large pot, put the cubes of taro root in 4 cups of water, bring to a boil, lower the heat, and simmer for 20 minutes. Remove the taro root, reserving the liquid, and mash. Add the cooking water and mashed taro root to the pot of coconut milk.

3. Add the sugar, lower the heat to a simmer, and cook for 5 minutes. Add the mashed fruit and noodles, and simmer for 5 more minutes before pouring into individual bowls. Serve hot or warm.

TEA, CHICKEN, AND DATE SOUP

This soup is recommended for children, pregnant women, and the elderly. It is consumed more in winter than summer, and can be made adding other dried fruits. A few cooks make theirs with another kind of green tea, but *longjing* is the local favorite. SERVES 8 TO 10

1 tablespoon *longjing* tea leaves
12 dried Chinese red seedless dates
12 dried gingko nuts
1 (5-pound) chicken, cut in eighths
½ cup *shaoxing* wine or another light Chinese wine
2 teaspoons salt
1 teaspoon light soy sauce
½ cup drained canned gingko nuts
4 fresh Chinese black dates, cut into small pieces
3 tablespoons minced fresh coriander (cilantro) leaves

1. Put the tea leaves and 3 cups of water in a pot and bring to a boil. Add the dried dates and dried gingko nuts, lower the heat, and simmer for 1 hour. Remove the dates, cut each in half, and return them to the pot.

2. Rub all sides of the chicken pieces with the wine and set aside for 20 minutes. Then put them into a separate pot with 3 quarts of water. Simmer for 30 minutes. Remove the chicken pieces, and discard their skin and bones. Shred the chicken.

3. Put the chicken into the tea mixture with the salt, soy sauce, canned gingko nuts, and Chinese black dates. Simmer for 30 minutes. Add the coriander and pour into a tureen to serve.

THIN NOODLES AND PORK SOUP

This soup can be made with bean thread noodles or the exceptionally thin Fujianese wheat noodles. By the time it is finished cooking, most of the liquid is absorbed. Hence some serve it as a casserole; others add additional boiling water and make it into a thin soup. **SERVES 10**

- 2 ounces bean thread noodles, soaked for 30 minutes then drained, or 3 ounces very thin wheat noodles, soaked for 5 minutes and drained
- 2 tablespoons sesame oil
- 4 dried Chinese black mushrooms (shiitake), soaked in 4 cups hot water, stems discarded, sliced
- 2 tablespoons vegetable oil
- 1 small onion, peeled and thinly sliced
- ¼ pound pork loin, thinly sliced, then slivered
- 1 carrot, peeled and cut into matchstick-size pieces
- ¼ cup water chestnuts, cut into matchstick-size pieces
- ¼ cup bamboo shoots, cut into matchstick-size pieces
- 4 cups boiling water
- 1 pound bean sprouts, heads and tails removed
- ¼ cup coarsely chopped fresh coriander (cilantro) leaves

1. Toss the noodles with the sesame oil, and set aside.

2. Squeeze the water from the soaked mushrooms, and set them aside. Heat the vegetable oil and stir-fry the onion slices for 1 minute. Add the mushroom slices and stir-fry for another minute, then add the pork loin and stir-fry until no longer pink. Add the carrot, water chestnuts, and bamboo shoots, and stir-fry for 2 minutes.

3. Add 4 cups of boiling water, lower the heat and simmer for 5 minutes. Add the noodles, bean sprouts, and coriander and simmer for another minute or two, then pour into a soup tureen to serve.

VEGETABLE CONGEE

This rice-based soup differs from many because the vegetables used are dried and not fresh. Some families do use a mixture of both, but my Fujianese friends prefer theirs dried because their parents made it that way. For them, the dried vegetables make it a comfort food. **SERVES 10**

- ¼ cup dried greens, such as kale, watercress, mustard greens, or any combination thereof
- 1 pound fresh pork or chicken bones
- ¼ cup shells from fresh shrimp
- ¼ cup red rice, soaked in water for 2 hours, then drained
- ¼ cup glutinous rice, soaked in water for 1 hour, then drained
- 1 cup long-grain rice, soaked in water for 30 minutes, then drained
- 1 (2-inch) piece dried tangerine peel, soaked in water for 15 minutes, then drained and minced
- 2 slices peeled fresh ginger, slivered
- ¼ teaspoon salt
- ⅛ teaspoon ground white pepper

1. Rinse the dried vegetables well, then soak in 2 quarts of cool water for 3 hours. Discard that water, rinse again, and cut the vegetables into 2-inch lengths.

2. In a large pot, bring 2 quarts of cold water to a boil, add the bones and shells, and boil for 5 minutes. Skim anything floating, then lower the heat and simmer for 1 hour. Remove the bones and shells and discard them, and strain the broth, if necessary.

3. Add the rinsed greens and three kinds of rice to the broth, and simmer for 2 hours, or until all of the rice is very soft. (The recipe can be made to this point one or two days before serving, and refrigerated until needed.)

4. When ready to serve, return the congee to a boil, lower the heat, add the tangerine peel, ginger, salt, and pepper, and simmer for 15 minutes before pouring into a soup tureen to serve.

WINTER MELON SOUP

At a banquet, this soup would be tripled and made in a medium whole winter melon. It would be steamed for an hour and a half and then served. It is so beloved that some families use small winter melons and make just enough for themselves. SERVES 8

1 (3-inch) wedge winter melon (about a pound), peeled and seeded, and cut into 1-inch cubes
1 tablespoon water-chestnut flour or cornstarch
1 tablespoon sesame oil
¼ pound minced or ground pork
2 slices peeled fresh ginger, minced
8 cups chicken or fish stock
1 salted duck egg, mashed with 2 tablespoons cold tea or water
¼ teaspoon salt
1 teaspoon fermented white rice

1. Mix the winter melon pieces with the water-chestnut flour.

2. Put the sesame oil in a large pot and heat over medium heat; after 15 seconds, add the pork and ginger, and stir-fry for 1 minute, then add the winter melon and stir-fry for another minute. Add the chicken stock. Lower the heat and simmer for 30 minutes.

3. Bring the soup mixture to just below the boiling point, add the duck egg, salt, and fermented rice, and stir well. Simmer for 5 minutes, then serve in a scooped out melon shell or put the soup directly into individual bowls.

FISH AND SEAFOOD

WITH ITS MILES AND MILES OF COASTLINE and hundreds of islands, the Fujian province has inspired many of its men to explore for foods from the sea—important components of this provincial cuisine. They are so important and so appreciated that they are eaten alone or with meat, served at almost every meal, and found in almost every dish.

Without question, fish is the culinary ingredient used most often in this province. Countless species have long been harvested and consumed. Recently, some have become commercially bred, making them more plentiful than ever, and even available for export.

No Chinese banquet is complete without a whole fish; no Fujianese meal is complete without two soups and several dishes made with fish. It is not unusual that some meals include many different foods of the sea. There are many varieties used in lunch and dinner dishes; some are served in straightforward fashion, others elaborately mixed or hidden within other foods and other dishes. Some fish are even used as all or part of wrappings for other ingredients such as meats and vegetables.

BEAN CURD, PORK, AND SHRIMP PASTE CASSEROLE

In Fujian, though soups are often served as casseroles, and vice versa, for reasons unknown, this particular recipe rarely comes to the table as a soup. **SERVES 6**

- 3 tablespoons vegetable oil
- 2 squares (about ½ pound) firm bean curd, cut into 1-inch cubes and patted dry with paper towels
- 2 cloves garlic, minced
- 1 to 3 teaspoons shrimp paste
- ½ pound roast pork, cut into 1-inch cubes
- 1 cup chicken, pork, or beef stock
- 1 tablespoon Chinese rice wine
- 1 tablespoon oyster or other fish sauce
- 1 teaspoon sugar
- 1 tablespoon cornstarch mixed with 1 tablespoon cold water
- 2 tablespoons minced Chinese chives

1. Heat the oil and fry the bean curd cubes, stirring constantly, until they are golden. Remove cubes from the pan and set aside. Pour out all but 1 tablespoon of the oil, reserve the rest for another purpose.

2. Reheat the tablespoon of oil and fry the garlic for 30 seconds, then add some shrimp paste and stir-fry for another 30 seconds. Add the pork cubes and stir-fry for 1 minute, then add 1 cup stock, the rice wine, fish sauce, and sugar, and simmer for 3 minutes.

3. Add the cornstarch mixture and boil for a minute or two, until thick. Add the chives, stir, and pour onto a deep serving platter.

BOILED CRABS

Simple this is, ancient as well. No fancy meal in Fujian is complete without crabs. Large ones are boiled and served with one or two dipping sauces. The liquid they are cooked in is often kept to use as a base for another soup or casserole dish. SERVES ONE CRAB PER PERSON

1 medium-to-large crab per person
3 tablespoons white rice wine lees
1 tablespoon Chinese white rice vinegar
1 cup coarsely shredded cabbage

DIPPING SAUCE:
2 tablespoons thin soy sauce
2 tablespoons peeled, minced fresh ginger
1 tablespoon minced scallion, green part only
1 teaspoon sesame oil

1. Put 2 cups of water in a pot large enough to hold the crabs. Add the wine lees, vinegar, and shredded cabbage. Bring to a boil, put the crabs on the cabbage, and cover tightly. Boil this for 10 minutes and then transfer the crabs to a serving platter. Serve with the following or any preferred dipping sauce.

2. For the dipping sauce, mix together the thin soy sauce, fresh ginger, minced scallion, and sesame oil. Serve in a small saucer.

BRAISED SEA CUCUMBER

In *The Taste of China*, published in 2000, Liang Qiongbai includes this Fujianese recipe that, like many others from this region, combines sea and land animals. She recommends choosing the seafood and meat according to personal preference. We make ours with shrimp, scallops, and pork or beef tripe. **SERVES 8 TO 10**

8 very small or 2 large sea cucumbers, soaked
1½ cups vegetable oil
1 scallion, minced
1 slice peeled fresh ginger, minced
2 tablespoons Chinese rice wine
2 cups chicken stock
1 boneless chicken breast half, cut into 1-inch squares
1 egg white
1 tablespoon cornstarch
¼ teaspoon coarse salt
8 small dried Chinese black mushrooms (shiitake), soaked for 20 minutes in warm water, stems discarded
½ fresh bamboo shoot tip, peeled and thinly sliced
¼ pound pork or beef tripe
1 tablespoon white rice wine lees
3 tablespoons thin soy sauce
¼ teaspoon salt
¼ teaspoon ground white pepper
1 teaspoon sugar
8 shrimp, peeled and deveined
4 scallops, quartered

1. Remove and discard the internal organs from the sea cucumbers, and rinse well. Cut into 1-inch pieces. Bring 2 cups of water to a boil and blanch the pieces for 2 minutes. Drain and discard the water.

2. In a wok or skillet, heat ½ cup oil, and fry the scallion and ginger pieces for 1 minute. Add the sea cucumbers, rice wine, and stock, and simmer for 30 minutes. Drain, reserving 1 cup of the liquid and putting aside the rest for another purpose.

3. Mix the chicken with the egg white, cornstarch, and coarse salt, and set aside for 10 minutes. Heat 1 cup of oil, and stir-fry the chicken mixture for 2 minutes, then drain and set the chicken aside, reserving 2 tablespoons of the oil.

4. Heat the reserved oil and stir-fry the mushrooms for 2 minutes, then add the bamboo shoots and tripe and stir-fry for 5 minutes. Add the chicken, reserved cup of stock, wine lees, soy sauce, salt, pepper, and sugar. Bring to a boil, add the sea cucumber, shrimp, and scallops and simmer for 5 minutes. Remove most of the sea cucumber pieces and place them around the rim of a platter. Strain out the other solids and place them in the middle of the dish. Boil the remaining liquid until reduced to about 3 tablespoons, and pour this over the middle of the platter.

BUDDHA JUMPS OVER THE WALL I

This dish is named as it is because people believe that any monk could be tempted, if he caught a whiff of this dish, to vault the wall and leave the monastery to follow the aroma, and indulge in a dish loaded with forbidden foods. (See pages 145 and 147 for two other versions of this recipe.) SERVES 10

- ½ pound pork ribs, cut into 1- to 2-inch lengths
- ½ pork leg, cut into 6 pieces
- 2 chicken legs, each chopped into 3 pieces
- 3 quarts chicken stock
- 10 napa cabbage leaves
- 12 dried Chinese black mushrooms (shiitake), soaked, their stems discarded
- 18 dried chestnuts, peeled with inner skins removed, then soaked for 1 hour and boiled for another hour
- 3 tablespoons mushroom soy sauce
- 3 tablespoons Chinese rice wine
- ½ pound piece of any firm white fish
- ½ presoaked and cleaned sea cucumber, cut into 16 pieces
- 6 ounces shark's fins, simmered for 20 minutes in 2 cups of chicken stock, then drained and the liquid reserved

1. Bring 3 quarts of water to a boil, then reserve 1 quart. Boil the pieces of pork ribs, pork leg, and chicken in 2 quarts of the water for 5 minutes. Drain, and discard the liquid. Pour the reserved 1 quart of boiling water over the meat, then drain and discard this liquid also. Put the 3 quarts of chicken stock in the pot, and bring to a boil. Add the meats, lower the heat, and simmer for 2 hours. Remove the meats and discard the bones, reserving the stock.

2. Line a stove-to-table casserole with cabbage leaves, pour in the reserved chicken stock, and bring almost to a boil before reducing the heat. Add the meats, mushrooms, chestnuts, soy sauce, rice wine, and salt and pepper to taste. Stir well, cover tightly, and simmer for 30 minutes.

3. Add the whole piece of fish, then the sea cucumber, and finally the shark's fins on top. (If the stock in the pot needs replenishing now or later, use some of the reserved shark's fin liquid.) Simmer this mixture for 1 hour, then check to see if the shark's fins are soft. If not, simmer for another 30 minutes and check again. Repeat until they are soft. DO NOT stir the casserole. When done, put the casserole on the table on a cloth or trivet and serve.

CRAB AND NOODLE CAKES

This recipe can be an appetizer or main course. As an appetizer, use half the crabmeat and fry two tablespoons at a time, making small patties, and cut each of these in half before serving. Minced fish or shrimp can replace the crabmeat, as can a mixture of any fish or seafood components. **SERVES 10**

- ½ pound spinach leaves, stems removed
- ½ pound thin egg noodles, cooked and rinsed in cold water
- 1 red chili pepper, seeded and minced
- 1 small red bell pepper, seeded and cut into slivers
- 1 pound cooked crabmeat, all cartilage discarded, minced
- ¼ cup minced fresh coriander (cilantro) leaves
- 1 tablespoon water-chestnut flour
- 2 eggs, beaten well
- 3 tablespoons vegetable oil

1. Blanch the spinach leaves for no more than 1 minute. Drain and coarsely mince, then squeeze out any remaining liquid.

2. Cut the noodles into 3- or 4-inch pieces.

3. Mix together the spinach, noodles, chili pepper, bell pepper, crabmeat, coriander, water-chestnut flour, and eggs.

4. Heat a large flat-bottomed wok or skillet, and heat the oil. Put in the noodle mixture, and gently press down just enough to evenly distribute it. Do not press hard. If no large wok or pan is available, do this in two or three batches. Fry the noodle mixture until golden, then turn over and fry the other side until golden as well. If making in several batches, heat additional oil for each of them.

5. Cut the cake(s) into small triangles and overlap the pieces on a platter. Serve.

CRABMEAT AND SHRIMP BALL CASSEROLE

In Fujian, they like to add several meats to this popular seafood mixture, making the dish even more flavorful. This casserole is more common in southwestern areas of Fujian, and in Fuzhou, the capital city of this province. **SERVES 6 TO 8**

¼ pound crabmeat, simmered for 5 minutes, then drained and coarsely chopped
½ pound raw shrimp, coarsely chopped
¼ pound minced or ground pork
½ teaspoon salt
½ teaspoon sugar
1 tablespoon ginger juice (page 232)
½ teaspoon sesame oil
1 tablespoon minced Chinese chives
1 egg white
¼ cup water-chestnut flour or arrowroot powder
1 cup chicken stock
1 teaspoon vegetable oil
½ teaspoon minced fresh ginger
½ teaspoon minced fresh garlic
1 teaspoon oyster sauce
2 tablespoons cornstarch mixed with 2 tablespoons cold water

1. Mix together the crabmeat, shrimp, and pork. Add the salt, sugar, ginger juice, sesame oil, Chinese chives, and egg white, and gently mix until all are incorporated.

2. Put the water-chestnut flour on a shallow plate. Wet your hands and form the seafood mixture into 1-inch balls, putting them on a second plate. After the balls are made, working with dry hands, roll the balls in the water-chestnut flour to coat. As they are made, put them on a third, dry plate. Let them rest for 15 to 20 minutes, then dust again with any remaining water-chestnut flour.

3. Heat the chicken stock in a medium pot and gently put in the balls. Simmer them for 5 minutes. Remove with a slotted spoon to a preheated serving bowl. Reserve the stock.

4. Heat the vegetable oil and stir-fry the ginger and garlic for 30 seconds, then add the reserved stock and oyster sauce, and reheat almost to the boiling point. Add the balls and simmer for 1 or 2 minutes, or until heated through, then add the cornstarch mixture and stir. As soon as the mixture shows signs of thickening, transfer it and all the contents to the preheated serving bowl.

CRABMEAT, BIRD'S NEST, AND EGG WHITES

This special dish, though expensive to make, is worth the cost and the time needed to prepare it. It is considered a special birthday, holiday, or any festive-occasion food. One crab per person is preferred. **SERVES 4**

6 to 8 tablespoons dried bird's nest	4 or 5 eggs, separated, whites and yolks each beaten well
4 or more whole fresh blue crabs	½ teaspoon salt
1 tablespoon vegetable oil	

1. Soak the bird's nest in 4 cups of warm water for 4 hours, drain and discard the water, and coarsely chop. Preheat the oven to 400°F.

2. Blanch the crabs in boiling water for 1 minute, remove, and let cool about 15 minutes. Remove the crabmeat, discarding any cartilage, and keeping the shells intact. Chop the crabmeat coarsely. Set the shells aside.

3. Heat the oil, mix together the crabmeat and chopped bird's nest, and stir-fry for 2 minutes. Add the egg whites and salt, and stir-fry for another minute. Divide the mixture evenly among the reserved crab shells; pour some egg yolk over the contents of each shell.

4. Put the crab-filled shells on a cookie sheet and bake in the preheated oven for 3 minutes, and then transfer them to a serving platter.

CRAB ROLLS

Swallow-skin wrappers are usually used for this recipe. A mixture of meat and flour, we have never found them commercially available outside of Taiwan and the Fujian province. For possible substitutes, spring or egg roll wrappers come to mind, as does caul fat, a favorite choice. **SERVES 10**

½ cup crabmeat, cartilage removed
½ cup finely shredded pork or pork floss (page 217)
½ cup water chestnuts, minced
2 scallions, minced
1 tablespoon thin soy sauce
1 teaspoon sugar
1 teaspoon sesame oil
¼ teaspoon ground white pepper
1 large piece of caul fat, cut into 6-inch squares, or 10 spring roll wrappers
1 egg white
1 tablespoon cornstarch
1 cup corn oil

1. Mix together the crabmeat, pork (or pork floss), water chestnuts, scallions, soy sauce, sugar, sesame oil, and white pepper. Put 3 tablespoons of the mixture on a wrapper and roll, folding in the sides. Seal with egg white, dust with cornstarch, and set aside. Repeat until all the filling is wrapped and sealed.

2. Heat the corn oil and deep-fry the rolls for 3 to 4 minutes, or until golden brown, turning them several times. It is best to fry a few at a time, and repeat until all are fried. Serve the crab rolls with a dipping sauce mixture of light soy sauce, sesame oil, and slivers of garlic, or another sauce of your choice.

EEL WITH HOISIN AND OYSTER SAUCES

Coating the eel only with cornstarch was once the preferred way to prepare this eel dish. More in keeping with the times, some folks use dried potato granules or potato flakes. Our testing determined a mixture of half cornstarch, half potato flakes was appreciated the most. **SERVES 8**

- 1 pound eel, skinned, boned, gutted, and cut into 2-inch pieces
- 3 tablespoons hoisin sauce
- 2 tablespoons oyster sauce
- ¼ teaspoon salt
- ¼ teaspoon ground white pepper
- 1 tablespoon dark or mushroom soy sauce
- 1 tablespoon minced, peeled fresh ginger
- ½ teaspoon sesame oil
- ½ teaspoon chili oil
- ½ cup cornstarch
- ½ cup instant potato flakes
- ½ cup corn oil

1. Pat the eel dry with paper towels.

2. In a glass or ceramic bowl mix together the hoisin and oyster sauces, then add the salt, pepper, soy sauce, ginger, and sesame and chili oils. Add the eel and stir until well-coated. Cover and allow to marinate in the refrigerator for 3 hours or overnight.

3. Mix the cornstarch and potato flakes together on a shallow plate. Remove the eel from the refrigerator and let rest at room temperature for 1 hour. Using a fork, take a piece of eel out of the marinade, let the excess liquid drip off, and roll the piece in the cornstarch mixture. Set aside on a dry plate. Repeat until all the pieces have been coated.

4. Heat the corn oil and add the eel, one piece at a time, until half have been put in the oil. Do this slowly so that they do not stick to one another. Gently stir-fry for 5 minutes. Remove from the oil and drain on paper towels. Repeat the process with the rest of the eel pieces. Mix both batches together in a deep serving bowl. Serve hot.

EEL WITH RED RICE WINE LEES

This recipe appeared in *Flavor and Fortune* in 2002. Several letters arrived soon after, praising it and the other eel recipes in that issue. Though new and appreciated by the magazine's readers, it is not a new dish to the Fujianese. **SERVES 6 TO 12**

3 tablespoons red rice wine lees
3 tablespoons dark soy sauce
2 tablespoons Chinese rice wine
1 teaspoon sesame oil
¼ teaspoon ground white pepper
¼ teaspoon garlic powder
2 eggs, separated
1 pound eel, skinned, boned, gutted, and cut into 6-inch lengths
½ cup water-chestnut or sweet-potato flour
1 cup corn oil

1. In a bowl combine the wine lees, soy sauce, rice wine, sesame oil, ground pepper, garlic powder, and egg yolks, and mix well. Marinate the eel pieces in this mixture for 30 minutes.

2. Beat the egg whites until stiff and then beat in the water-chestnut flour, making an egg-white batter.

3. Heat the corn oil and dip six to eight pieces of eel, one by one, into the batter. Carefully drop each as it is coated into the hot oil. When lightly browned, remove and set on paper towels to drain. Repeat until all the eel pieces are battered, fried, and drained. Transfer to a platter and serve with a dipping sauce of your choice or a salt-pepper mix.

FIRECRACKER SHRIMP WITH LITCHI

While the title of most dishes names their main ingredient first, a few are known for their visual impressions, as is this one. Many Chinese keep a poster in their kitchen depicting the Kitchen God. This dish is often served on the day the Kitchen God's lips are sealed with sugar or maltose before his picture is burned and sent to heaven. On that day, firecrackers simulate the sound of horses' hooves speeding him on his journey. **SERVES 5 TO 10**

- ½ pound fresh shrimp, peeled, deveined, and minced
- 2 tablespoons minced fresh pork belly (raw unsmoked bacon)
- 6 canned or fresh litchi fruits, coarsely minced
- ½ teaspoon salt
- ½ teaspoon sugar
- 1 tablespoon cornstarch
- 1 teaspoon sesame oil
- 10 small whole canned water chestnuts
- 2 tablespoons minced Yunnan or Smithfield ham
- 2 coriander (cilantro) stems, each cut into 5 small pieces
- 1 teaspoon vegetable oil

1. Mix together the minced shrimp and pork thoroughly. Gently mix in the minced litchi fruit, and then gently stir in the salt, sugar, cornstarch, and sesame oil. Divide into ten parts, and roll each portion around one water chestnut.

2. Roll each covered water chestnut into one-tenth of the ham, and poke one cilantro stem into its top.

3. Use the vegetable oil to brush the bottom of a flat, heatproof plate or platter that will fit into a steamer. Set the firecracker balls on it, none touching another.

4. Steam the balls for 5 minutes over rapidly boiling water, then remove and serve.

FISH BALL CASSEROLE

The Fujianese make plain fish balls and then add minced meat either by mixing it in, or more commonly by making a tiny meatball and enclosing that in the fish paste mixture. This dish can be made both ways. Increase the amount of fish when using it to enclose the meat. **SERVES 6 TO 8**

½ pound skinless, filleted white-fleshed fish
1½ teaspoons sesame oil
Pinch of ground white pepper
1 tablespoon cornstarch
2 eggs, beaten
1 cup vegetable oil
2 slices peeled fresh ginger, slivered
1 teaspoon thin soy sauce
1 teaspoon sugar
1 teaspoon oyster sauce
½ pound Shanghai or other Chinese cabbage, cut into 1-inch pieces
¼ carrot, peeled and thinly sliced

1. Mince the fish, then add ½ teaspoon of the sesame oil, the white pepper and cornstarch. Mix well, add the beaten eggs, and stir again until the texture feels sticky.

2. Use a tablespoon of vegetable oil to lubricate two Chinese soup spoons or another type of large tablespoon. Preheat a casserole.

3. In a wok or large pot, heat the remaining vegetable oil, and using the oiled spoons, put a heaping spoonful of the fish mixture on one spoon and use the other spoon to help gently drop three or four fish balls at a time into the hot oil. Fry them until lightly browned, and then drain on paper towels. Repeat until all the fish paste is made into balls and fried. Retain 1 tablespoon of the oil in the wok, and pour off the rest to keep for another use.

4. Reheat the wok and stir-fry the ginger slivers in the remaining oil for about 30 seconds. Add the soy sauce, sugar, oyster sauce, and remaining teaspoon of sesame oil and stir-fry for 1 minute. Add 1 cup of water and the cabbage and carrot slices, and simmer for 2 minutes, then add the fish balls and simmer for another minute. Pour into the preheated casserole to serve.

FISH CAKES

Traditionally made with shark, these fish cakes can be made with virtually any white-fleshed sea creature. They are good with cod, catfish, scallops, a mixture of shrimp and scallops, etc. A small amount of meat can be added, if desired, and many Fujianese families like that addition. **SERVES 10**

- 1 pound skinless, boneless fresh fish fillet, minced
- ¼ pound minced or ground pork
- 2 scallions, minced
- 1 tablespoon Fujianese rice wine or white rice wine lees
- Pinch of ground white pepper
- ½ teaspoon coarse salt
- ½ teaspoon sugar
- 1 tablespoon vegetable oil
- 2 tablespoons Chinese red rice wine
- 2 tablespoons thin soy sauce
- 1 tablespoon cornstarch

1. Combine the fish with the pork and scallions. Gently mix in the rice wine, pepper, salt, and sugar. Shape into five large balls and slightly flatten each one.

2. Heat a wok or heavy pan, then add the oil. When heated, add the fish cakes and fry on one side until golden. Turn over, and fry until golden on the other side.

3. Mix together the wine, soy sauce, and cornstarch and pour over the fish cakes. Cook until the liquid is reduced by half, about 2 minutes. Cut each fish cake into two or four pieces, and transfer them and the sauce into a serving bowl.

FISH SLICES WITH SWEET AND SOUR WINE SAUCE

This Fujianese recipe is adapted from one by Pei Mei Fu, thanks to permission from her daughter Angela. It is in Madam Fu's *Best Selections Chinese Cuisine I*. Put the fish on the plate or platter first, then pour the sauce over it. The fish must be handled carefully, as it breaks apart easily. **SERVES 10**

4 ounces bean thread noodles
1 tablespoon vegetable or sesame oil
2-pound whole freshwater fish
2 scallions
2 slices peeled fresh ginger
1 teaspoon coarse salt
3 tablespoons vegetable oil
2 large cloves garlic, peeled and coarsely minced
¼ red chili or sweet red pepper, coarsely minced
1 to 2 tablespoons dried shrimp, soaked for 10 minutes, then coarsely minced
2 tablespoons Chinese rice wine
½ cup chicken broth
3 tablespoons Chinese black rice vinegar
2 tablespoons sugar
1 tablespoon black soy sauce
1 tablespoon thin soy sauce
1 tablespoon cornstarch mixed with 2 tablespoons of cold water
1 teaspoon salt
¼ teaspoon ground white pepper
¼ teaspoon ground black pepper
1 teaspoon hot oil

1. Cook the bean thread noodles in boiling water for 1 to 2 minutes, drain very well, mix with 1 tablespoon of vegetable or sesame oil, and set out on a deep platter with 1-inch sides.

2. Remove the scales from the fish, then skin and gut, remove the center and fin bones, and divide the flesh into ten pieces. Cut 1 inch of white from each scallion and then tie the 2 long pieces in knots. Bring 3 to 4 cups water to a boil, add the knotted scallions, ginger, and coarse salt, and lower the heat. Gently immerse the fish pieces in this liquid and simmer for 3 minutes. Carefully remove the fish and place on top of the bean thread noodles.

3. Mince the reserved white parts of the scallions. Heat the vegetable oil, add the minced scallions, minced garlic, red pepper, and dried shrimp, and stir-fry for 1 minute. Add all the remaining ingredients. Bring to a boil, stirring until thick and somewhat clear. Pour the sauce over the fish and serve.

FISH-STUFFED BEAN CURD IN CASSEROLE

This recipe is typical of a dish that can be used as a soup or a casserole. All or part of the bean curd can be used in this casserole, as can other protein ingredients such as meatballs or chicken wings. **SERVES 8 TO 10**

- 4 or 5 leaves Chinese cabbage, each cut into 4 pieces
- 1 recipe Fish-stuffed Bean Curd (see page 23)
- 5 dried Chinese black mushrooms (shiitake), soaked for 20 minutes, stems removed, cut in half
- 1 teaspoon sugar
- 1 tablespoon oyster sauce
- 2 teaspoons thin soy sauce
- 1 teaspoon sesame oil
- 2 tablespoons minced Yunnan or Smithfield ham
- 1 cup chicken broth
- 2 tablespoons cornstarch mixed with 2 tablespoons cold water

1. Line a casserole, clay pot, or Yunnan pot with the cabbage leaves, and put the fish-stuffed pieces of bean curd on them, preferably in a single layer.

2. Distribute the mushrooms around and on the bean curd.

3. Mix together all the remaining ingredients except the cornstarch mixture and pour over the tofu. Cover and steam for 10 minutes, then add the cornstarch mixture, gently stirring it into the pot. Cover and steam for another 10 minutes. Set the pot on a trivet and serve.

FIVE FOR FIVE OYSTER CAKES

Where or when this dish received this fanciful name, I never could learn. One variation appeared in *Flavor and Fortune* and is on the magazine's Web site. Different chefs and different families make different quantities of oyster cakes, depending upon the number of people to be served, and most of them make the cakes small in size. **SERVES 8 TO 10**

- 5 tablespoons chopped oysters (about 5 large or 10 small ones)
- 5 tablespoons shredded, peeled fresh taro root or carrots
- 5 tablespoons shredded Chinese celery cabbage, or shredded spinach
- 5 cloves garlic, minced
- 5 scallions, slivered
- 1 teaspoon thin soy sauce
- ½ teaspoon sugar
- ¼ teaspoon ground white pepper
- ¼ teaspoon five-spice powder
- ½ cup all-purpose flour
- ½ cup cornstarch
- 1 cup corn oil

1. Combine the oysters, taro root, cabbage, garlic, scallions, soy sauce, sugar, pepper, and five-spice powder.

2. Mix together the flour, cornstarch, and 2 tablespoons of cool water, then mix this into the oyster mixture.

3. Heat the oil. Immerse an empty ladle in the oil until it is hot. Take it out and fill the ladle half full with some of the oyster mixture. Immediately immerse the ladle and its contents under the surface of the oil until the mixture starts to set. At that point, tip the partially set contents into the oil and fry until golden, turning several times. Remove with a slotted spoon and drain on paper towels, immediately flattening it into a cake. Transfer to a heatproof plate in a warm, not hot oven. Repeat until all the oyster mixture has been fried. These oyster cakes can be served with or without a dipping sauce of your choice.

FRIED SQUID IN SHRIMP PASTE

Liang Qiongbai writes that seafood is a specialty of Fuzhou cooking, and that this recipe, adapted here from her book, *The Taste of China*, is made with staples found in most Fujianese homes. Commercially prepared shrimp paste must be stored in the refrigerator and keeps for about a year. Homemade shrimp paste keeps only two or three days. **SERVES 8 TO 10**

- 2 dried whole squid, soaked overnight in cold water, changing the water several times
- 2 cups vegetable oil
- ½ tablespoon minced, peeled fresh ginger
- ½ tablespoon minced garlic
- 2 tablespoons shrimp paste
- 1 tablespoon Chinese rice wine
- 1 teaspoon sugar
- 4 stalks coriander (cilantro), washed and then cut into ½-inch sections with their leaves

1. Drain the squid and discard the soaking water. Dry with paper towels, then remove and discard any membranes. Cut each squid lengthwise into three long sections, then across into 1-inch pieces. Score each piece lengthwise and crosswise, making the cuts as close together as possible without cutting through each small piece.

2. Heat the oil in a wok or a small deep pan and fry half the squid until it curls slightly, flowers out, and looks lovely. Remove and drain. Repeat with the rest of the pieces. Remove all but 1 or 2 tablespoons of the oil, and discard or reserve the rest for another use. Preheat a platter.

3. Reheat the oil remaining in the pan, fry the ginger and garlic for 30 seconds, then add the shrimp paste, wine, and sugar, and stir well. Add all of the squid and stir well, then add the coriander and mix well. Transfer to the preheated platter.

LOTUS ROOT WITH OYSTERS

This dish, like many others, can be an appetizer or a main course. If used as a main course, make the patties larger. The patties can be quartered and added to soup, or used as filler in any number of casseroles. Some children like to take them to school for lunch, and do so, but only in cold weather. **SERVES 6 TO 8**

- 1 cup peeled and minced lotus root
- ½ cup minced fresh oysters
- 2 dried Chinese black mushrooms (shiitake), soaked, stems removed, minced
- 2 eggs, beaten
- ½ teaspoon chicken bouillon powder
- 1 teaspoon salt
- 3 tablespoons sweet-potato flour
- 2 tablespoons cornstarch
- 3 tablespoons vegetable oil

1. Mix together the lotus root, oysters, mushrooms, eggs, chicken bouillon, salt, and sweet-potato flour. Shape into patties, and dust them on both sides with the cornstarch. Preheat a platter.

2. Heat the oil in a wok or skillet, and fry half the patties for 2 minutes or until lightly browned, turn over, and fry them for another minute. Drain and transfer to the preheated platter. Repeat until all are fried and drained. Serve hot.

OYSTER OMELET

This is one of the most popular Fujian dishes. There are many variations; it can be made adding or eliminating a plethora of other foods of the sea or land, including vegetables. Various milks, such as cow, soy, yak, or evaporated milk, can be added to the variations. Canned oysters can be used, but fresh ones are preferred. **SERVES 6 TO 8**

1 tablespoon oil
¼ cup ground or minced pork
4 eggs, beaten until light in color
½ cup milk or water
2 tablespoons sweet-potato flour
1 teaspoon oyster sauce
½ teaspoon salt
1 scallion, minced
8 fresh, shucked oysters, dried on paper towels and cut in half
2 tablespoons coarsely diced fresh or dried and soaked mushrooms
2 tablespoons coarsely diced water chestnuts

1. Heat a wok or skillet, then heat the oil. Stir-fry the pork for 1 minute or until it just begins to lose its pink color.

2. Mix together the beaten eggs, milk, flour, oyster sauce, salt, and scallion, and pour into the pan. As the mixture starts to set, add the oysters, mushrooms, and water chestnuts. Then tilt the pan so some of the egg mixture slides under the setting eggs.

3. When the egg mixture is firm around the edges and only a little liquid remains, turn the omelet, and after 1 minute, slide it onto a platter. Cut in six to eight triangular pieces and serve.

RAZOR CLAMS WITH BLACK BEAN SAUCE

There are many variations of this popular dish in Fujian and throughout China. While its name may say "Cantonese" to some, the inclusion of rice wine lees makes it distinctively Fujian. SERVES 4 TO 6

- 1 pound razor clams, blanched in boiling water for 1 minute, clams removed and shells discarded
- 1 tablespoon fermented black beans, rinsed and mashed
- 1 teaspoon sugar
- 2 tablespoons red rice wine lees
- 2 tablespoons oyster sauce
- 1 tablespoon thin soy sauce
- ¼ teaspoon salt
- 2 tablespoons vegetable oil
- 2 tablespoons minced or ground pork
- 2 scallions, minced

1. Slice the razor clams in half the long way, and set them aside.

2. Mix together the mashed black beans, sugar, wine lees, oyster and soy sauces, and salt, and set aside.

3. Heat a wok or skillet, heat the oil, add the ground pork, and stir-fry for 1 minute. Add the black bean mixture and stir-fry for 1 minute. Add the razor clams and stir-fry another minute. Transfer this to a serving platter and sprinkle the scallions on top.

SEA CUCUMBER, SPARERIBS, AND SWEET POTATO

This recipe is a variation of one made at Hsin-Nan-Hsuan, a famous restaurant. It was first reported by Pei Mei Fu, whose well-known version is made with more spareribs than sea cucumber and a combination of white and sweet potatoes. My Fujianese friends prefer theirs made only with sweet potatoes. One of them shared this recipe. **SERVES 10**

1 cup vegetable oil
1 pound sweet potatoes, peeled and cut into 2-inch pieces
2 pounds spareribs, pork preferred, cut into 2-inch pieces
2 tablespoons cornstarch mixed with 1 tablespoon cold water
6 scallions, cut in 2-inch lengths
¼ cup red rice wine lees
¼ cup thin soy sauce
2 cups stock
2 pounds sea cucumbers, soaked in water in the refrigerator overnight, any inside matter removed
2 tablespoons Chinese black rice vinegar
½ cup coarsely chopped coriander (cilantro) leaves
1 tablespoon mixed ground white and black pepper

1. Heat a wok or pan, heat the oil, and deep-fry the sweet potatoes for 3 or 4 minutes, just until the outsides are crisp. Remove with a slotted spoon and drain on paper towels, then set aside.

2. In the same oil, deep-fry the spareribs for 10 minutes; drain them and reserve 2 tablespoons of their oil. Remove or leave the meat on the bones. Put the spareribs in a heatproof bowl that will fit in a steamer. Toss them with the cornstarch mixture.

3. Heat the reserved 2 tablespoons of oil, and stir-fry the scallions for 1 minute, then add half the wine lees, half the soy sauce, and half the stock, mixing well. Put into the bowl with the spareribs, place the uncovered bowl in a steamer, cover the steamer and steam for 1 hour.

4. Add the sweet potatoes to the center of the bowl and steam for another 20 minutes. Uncover and allow to rest until needed.

5. Put the sea cucumber pieces into a pot with the remaining wine lees, soy sauce, and stock, and bring to a boil. Lower the heat, cover and simmer for 1 hour.

6. Take out the sea cucumbers and slice each once lengthwise and three or four times widthwise. Return them to the pot, add the vinegar and coriander, and simmer 10 minutes longer.

7. To serve, drain the sea cucumber pieces and put around the rim of a large, deep platter. Unmold the sparerib mixture in the center of the platter, and sprinkle ground pepper over all.

SHARK'S FIN AND EGGS

This dish is commonly made using oiled Chinese soup spoons as the holders when steaming. If not available, use small smooth-edge ramekins that can go into a steamer, and coat them with oil before filling them. (Ramekins with scalloped edges are difficult to use because the contents do not come out easily.)
SERVES 10

1 tablespoon oil
4 eggs, beaten
¼ cup ½-inch pieces shark's fin
¼ cup dried Chinese black mushrooms (shiitake), soaked, stems discarded, minced coarsely
¼ cup coarsely minced bamboo shoots
¼ cup minced fresh scallops
1 tablespoon minced fresh coriander (cilantro) leaves
1 teaspoon sesame oil
1 cup chicken broth
1 teaspoon salt
½ teaspoon sugar
Pinch of ground white pepper
1 teaspoon cornstarch

1. Oil twenty Chinese ceramic soup spoons or small ramekins. Set the remaining oil aside.

2. Mix together the beaten eggs, shark's fin, mushrooms, bamboo shoots, scallops, and coriander. Pour equal amounts of this mixture into the oiled spoons or ramekins and carefully set them in a steamer. Steam for 7 minutes or until set. Ease the mixture out from each spoon with a skewer or thin knife onto a lightly oiled plate.

3. Pour the sesame oil into an unheated pan, add the egg ovals, turn the heat to high, and fry them on one side until lightly browned. Transfer them to a serving plate with low sides. Serve.

4. In a small pot, mix together the broth, salt, sugar, pepper, and cornstarch. Bring to a boil, and pour over the ovals.

SHRIMP WITH SEAWEED

This dish is made with slivered green seaweed. The Japanese call this type of seaweed *nori*. Once I used half green, half purple seaweed, alternating them, and that dish received rave reviews. When presenting as a first or last course, add a teaspoon of sugar to the cornstarch before incorporating it. **SERVES 10**

- 20 large shrimp, deveined, shelled, heads and tails left on, the shrimp bodies slit open but not cut through (butterflied)
- 1 tablespoon white rice wine lees
- 1 tablespoon Chinese white rice wine
- 2 teaspoons sesame oil
- 1 teaspoon thin soy sauce
- 2 tablespoons cornstarch
- 2 egg whites, beaten until frothy
- 2 to 3 tablespoons slivered green or other color seaweed, or some of both
- 1 tablespoon minced fresh ginger
- 2 cups vegetable oil
- ¼ cup coarsely chopped coriander (cilantro) leaves or any edible flower

1. Put the shrimp in a bowl with the wine lees, rice wine, sesame oil, and soy sauce; mix well, then cover and marinate for 30 minutes in the refrigerator. Remove the shrimp from the marinade, then coat with cornstarch.

2. Mix the shrimp with the beaten egg whites, then coat each tail section on both sides with one or the other seaweed, shaking off any excess. Sprinkle with the ginger and press it on.

3. Heat the oil and deep-fry half the shrimp for 1 minute. Using a slotted spoon, drain on paper towels. Repeat with the rest of the shrimp.

4. Put the coriander in the center of a platter. Place the shrimp around the rim.

SHRIMP WRAPPED IN ALMONDS

Almonds, usually sliced, and pine nuts, commonly crushed coarsely, are popular coatings for fish and seafood. They are used for both deep-frying and sautéing. These nuts may be mixed with the fish or shrimp paste. They can also be used on other foods when braising them. **SERVES 8 TO 10**

1 pound shrimp, peeled and deveined
¼ pound beef or fatty pork, minced or ground
1 egg white
2 tablespoons sweet-potato flour
½ teaspoon salt
⅛ teaspoon ground white pepper
¼ teaspoon sugar
3 tablespoons minced coriander (cilantro) leaves
1 small piece (about 1-inch by 1-inch) soaked dried tangerine peel, minced
1 cup sliced almonds, peeled if available, or coarsely chopped pine nuts
1 cup vegetable oil

1. Mince half the shrimp coarsely and set aside. Finely mince the other half, and mix with the beef, egg white, sweet-potato flour, salt, pepper, and sugar. Shape the mixture into small balls.

2. Roll each ball in the coarsely chopped shrimp, then in the minced coriander, then in the minced tangerine peel, and finally in the chopped almonds. Flatten each roll gently and allow to dry for an hour, turning each ball once. Preheat a platter.

3. Heat a wok or skillet, heat the oil, and fry half the shrimp over medium heat until golden and crisp, then turn and fry the other side. Remove with a slotted spoon and drain on paper towels. Transfer to the preheated platter. Repeat with the second batch. Serve hot.

SPICY CLAMS WITH BASIL

Small clams are preferred, as they will remain softer and juicier in this recipe; large clams often toughen more quickly. The basil used in the Fujian province is Thai basil which is milder than the Italian variety. **SERVES 6 TO 8**

- 1 tablespoon vinegar
- 1 tablespoon cornstarch mixed with 2 cups cold water
- 1 pound small clams, less than 2 inches across, shells scrubbed with a brush
- 2 tablespoons vegetable oil
- 2 scallions, cut into ½-inch pieces
- 2 cloves garlic, peeled and cut into 4 pieces each
- 1 teaspoon Chinese barbecue sauce (*sacha*), or other fermented fish sauce
- 1 tablespoon Fujianese rice wine
- 2 tablespoons thin soy sauce
- Pinch of ground white pepper
- 2 tablespoons coarsely chopped Thai basil leaves
- ½ cup thinly sliced and seeded red and green bell pepper

1. Mix together the vinegar and cornstarch water, and soak the clams in this mixture for 1 hour. Drain and discard the liquid. Preheat a platter.

2. Heat the oil and stir-fry the scallions, garlic, and *sacha* sauce for 1 minute, then add the clams, rice wine, soy sauce, and white pepper, and stir-fry until the clam shells open, about 2 or 3 minutes. Discard any clams that do not open. Add the basil and peppers, and stir-fry for another minute before transferring to the preheated platter. Serve.

Steamed Fish in Sweet-Potato Flour

Using a wrap or a coating for foods is common in the Fujian province. So is changing a food's texture by chopping it. Vegetables are chopped finely on some occasions and chopped coarsely on others. **SERVES 4 TO 6**

- 1-pound fish fillet (such as flounder or sea bass), cut into 4 pieces
- 1 teaspoon hot sauce
- 1 teaspoon light soy sauce
- 1 teaspoon Fujianese white rice wine or white rice wine lees
- ½ teaspoon sugar
- ½ teaspoon sesame oil
- 1 cup sweet-potato flour
- ¼ cup coarsely chopped pickled mustard greens

1. Dry the fish, using paper towels. Mix together in a medium bowl the hot and soy sauces, wine, sugar, and oil. Add the fish, cover and marinate in the refrigerator for 1 hour or overnight.

2. Remove the fish from the marinade and coat it with the sweet-potato flour. Set aside for 30 minutes on a heatproof plate that can be used in a steamer. The flour coating should seem wet by that time.

3. Top the fish with the pickled mustard greens and place in a steamer over rapidly boiling water for 8 to 10 minutes. The amount of time depends upon the thickness of the fish (e.g., flounder needs less time, sea bass needs more). Preheat a platter. Remove the fish to the preheated platter and serve.

STEAMED FISH WITH LITCHI

These fish rolls can be made sweet, as in this recipe, or piquant. They can also be served without a sauce. If the latter, make the pieces of fish larger, slicing them widthwise. SERVES 6

3 skinless, boneless pieces of a white fish, each about half a pound
1 tablespoon Fujianese white rice wine
1 egg white
1 tablespoon sweet-potato flour
6 fresh or canned litchi fruits, peeled and pitted
2 slices fresh or canned pineapple
2 tablespoons vegetable oil

SWEET SAUCE:
¾ cup chicken stock
4 teaspoons rice vinegar
1 tablespoon tomato sauce
1 tablespoon cornstarch mixed with 2 tablespoons water or canned litchi juice

1. Cut each piece of fish in half lengthwise, and twice widthwise, making six pieces from each. Mix together the rice wine, egg white, and flour and then marinate the fish in this mixture for 30 minutes. Preheat a platter.

2. Quarter the litchi fruits. Cut the pineapple into thin strips. Oil a heatproof plate that will fit in a steamer. Put some pieces of each fruit on the short end of a fish piece and roll. Place the rolled fish seam side down on the oiled plate. Repeat until all fish pieces are rolled. Place in a steamer and steam for 6 minutes (8 if using large fish pieces). Remove to the preheated platter. Serve with the sweet sauce on the side.

SWEET SAUCE: Heat together chicken stock, rice vinegar, and tomato sauce, add cornstarch mixed with an equal amount of cold water, and heat and stir until thickened.

Stewed Eel with Mushrooms and Pork

This recipe first appeared in *Flavor and Fortune* in 2002. It was given to the magazine by a reader who lived in Amoy, now called Xiamen. She said her grandmother made it often and that the people of her grandmother's generation loved it, as does she. **SERVES 6 TO 8**

- 1 pound eel, skinned, boned, and gutted, and cut into 2-inch sections
- 6 dried Chinese black mushrooms (shiitake), soaked for 30 minutes, stems removed, then quartered
- ¼ pound pork belly (fresh bacon) cut into 3-inch pieces
- 1 cup corn oil
- 6 whole cloves garlic
- ¼ cup soaked tangerine peel, slivered
- 4 scallions, cut into 1-inch pieces
- 2 slices peeled fresh ginger, slivered
- 3 cups chicken broth
- ¼ teaspoon ground white pepper
- ½ teaspoon salt
- 2 tablespoons dark soy sauce
- 2 tablespoons Chinese rice wine
- 2 tablespoons cornstarch mixed with 2 tablespoons cold water
- 2 tablespoons sesame oil

1. Mix together the eel, mushrooms, and pork belly, and blanch them in boiling water for 1 minute, then drain. Meanwhile, heat the corn oil in another pot. Blanch the eel mixture again, this time in the hot oil, for 1 minute. Drain well. Reserve 1 teaspoon of the oil and keep the rest for another use. Preheat a serving bowl.

2. Heat the 1 teaspoon of reserved oil and fry the garlic, tangerine peel, scallions, and ginger for 30 seconds, then add the broth, pepper, salt, soy sauce, and wine, and bring to a boil. Add the eel mixture, lower the heat, and simmer for 20 minutes.

3. Increase the heat and add the cornstarch mixture. Stir until the sauce thickens and clears, then add the sesame oil and transfer to the preheated bowl.

STUFFED FISH

Sweet potatoes are popular in Fujian. They are used here to stuff a fish, a unique way to cook and serve it in this part of China. Also unique is simmering the fish in soy sauce and water so it is tinted red and loaded with flavor. **SERVES 8 TO 10**

½ cup vegetable oil
1 (12- to 18-inch) *yaotai* (fried dough stick), sliced into ½-inch pieces
1 (2-pound) whole fish (such as sea bass, red snapper, or grouper), gutted and scaled
1 tablespoon cornstarch
4 ounces ground pork
½ cup cooked mashed sweet potato
1 egg, beaten
1 teaspoon rice wine
¼ teaspoon ground white pepper
½ cup preserved mustard greens, rinsed and minced
3 slices peeled fresh ginger, minced
3 scallions, minced
1 small fresh hot chili pepper, minced
3 tablespoons sweet-potato flour
2 tablespoons dark soy sauce
½ cup fish stock

1. Heat the oil and deep-fry the dough stick pieces for about 2 minutes, or until crisp and golden. Remove using a slotted spoon, drain on paper towels. Reserve the leftover oil.

2. Rinse and dry the fish. Dust the cavity with cornstarch.

3. Mix together the pork, mashed sweet potato, egg, rice wine, and ground pepper, and use this to stuff the cavity of the fish.

4. Place the fish on a heatproof platter that fits into a steamer.

5. Mix together the mustard greens, ginger, scallions, and chili pepper, and place them on top of the fish. Then cover the steamer and steam the fish for 15 minutes over rapidly boiling water. Remove the platter, and put the fried dough stick pieces around the fish.

6. Heat a wok, pouring in the reserved oil. Mix together the sweet-potato flour, soy sauce, and stock, and add to the hot oil. Pour over the fish and serve.

SQUID WITH GREENS

The squid in this dish can be served separately from the vegetables or they can be stirred together before serving. They can be put under or on top of any sauce. Chinese spinach, celtuce, Chinese chives, and bok choy are a few examples of possible vegetables. SERVES 6 TO 8

- ½ pound squid, cleaned and cut into 1-inch pieces, then scored on the top sides
- 1 tablespoon sesame oil
- 1 tablespoon corn or other vegetable oil
- 6 slices peeled fresh ginger, slivered
- 1 pound Chinese green vegetables (see above), cut into 2-inch lengths
- 1 tablespoon red rice wine lees
- 1 tablespoon white rice wine lees
- 1 teaspoon Chinese white rice vinegar
- ¼ teaspoon sugar
- ¼ teaspoon salt
- ⅛ teaspoon ground white pepper

1. Blanch the squid in boiling water for 30 seconds, then remove and drain well, spreading out the pieces so they do not touch one another on a plate.

2. Heat the oils, and fry the ginger for 1 minute. Add the vegetables and stir-fry them just until wilted (usually a minute), then add both wine lees, the vinegar, sugar, salt, and white pepper, and stir well. Add the squid and stir-fry for just a minute more. Serve.

UP AND DOWN SHRIMP

Fujian has many well-populated mountainous areas. A plethora of herbs grow at all elevations and are gathered for personal use and/or to sell in local, regional, and distant marketplaces. This recipe reflects the bounty of these regions and the provincial coastal areas. SERVES 10

- 1 pound extra-large shrimp, peeled and deveined, leaving on their tail shells
- 2 tablespoons dried Chinese wolfberries (goji berries)
- 5 pitted dried Chinese black dates, cut in half
- 2 dried Chinese brown dates, soaked for 10 minutes, then coarsely chopped
- 5 pitted dried Chinese red dates, cut in half
- 2 pieces dried licorice
- 1 (2-inch) stick cinnamon
- 4 tiny dried shrimp, minced
- ¼ cup Chinese red rice wine
- 1 teaspoon white or red rice wine lees
- ½ teaspoon Chinese black rice vinegar
- ½ teaspoon salt

1. Cut the shrimp lengthwise including through the tail shell and soak in cold water.

2. Put the wolfberries, dates, licorice, cinnamon stick, and dried shrimp in a pot with 2 cups of water. Simmer for 20 minutes. Remove the licorice and cinnamon stick and then simmer for another 10 minutes.

3. Add the wine, wine lees, vinegar, salt, and large shrimp. Turn off the heat, cover, and let steep for 15 minutes. Preheat a bowl during this time. Uncover the shrimp mixture and transfer to the preheated bowl. Serve.

SEAFOOD CASSEROLE

Any number of seafood items can be used in this winter recipe. This dish is always served with plain white rice, very thin noodles, or both. Sometimes, leftover rice is added at the last minute just before it is served. **SERVES 10**

5 large or 10 small scallops
10 medium shrimp, peeled, deveined, and cut in half
10 shucked medium clams, or 6 shucked razor clams, cut in half the short way
10 shucked medium mussels
¼ cup white rice wine lees
6 slices peeled fresh ginger, each cut in half
3 cloves garlic, peeled, each cut in half
1 tablespoon sesame oil
1 cup shredded cabbage
2 scallions, cut into 2-inch pieces
1 ounce bean thread noodles, soaked for 15 minutes in warm water, then drained
2 cups chicken broth
2 tablespoons Chinese black rice vinegar
½ cup coarsely minced fresh coriander (cilantro) leaves, plus 2 whole sprigs for garnish

1. Put the scallops, shrimp, clams, mussels, wine lees, ginger, garlic, and sesame oil in a bowl and let marinate for 30 minutes.

2. Put the cabbage in a large stove-to-table casserole, add the scallion pieces, and put the bean thread noodles on top.

3. Heat the broth, add the vinegar, and pour this over the cabbage mixture. Add the seafood mixture. Do not stir, simply bring it to a boil, lower the heat, and simmer for 10 minutes. Gently mix in the chopped coriander and then decorate with the whole sprigs. Serve.

CHICKEN AND CHESTNUTS

This is a popular everyday dish. Leftovers can be added to a breakfast congee or served as a snack during the day. It does not need reheating as it is enjoyed cold. This dish can be and often is made with duck, rabbit, frog's legs, or most other meats. **SERVES 6 TO 8**

¼ pound cooked and peeled chestnuts
1 tablespoon vegetable oil
1 clove garlic, minced
½ chicken with skin, chopped into 2-inch pieces (can be boneless or on the bone, the preferred way)
1 teaspoon dark soy sauce
1 teaspoon thin soy sauce
1 teaspoon oyster sauce
1 teaspoon yellow bean paste
1 teaspoon sugar
1 teaspoon sesame oil
2 tablespoons white rice wine lees
1 tablespoon cornstarch mixed with 1 tablespoon cold water
2 scallions, minced

1. Heat a wok, put in the chestnuts, and stir-fry in the dry wok for 1 minute. Carefully add the oil and garlic and stir-fry another minute. Add the chicken and stir-fry for 2 minutes more. Add both soy sauces, the oyster sauce, yellow bean paste, sugar, sesame oil, wine lees, and 1 cup of water. Stir well, cover, and simmer for 20 minutes.

2. Remove the cover, add the cornstarch mixture and scallions, and stir until the mixture thickens. Transfer to a serving bowl.

CHICKEN CUBES IN THREE SAUCES

This recipe, from Fujian's Amoy Food Company, uses their Gold Label dark and thin soy sauces, black bean and chili sauce, and sesame oil. It has been modified with their permission; brand names have been eliminated. **SERVES 6 TO 8**

- 1 tablespoon plus ½ teaspoon thin soy sauce
- ½ tablespoon plus ½ teaspoon dark soy sauce
- 1½ teaspoons sesame oil
- 2 teaspoons sugar
- 1 tablespoon cornstarch
- 1 pound boneless chicken leg meat, cut into 1-inch cubes
- 2 tablespoons vegetable oil
- 2 tablespoons black bean and garlic sauce
- 1 red chili pepper, seeded and cubed
- 2 scallions, cut into small pieces

1. Mix together the thin and dark soy sauces, 1 teaspoon each of the sesame oil and sugar, and 2 teaspoons of the cornstarch. Stir this mixture into the chicken cubes and set aside for 10 minutes.

2. Heat the wok, heat the vegetable oil, then stir-fry the cubes of chicken for 2 minutes leaving them about three-quarters cooked. Stir in the black bean and garlic sauce, the chili pepper pieces, and scallions. Stir-fry about 1 minute longer, then add 5 tablespoons of water mixed with the remaining teaspoon of sugar and the remaining teaspoon of cornstarch. When slightly thickened, pour into a large serving bowl.

CHICKEN LIVERS WITH SCALLOPS

People from Fujian love dishes combining fish or seafood with meat, and this one is unusual because the meat is chicken livers. Be careful not to overcook them. For best results, do not substitute beef or pork liver because they are not as delicious. **SERVES 6 TO 8**

½ pound chicken livers, fat and veins removed, each cut into 3 or 4 pieces
½ pound sea scallops, each sliced across the center into semicircles
5 tablespoons cornstarch
2 tablespoons Chinese rice wine
1 egg white
½ teaspoon salt
2 teaspoons sesame oil
2 tablespoons oyster sauce
¼ teaspoon ground white pepper
1 cup vegetable oil
3 slices peeled fresh ginger, minced
3 cloves garlic, minced
3 scallions, white ends sliced and reserved, green ends cut into 1-inch pieces
½ teaspoon sugar
2 tablespoons coarsely minced fresh coriander (cilantro) leaves

1. Keeping them separate, dry the chicken livers and scallops. Mix each of them with 1½ tablespoons of cornstarch and set them aside.

2. Mix together the rice wine, egg white, salt, sesame oil, oyster sauce, and white pepper, and set this mixture aside.

3. Heat the vegetable oil in a wok or pan, and stir-fry the scallops for 2 minutes. With a slotted spoon, drain them and set them aside.

4. Reheat the oil and drippings, and stir-fry the chicken livers for 2 minutes. With a slotted spoon, drain them and set them aside.

5. Discard all but 1 tablespoon of the oil and drippings, and fry the minced ginger and garlic for 30 seconds; add the white slices of scallions, and stir-fry for another minute. Then add the scallops, chicken livers, sugar, and scallion greens and stir-fry for 1 minute before adding the coriander leaves. Stir well and put in a serving bowl.

CHICKEN WITH BASIL

Taiwanese and Fujianese people love this dish. In restaurants, it is often made and served in a small metal crock that is cooked directly in the flames. Large families make theirs in large ceramic stovetop casseroles. Both prefer using thigh meat on the bone. **SERVES 6 TO 8**

- 4 chicken thighs, on the bone, each chopped into 2-inch pieces
- 3 tablespoons sweet-potato flour
- 1 tablespoon vegetable oil
- 3 cloves garlic, peeled and slivered
- 3 slices peeled fresh ginger, slivered
- 3 fresh chili peppers, cut in half, seeded, and then cut into very thin strips
- 2 teaspoons sesame oil
- 3 tablespoons black sesame oil
- 1 tablespoon dark soy sauce
- 1 tablespoon thin soy sauce
- 1 tablespoon mushroom soy sauce
- 2 tablespoons Chinese red rice wine
- 1 tablespoon white rock sugar
- 6 to 8 sprigs fresh basil, each sprig cut into 3 or 4 pieces

1. Blanch the chicken for 3 minutes in boiling water, drain, and discard the water. Coat each piece with sweet-potato flour and set aside on a plate in a single layer to dry for 30 minutes.

2. Heat a wok or skillet, then heat the vegetable oil for 30 seconds. Add the garlic, ginger, and chili peppers, and fry for 1 minute. Add the chicken and the sesame oils, and stir-fry for 5 minutes.

3. Add the soy sauces, rice wine, and rock sugar, and simmer for another 5 minutes, and then add 2 to 3 tablespoons of water.

4. Add the basil and stir for 30 seconds, then transfer to a platter and serve.

CHICKEN WITH RED FERMENTED BEAN CURD

Usually deep-fried, this recipe can also be braised after the poultry is blanched in oil and marinated. Other meat, fish, and shellfish can be prepared in this manner. Other fermented bean curd products can be used, but locals prefer theirs with red fermented bean curd. **SERVES 8 TO 10**

- 6 skinless, boneless chicken thighs, cut into 2-inch pieces
- 1 (2-inch) cube red fermented bean curd, mashed and mixed with 1 tablespoon prepared tea
- 1 tablespoon Fujian rice wine
- 1 teaspoon sugar
- 2 teaspoons cornstarch
- 1 cup vegetable oil
- 2 cups shredded cabbage

1. Mix the chicken with the mashed red bean curd, and allow to rest for 30 minutes before adding the rice wine, sugar, and cornstarch.

2. Heat the oil and blanch the chicken pieces in the oil a few at a time for 2 minutes. Remove them with a slotted spoon, drain, and set on paper towels. Repeat until all are blanched, drained, and set aside. Reserve the oil.

3. Bring 4 cups of water to a boil. Blanch the cabbage in this for 30 seconds, then drain and place in 4 cups of cold water for 1 minute. Drain well. Set the cabbage out on a platter, leaving 1 inch along the rim uncovered.

4. Reheat the oil and stir-fry the chicken for 20 minutes, drain, and put in the center of the platter. Serve.

CHICKEN WITH RED RICE

Oiling the casserole is unusual but important when making this recipe. It keeps the rice from sticking as it boils. This recipe uses green soybeans (known sometimes when raw or boiled by their Japanese name of *edamame*). Please note that they can be added to many other recipes that cook for 20 minutes or more. Soybeans should never be eaten raw. **SERVES 6 TO 8**

½ cup red rice
½ chicken (with skin and bone), cut into 2-inch pieces
2 cloves garlic, peeled and minced
½ chili pepper, seeds removed, minced
2 tablespoons vegetable oil
6 dried Chinese black mushrooms (shiitake), soaked, stems discarded, then quartered
6 tablespoons fresh soybeans without their pods
1 tablespoon thin soy sauce
1 tablespoon dark soy sauce
1 teaspoon sesame oil

1. Soak the rice in 8 cups of warm water for 2 hours, then drain and rinse with cold water, and put in a large, oiled, heatproof casserole or pot you can serve from.

2. Mix the chicken with the garlic and chili peppers, and set aside for 20 minutes.

3. Heat a wok, and add the vegetable oil. When oil is hot, stir-fry the chicken mixture for 1 minute and then add the mushrooms. Stir-fry for 2 more minutes, or until the chicken is golden and crisp. Remove to the casserole.

4. Add the soybeans, soy sauces, and 1 cup of water to the casserole. Bring to a boil, then lower the heat, cover, and simmer for 20 minutes. Remove the cover and simmer for 10 minutes more. Let rest 15 minutes, then put the casserole on a trivet, add the sesame oil and serve.

CRISPY-COATED CHICKEN

In Fujian they like this preparation salty. Today's focus on health now has families preparing theirs with less salt than when it was traditionally made. Either way is good, so suit your own health needs and tastes. SERVES 8 TO 10

6 chicken thighs on the bone, chopped into 2-inch pieces
3 tablespoons cornstarch
¼ teaspoon coarse black pepper
½ cup sweet-potato flour
2 tablespoons Chinese red rice wine
1 egg, beaten until it turns light lemon color
½ cup vegetable oil
2 scallions, chopped coarsely
2 cloves garlic, peeled and chopped coarsely
½ to 2 teaspoons coarse salt
1 teaspoon black rice vinegar

1. Boil the chicken for 5 minutes, drain and toss with the cornstarch. Set aside for 20 minutes.

2. Stir together the black pepper and sweet-potato flour, and mix with the chicken. Add the rice wine and egg.

3. Heat a wok or skillet, heat the vegetable oil, and stir-fry the chicken for 10 minutes, until crisp and golden. Remove with a slotted spoon and drain on paper towels, discarding all but 1 tablespoon of the drippings.

4. Reheat the drippings and stir-fry the scallions and garlic for 1 minute, then add the chicken and stir-fry for 5 minutes. Transfer to a serving bowl, toss with the salt and vinegar, and serve.

DUCK AND TARO IN OYSTER SAUCE

This is made with cooked fresh or roasted duck, even leftovers of boiled duck. The taro root in this dish can be boiled, roasted, pan-fried, or deep-fried. Other vegetables, particularly sweet potatoes, can also be used in this versatile home-cooked dish that can be stewed or baked. It reheats very well. **SERVES 4 TO 10**

1 tablespoon vegetable oil
1 to 3 cloves garlic, peeled and minced
2 tablespoons red rice wine lees
3 tablespoons oyster sauce
1 tablespoon thin soy sauce
1 tablespoon sugar
¼ teaspoon ground black pepper
½ to 1 cup boiling water
¼ to ½ roast duck on the bone and with the skin, cut into six to ten 2-inch pieces
1 cup (1-inch cubes) fresh, peeled taro root, deep-fried or pan-fried
1 scallion, cut into 1-inch pieces

1. Heat a wok or large pan, heat the oil, and stir-fry the garlic for 1 minute. Add the wine lees, oyster and soy sauces, sugar, and black pepper. Simmer for 1 minute, then add ½ cup of boiling water, the duck, and taro root. Cover and simmer for 30 minutes, checking the liquid after 10 minutes. If no liquid remains, add another ½ cup of boiling water.

2. Remove the cover, stir in the scallion pieces and serve.

DUCK, BITTER MELON, AND SALTED DUCK EGGS

Most Chinese recipe names use ingredients listed in order of quantity used. This recipe's name is misleading, as the main ingredient really is the melon, not its poultry. No one seems to know how the name evolved for this much-loved dish. Perhaps a reader can find the answer and educate us all. **SERVES 4 TO 6**

- 3 salted duck eggs, simmered for 7 minutes
- ¼ roasted duck, chopped into 2-inch pieces
- 2 bitter melons, cut in half and seeded, then thinly sliced
- 1 tablespoon vegetable oil
- 2 cloves garlic, peeled and minced
- ½ pound ground pork
- 2 tablespoons Fujianese rice wine
- 1 tablespoon thin soy sauce
- 3 tablespoons sugar
- ¼ teaspoon ground black pepper

1. Peel the duck eggs and slice in half. Mash the yolks and add 1 tablespoon of water to them. Mince the whites and keep them separate from the yolks.

2. Boil 2 quarts of water. Place the duck pieces in a large pot, pour in 1 quart of the boiling water, and add the bitter melons. Simmer for 2 minutes, then discard the water. Add the second quart of boiling water and simmer for 2 more minutes. Discard this water, as well.

3. Heat a wok, heat the oil, and fry the garlic for 30 seconds, then add the pork and fry until almost all pink is gone. Add the wine, soy sauce, sugar, pepper, bitter melon, and minced egg whites. Stir-fry this mixture for 2 minutes, add the duck, and stir-fry for 4 minutes.

4. Add the egg yolks and stir-fry for another minute, then transfer to a serving bowl.

DUCK IN RED RICE WINE LEES

This is considered a holiday dish, probably because ducks are expensive and this recipe takes several days to prepare. Large families might make an entire duck; smaller or poorer ones use less than a quarter of one. SERVES 4 OR MORE

½ duck, cut in half
2 scallions, each tied in a knot
2 slices peeled fresh ginger, plus 3 tablespoons minced fresh ginger
1 cup red rice wine lees
1 cup Fujianese rice wine
2 tablespoons sugar

1. Discard any innards left in the duck, blanch the duck in boiling water for 2 minutes, rinse in cold water, and set aside for 15 minutes so the skin tightens.

2. Bring 4 cups water to a boil, add the scallions, sliced ginger, and duck pieces, lower the heat, and simmer for 40 minutes. Transfer the duck to a bowl. Use the liquid for duck soup, or discard.

3. Mix together the wine lees, rice wine, sugar, and minced ginger, and pour over the duck. Cover tightly and refrigerate for two days.

4. Remove the duck and chop the meat into small pieces. It can be reheated in its own liquid or served at room temperature. Some liquid can be thickened with cornstarch, if a sauce is desired.

FLAVORED DUCK

It used to be common for Fujian families to make lots of something they call rice wine lees. It lasts a week or two, and is used in this and many other dishes. Rare is the urban family that makes theirs today though. However, purists and mountain folk still do. SERVES 8 TO 10

1 whole duck, quartered
2 tablespoons salt
1 tablespoon Chinese white rice wine
2 slices peeled fresh ginger, minced
1 (1-pound) jar red rice wine lees
2 tablespoons sugar

1. Dry the duck quarters with paper towels, then rub with salt inside and out. Put into a bowl or casserole and sprinkle the rice wine over the duck. Set aside for an hour. Then put the duck into a deep heatproof bowl and cover with the minced ginger, wine lees, and sugar.

2. Steam the duck over rapidly boiling water for 1 hour. Check every 10 to 15 minutes to make sure there is water in the bottom of the steamer. Transfer the duck quarters to a deep plate and let them cool for 30 minutes. Cover them with the wine lees. Wrap with plastic wrap and refrigerate for two days.

3. Chop the duck into serving-size pieces. Reheat to remove the chill but not to heat through.

GAME HEN WITH RICE WINE LEES

Though better when made with the homemade mock wine lees (see page 214), this recipe works well with the commercially prepared product found in jars in refrigerator sections of Asian supermarkets. This recipe is from my friend Wonona, and I added additional vegetables. **SERVES 6 TO 8**

- 1 tablespoon glutinous rice wine
- ½ teaspoon salt
- 1 teaspoon sugar
- 2 teaspoons cornstarch
- 2 whole (1-pound) game hens, cut into 8 pieces
- 1 tablespoon dark soy sauce
- ¼ cup chicken broth
- 1 tablespoon vegetable oil
- 2 teaspoons peeled and finely minced fresh ginger
- 2 teaspoons peeled and finely minced fresh garlic
- 2 scallions, finely minced
- 1 cup red or white rice wine lees
- 2 scallions, cut into 2-inch pieces
- ½ cup melting mouth or snow peas, ends and attached strings removed

1. Mix together the rice wine, salt, sugar, and cornstarch, and stir in the game hen pieces. Allow to rest for 30 minutes.

2. Stir together the soy sauce and chicken broth, and set aside.

3. Heat a wok or skillet, heat the oil, then add the pieces of game hen and stir-fry for 15 minutes. Remove from the pan and drain on paper towels.

4. In the same pan, stir-fry the ginger and garlic for 1 minute, add the minced scallions and stir-fry another 30 seconds, then add the wine lees. Stir well and add the game hen pieces. Cover and simmer for 3 minutes, then add in the soy sauce mixture, scallion pieces, and peas. Recover and simmer 1 minute, then transfer to a serving bowl.

GRILLED CHICKEN WINGS

These wings, appetizers to some, can be used anywhere in a meal, start to finish. Add lots of broth and thicken it, and then add sweet potatoes, and it is a casserole. Add lots of broth without thickening it, and it is a soup. **SERVES 10**

- 10 chicken wings, tips discarded, each cut apart at the joint
- 3 tablespoons Chinese barbecue sauce (also known as *sacha* sauce)
- 1 tablespoon dark soy sauce
- 1 tablespoon thick soy sauce
- 6 cups chicken broth (optional)
- 2 tablespoons cornstarch mixed with 2 tablespoons cold water (optional)

1. Poke a few holes in the skin of the wings with a skewer or fork, then marinate in a mixture of barbecue sauce, dark soy sauce, thick soy sauce, and 1 tablespoon of water. Cover the wings and refrigerate for 4 hours. Then drain, and reserve the marinade.

2. Preheat the oven to 425°F or heat a charcoal barbecue grill. Cook the wings for 30 minutes turning every 5 minutes and brushing them with the reserved marinade after each turn. Transfer to a platter.

NOTE: If using as a casserole, put the wings and remaining marinade in a pot along with chicken broth and bring to a boil. Lower the heat and simmer for 30 minutes, then add the cornstarch mixture and simmer until somewhat thickened. (If using as a soup don't add the cornstarch mixture.)

PIGEON AND TANGERINE IN CASSEROLE

Pigeon, partridge, and quail, though distinctive in taste to those who eat them often, can be used in place of each other—and they frequently are. No Fujianese person queried could explain why one or another is almost never mixed with chicken or why several kinds of game birds are never found in the same dish. **SERVES 6 TO 8**

- 3 or 4 pigeons, entrails removed, each cut in half
- 1 tablespoon ginger juice (page 233)
- 1 teaspoon salt
- 1 tablespoon thin soy sauce
- 1 teaspoon maltose syrup or a sugar paste, thinned with equal amount of boiling water
- ½ teaspoon ground white pepper
- 2 tablespoons vegetable oil
- 8 shallots, peeled and cut in half
- 2 scallions, cut into ½-inch pieces
- 3 thin slices peeled fresh ginger
- 1 tangerine, peel removed and excess pith removed, cut into 3-inch strips; segments pitted, any white strands removed
- 1 tablespoon fermented white rice
- 1 cup baby Chinese cabbage or baby spinach
- 1 tablespoon oyster sauce
- 2 teaspoons water-chestnut flour or potato starch

1. Mix the pigeons with the ginger juice, salt, thin soy sauce, maltose, and white pepper. Set aside for 15 minutes.

2. Heat the vegetable oil in a wok or deep skillet. Brown the pigeons, then remove them to a plate.

3. Reheat the oil and stir-fry the shallots, scallions, and ginger for 1 minute, then add the tangerine peel and pigeons along with 2 cups of water and the fermented rice. Bring almost to a boil, lower the heat, and cover the pan. Simmer for 15 minutes, and then remove the pigeon halves. Add the tangerine segments, baby cabbage, and oyster sauce, and simmer for 5 minutes, then add the water-chestnut flour and stir-fry for 2 minutes. Transfer to a deep platter.

4. Chop each pigeon half into four pieces, and put on top of the vegetables.

RED RICE RABBIT ON CABBAGE SHREDS

This dish is also known as "Hopping Chicken," and is not to be confused with a dish made with frog's legs. In China, frogs are often called "field chickens." The red seasoning sauce for this recipe is divided into two batches: one to marinate the meat, the other as a final dipping sauce. SERVES 8 TO 10

- 2 tablespoons fermented red bean curd, mashed with 1 tablespoon cold tea
- 3 tablespoons red rice wine lees
- 2 tablespoons brown sugar
- 2 tablespoons sweet-potato flour mixed with 2 tablespoons cold water
- 1 teaspoon cornstarch
- ½ cup Chinese red rice wine
- 1 tablespoon Chinese black rice vinegar
- 1 rabbit, skinned, on the bone, and chopped into 8 to 10 pieces
- 2 tablespoons vegetable oil
- 1 pound Chinese cabbage, shredded

1. Mix together the mashed red bean curd, red rice wine lees, brown sugar, sweet-potato flour mixture, and cornstarch. Divide the mixture into two portions. Set one half aside for use as a dipping sauce. Mix the other half with the wine and vinegar, and marinate the rabbit in it for 30 minutes. Drain, and discard this marinade.

2. Heat a wok or skillet, heat the oil, and stir-fry the rabbit until browned and fully cooked, 20 to 25 minutes. Remove and drain on paper towels.

3. Using the same oil, stir-fry the shredded cabbage for 1 minute until wilted, drain well, and arrange along the rim of a platter.

4. In a small pot, bring the reserved unused marinade to a boil and pour it into a small, deep dish. Set it in the center of the platter and place the fried rabbit pieces around it.

RED WINE AND CHICKEN LEGS

People like the flavor of red rice wine lees and its red color. Using it with chicken is said to bring prosperity. The Chinese know that meat next to the bone is sweeter and more flavorful than if the dish is prepared boneless, so they leave the chicken on the bone in this and most other recipes. **SERVES 8 TO 10**

- 6 chicken legs, with skin and bones, ends chopped off, chopped into 2-inch pieces
- ¼ cup vegetable oil
- 1 tablespoon peeled and slivered fresh ginger
- 3 tablespoons red rice wine lees
- 2 tablespoons Chinese red rice wine
- 1 teaspoon red rice vinegar
- 1 tablespoon sugar
- ½ teaspoon salt
- 2 teaspoons thin soy sauce
- ½ cup boiling water
- 1 ounce mung-bean noodles, soaked for 30 minutes in 3 cups hot water
- 2 tablespoons cornstarch mixed with 1 tablespoon cold water
- 1 tablespoon sweet-potato flour

1. Boil the chicken pieces in a quart of water for 15 minutes, drain, and set aside for 15 minutes. Use the liquid for soup or other purposes.

2. Heat the oil in a wok or skillet, and fry the chicken pieces until crisp. Drain them on paper towels, and leave 1 tablespoon oil in pan. Discard the rest of the oil.

3. Reheat the oil, add the ginger slivers and stir once, then add the red rice wine lees, rice wine, vinegar, sugar, salt, and soy sauce. Stir-fry for 2 minutes and transfer to a bowl. Do not clean the wok, just add ½ cup of boiling water and the drained mung-bean noodles, and stir for 1 minute. Return the chicken and sauce to the pan, stir once or twice, then add the cornstarch mixture and sweet-potato flour, and stir for 1 minute. When the mixture thickens somewhat, pour into a serving bowl.

SLICED CHICKEN WITH FRUIT

Chinese cooking usually uses same-size pieces of food to keep cooking even and visuals similar. Such is the case in this dish. The chicken can be white or dark meat, the latter preferred. The color and texture of the main items, in this case chicken and fruit, are kept uniform by cutting the chicken the same size as the apples, and using red-skinned apples. **SERVES 6 TO 8**

1 egg white
2 cups skinless, boneless chicken, thinly sliced; do not cut into strips
1 teaspoon salt
1 teaspoon white rice wine lees
1 tablespoon cornstarch
Pinch of ground white pepper
1 red apple
½ teaspoon salt or lemon juice
1 tablespoon vegetable oil
4 slices peeled fresh ginger, each cut in half
2 scallions, cut into 1-inch pieces

1. Lightly beat the egg white, add the chicken slices, salt, wine lees, cornstarch, and pepper, and set aside for 15 minutes.

2. Peel the apple, slice, and mix with salt or lemon juice to prevent discoloration.

3. Heat a wok or a pan, heat the oil, and stir-fry the ginger and scallions for 1 minute. Add the chicken mixture. Cook until the chicken is no longer pink. Add the apple slices, stir, and transfer to a bowl or deep platter. Serve.

STEAMED CHICKEN AND EGG WHITES

This dish takes time to make, is made in layers, and is cut into triangular or diamond shapes before serving. Cut in small pieces, it can be an appetizer or used in a soup or a casserole. SERVES 6 TO 8

- ½ pound shrimp, peeled, deveined, and finely minced
- 2 tablespoons melted lard or other minced pork fat
- 1 tablespoon Fujianese rice wine
- 1 tablespoon cornstarch
- ½ pound chicken breast meat, cut in 3-inch slices
- 1 teaspoon sesame oil
- 1 tablespoon melted chicken fat
- 5 egg whites, beaten stiff
- 2 cups pea, sweet potato, or spinach leaves, steamed for 1 minute
- 2 tablespoons minced ham

1. Mix the shrimp with the lard, wine, and cornstarch, and let rest for 15 minutes.

2. Line a square heatproof container that will fit in a steamer with the chicken slices brushed with sesame oil. Spread the shrimp mixture evenly over them and steam over boiling water for 10 minutes. Remove from the steamer and gently brush some of the chicken fat over the shrimp paste. Reserve the rest of the chicken fat.

3. Spread the beaten egg whites over the shrimp mixture and return to the steamer for 2 or 3 minutes, or just until the egg whites look set. Turn off the heat and remove the steamer cover. Allow to cool for 30 minutes and then remove the container from the steamer.

4. Put the steamed green leaves onto a heatproof platter. Invert the chicken mixture onto the steamed leaves. Cut the layered mixture into square or diamond-shaped pieces and gently lift each one with some of the greens onto a clean platter. Garnish with the minced ham, and brush any leftover chicken fat on the ham.

STEAMED CHICKEN WITH GINGER AND SCALLIONS

Fujianese cooks take pride in their flexibility in selection of ingredients. This dish is often made with just chicken legs or thighs, or both white and dark meat. Some make theirs with scallions and/or sweet potatoes; others, as in this recipe, use only scallions and lots of shredded ginger. **SERVES 6 TO 8**

- 2 scallions, minced or finely shredded
- ½ cup peeled and finely shredded young ginger
- 2 tablespoons Chinese white rice wine lees mixed with 1 small ice cube
- ½ chicken, preferably on the bone, skin left on and chopped into 2-inch pieces
- 1 tablespoon cornstarch
- 1 tablespoon sesame oil

1. Mix together the shredded scallions, ginger, and wine lees. Mix 2 tablespoons of this mixture with the chicken pieces and set aside for 1 hour on a heatproof deep plate.

2. Bring water in a steamer bottom to a rolling boil, put the plate with the chicken mixture in the steamer, cover, and lower the heat to a simmer. Steam for 20 minutes, and then remove from the steamer, pouring off and reserving the liquid in the plate.

3. Mix the cornstarch with the sesame oil and 5 tablespoons of the reserved liquid. Put this into a small pot with the remaining scallion mixture, and stir continuously for 1 minute until thickened. Pour over the chicken and serve.

STEWED CHICKEN WINGS

Chicken wings highlight the sweetness of meat, because so much of the meat is close to bone. This recipe uses both single- and double-bone wing sections. Some prefer only using 20 double-bone ones and reserving the single-bone wing sections to use as appetizers. Leftovers are also appreciated at room temperature. **SERVES 10**

2 cups corn oil
20 chicken wings, cut apart at the joints, the tips ends discarded
2 tablespoons mushroom soy sauce
3 or 4 pieces brown rock sugar
1 tablespoon Chinese black rice wine
6 slices peeled fresh ginger
2 cloves garlic, minced
2 scallions, cut into ½-inch pieces
3 tablespoons hoisin sauce
1 tablespoon fermented rice
1 cup chicken broth
1 tablespoon cornstarch mixed with 1 tablespoon cold water

1. Heat the oil, and deep-fry half the wing pieces for 3 minutes. Remove and drain the wings, and repeat with the remaining wings. Set the oil aside.

2. Simmer the mushroom soy sauce, rock sugar, and rice wine just until the sugar dissolves. Pour this into a heatproof casserole and put the fried wing pieces into it. Marinate for 30 minutes, turning the wings two or three times.

3. In a wok or pan, heat 1 tablespoon reserved oil, then fry the ginger and garlic for 30 seconds. Add the scallions, and stir-fry for another 30 seconds. Stir these into the chicken wing mixture and add the hoisin sauce, fermented rice, broth, and cornstarch mixture. Stir-fry, turning three or four times until the sauce starts to thicken, then lower the heat and simmer covered for 10 minutes. Serve.

STUFFED CHICKEN

Traditionally, this dish is cooked as explained below. However, it can also be wrapped in aluminum foil and roasted in an oven. Some folks even steam it for half of the given time, then wrap and roast it in the oven for an additional hour.
SERVES 10 OR MORE

- 1 large (5- to 8-pound) whole chicken
- 1 tablespoon salt
- 1 tablespoon dried shrimp, soaked in warm water for 30 minutes
- 5 dried Chinese black mushrooms (shiitake), soaked in warm water, stems discarded, mushroom caps diced
- 1 tablespoon vegetable oil
- 3 slices peeled fresh ginger, minced
- 5 scallions, sliced
- 3 fresh scallops, diced coarsely
- 6 shrimp, peeled, deveined and diced
- 1 small Chinese cabbage, diced coarsely
- 1 cup cooked glutinous rice
- ½ small taro root, peeled, and diced
- 1 cup grated taro root or grated sweet potato, mixed with 1 tablespoon black rice vinegar
- 2 tablespoons fermented white rice
- 1 tablespoon Chinese rice wine

1. Rub the inside of the chicken with salt and let it rest for 15 minutes.

2. Drain the soaked dried shrimp and mince them. Mix together the dried shrimp and mushrooms.

3. Heat a wok, heat the vegetable oil, and fry the ginger and half the scallions for 1 minute. Add the dried shrimp mixture, and fry for another minute. Add the diced scallops and shrimp and fry for another minute; then add the cabbage and fry for another minute, or until wilted. Remove from the pan and set aside for about 30 minutes. Mix with the glutinous rice, diced taro root, and grated taro root mixture.

4. Dry the inside of the chicken with a paper towel, pouring off any salt water. Stuff it with the shrimp mixture. Skewer or sew the opening closed, and rub the outside with a mixture of the fermented rice and rice wine. Place the chicken in a bowl in a steamer over simmering water, and steam for 2 hours.

5. Carefully remove the chicken from the steamer and bowl, and discard the skewers or thread. Place the stuffing in the center of a large platter. Chop the chicken into 2-inch pieces and put them around the stuffing, scattering the remaining scallions about. Serve.

SWEET-POTATO LEAVES WITH RABBIT

Be sure to use large yam leaves; they are sweeter than the smaller ones. Or substitute spinach or any other dark leafy green vegetable. When rabbit is hard to find, minced duck, chicken, or even frog's legs are used. This mountain dish is preferred in winter. Families with vegetarian members serve the meat on the side, not on top of the greens. **SERVES 6**

- 1 cup rabbit meat, minced coarsely
- 3 tablespoons white rice wine lees
- 1 pound sweet-potato leaves or other greens, stems discarded, cut in half
- 2 tablespoons plus 2 teaspoons sesame oil
- 3 cloves garlic, peeled and minced
- 3 slices peeled fresh ginger, minced
- 1 fresh chili pepper, seeded and minced
- ¼ cup coarsely chopped taro root
- 1 tablespoon Chinese black rice vinegar
- 2 tablespoons thin soy sauce
- 2 teaspoons sugar

1. Mix the rabbit meat with the wine lees and set aside for 15 minutes, then drain and discard all liquid.

2. Blanch the greens in 4 cups of boiling water for 1 minute, drain well. Mix the greens with the 2 tablespoons of sesame oil, and spread on all sides of a small, deep bowl.

3. Heat the remaining sesame oil, stir-fry the garlic for 30 seconds, then add the ginger and chili pepper pieces, and stir-fry for 1 minute. Add the minced rabbit and stir-fry for 3 minutes. Add the taro root and vinegar, and stir-fry for another minute, then add the soy sauce and sugar, and stir-fry for one more minute before transferring on top of the sweet potato leaves. Serve.

THREE-CUP CHICKEN CASSEROLE

Both Taiwanese and Fujianese make this dish, named for one cup each of sesame oil, soy sauce, and wine lees. While chicken may be the most common meat used, it is also made with duck, rabbit, squid, and even eel. During winter, herbal medicines are added to this popular dish to ward off winter chills and illnesses of the season. SERVES 10

- 2 tablespoons vegetable oil
- 6 whole cloves garlic, peeled
- 12 slices peeled fresh ginger
- 1 small fresh red chili pepper, seeded and coarsely chopped
- 1 whole chicken, with skin and bones, cut into about 30 pieces
- 1 cup sesame oil
- 1 cup white rice wine lees or Chinese white rice wine
- 1 cup thin soy sauce
- 1 cup fresh Thai basil leaves

1. Heat a large heatproof casserole, heat the vegetable oil, and then add the garlic and ginger, and stir-fry for 1 minute. Add the chili peppers. Stir once, then add the chicken and stir-fry until the chicken is browned on all sides.

2. Slowly add the sesame oil, wine lees, and soy sauce, lower the heat, cover, and simmer 20 minutes. Stir in the basil, simmer for 3 more minutes, and place the casserole on a trivet to serve.

MEATS

THROUGHOUT CHINA, "MEAT" MEANS PORK; it is the country's most consumed animal food. In the Fujian province, however, all kinds of meat are eaten but consumed in lesser quantities, and fish is more important than meat. The Fujianese like their land animal products mixed with those of the sea. They prepare them in ever-so-many dishes, incorporating a small amount of foods of the sea. Meatballs are often mixed with some fish, and even fish balls may have a tiny core of meat surrounded by much more minced or ground fish.

Beef is quite popular and plentiful, raised on lowlands near the mountains, while yaks and goats roam or are raised in mountainous regions, and also used as food. All of the province's land mammals are consumed from head to tail, including all of their innards. (The Chinese use the term "innards," more commonly known in the West as "organ" or "variety" meats.) Tripe is one of the more popular of these varietals. It and all others are enjoyed simmered in water or broth, "red-cooked" (a name given to simmering or braising in soy sauce), stir-fried, deep-fried, and indeed prepared in every cookery technique imaginable.

Many meats are cooked with this province's beloved red rice or white rice wine lees, and others are made sweet and sour, or piquant and sour. Vegetables are almost always combined and prepared with the meat; if not, they certainly are served alongside it.

In Fujian, stuffing vegetables with meat is a common preparation, with fillings ranging from pork and beef to yak, goat, and other creatures. One of the most popular meat dishes, not stuffed but layered, is one that combines meat with foods of the sea: Buddha Jumps Over The Wall. There are many variations of this most beloved dish, often each word capitalized emphasizing its importance to the culture. Therefore one is in the appetizer section (page 81) and two are included in this chapter (pages 145 and 147). The first is a home version, the second is made restaurant-style.

BEEF CAKES WITH WATERCRESS

Lean meat is not a high priority in Fujian nor is it in most of China, because the Chinese believe fattier meat creates a softer, smoother, and tastier dish. These days though, lean meats are becoming popular. Many people are adding only a little minced fat or incorporating only a few tablespoons of lard into this and other dishes, while years ago many tablespoons was the general rule.
SERVES 5 TO 10

- ½ pound minced beef, chuck preferred, with 1 tablespoon lard added
- ½ cup minced watercress
- Peel from ½ dried tangerine, soaked in ¼ cup warm water, then minced
- ⅓ teaspoon ground white pepper
- 1 teaspoon sugar
- 2 tablespoons oyster sauce
- 1 teaspoon mushroom soy sauce
- 1 teaspoon sesame oil
- 1 teaspoon chili oil
- 3 tablespoons cornstarch
- ½ teaspoon corn oil
- 1 lettuce or cabbage leaf

1. Mix together the beef, watercress, tangerine peel, white pepper, sugar, oyster sauce, mushroom soy sauce, sesame and chili oils, and cornstarch. Allow to rest for 20 minutes, then shape into ten small disks.

2. Oil a flat plate and put the disks on it. Cover with the lettuce leaf and steam over boiling water for 7 minutes. Discard the leaf and any liquid before serving.

BEEF SHORT RIBS

The Chinese love the ribs of pork and beef. A friend from Fuzhou offered a family recipe for this book, using pork ribs. This version of the same recipe is prepared with beef ribs. Many families have their own traditions, and some use both meats in the same dish. **SERVES 6**

6 beef short ribs, each one cut in half
2 tablespoons dark soy sauce
2 tablespoons Chinese black rice vinegar
2 tablespoons white rice wine lees
1 tablespoon sugar
1 teaspoon chili paste with garlic
2 tablespoons minced onion
2 cloves garlic, peeled and minced
2 slices peeled fresh ginger, minced
2 tablespoons white sesame seeds
1 teaspoon sesame oil

1. Crosshatch the meat on the top of each rib, in cuts ½ inch apart and not quite down to the bone. Be careful not to allow any meat to fall off the bone. Then put ribs, cut side up, in a shallow glass or ceramic dish.

2. Stir together the soy sauce, vinegar, wine lees, sugar, chili paste, onion, garlic, ginger, sesame seeds, and sesame oil. Pour this mixture over the meat and then turn the ribs cut side down. Cover with plastic wrap or a tight-fitting lid and allow them to marinate for 2 hours or overnight, turning them several times.

3. Drain the ribs, and reserve the marinade. Preheat the oven to 450°F or heat a charcoal grill. Cook the meat for 30 minutes, turning several times, and basting each time with the marinade. Transfer to a platter and serve.

BRAISED LEG OF PORK

Almost every region of China has a dish similar to this one, but each region's version tastes different. In Shanghai, theirs is made sweeter, whereas this one from Fujian uses two types of fermented rice wine lees. **SERVES 10 OR MORE**

4 cups vegetable oil
1 (3-pound) pork leg, exterior skin left on and edges scored 1 inch apart, patted dry
10 slices peeled fresh ginger
6 scallions, trimmed, each tied in a knot
¼ cup thin soy sauce
2 tablespoons dark soy sauce
1 tablespoon Chinese rice wine
2 tablespoons red rice wine lees
3 tablespoons white rice wine lees
2 teaspoons sugar
20 dried Chinese black mushrooms (shiitake), soaked for 20 minutes in 2 cups warm water, stems discarded
½ pound Chinese broccoli
1 teaspoon sesame oil
3 tablespoons cornstarch mixed with 2 tablespoons cold water

1. Heat the oil in a very large deep pot and fry the pork leg for 5 minutes, turning three or four times. As it will spatter, cover the pot with a spatter shield. Remove the leg and set it aside. Reserve all but a tablespoon of oil for other purposes.

2. Using the same pot, fry the ginger and scallions until aromatic, about 30 seconds, and then add both soy sauces, the rice wine, both wine lees, and the sugar. Mix well, then add the leg of pork, turning it three or four times until all sides are coated with the liquid.

3. In another pot, bring 8 cups of water to a boil, lower the heat, add the pork leg, cover, and simmer for 1 hour. Turn the pork and simmer for 3 hours more, turning it once or twice each hour.

4. Take the meat out of the pot, remove and discard the bones. Put the meat back into the pot, add the mushrooms, and simmer for another 2 hours, turning every 30 minutes. Test the meat and when very tender, transfer to a bowl and with chopsticks or two forks pull it apart into smaller pieces. (If not tender, return the meat to the pot and simmer for another 30 minutes or more, until it is fork-tender.)

5. When the pork is done, steam the broccoli for 3 minutes, drain, and put it around the rim of a large, deep platter. Sprinkle with sesame oil, then put the meat and mushrooms in the center. Bring 1 cup of the remaining pork liquid to a boil, stir in the cornstarch mixture, and continue stirring until thickened. Pour this over the meat and mushrooms and serve.

BRAISED MEATBALLS WITH VEGETABLES

This recipe has been graciously provided by the Amoy Foods Company of Fujian. It is used with their permission; brand names have been eliminated.
SERVES 4 TO 8

10 ounces minced pork
1 tablespoon dark soy sauce
1 tablespoon plus 1 teaspoon thin soy sauce
1 tablespoon sesame oil
3 tablespoons cornstarch
1½ egg whites, slightly beaten
¼ cup chopped water chestnuts
½ tablespoon minced ginger
2 cups vegetable oil
1 tablespoon oyster sauce
1 teaspoon sugar
4 ounces bamboo shoots, thickly sliced (if fresh, boil them first for 10 minutes)
4 slices peeled fresh ginger
8 dried Chinese black mushrooms (shiitake), soaked for 20 minutes, stems discarded
8 stalks Shanghai cabbage, washed and trimmed
2 teaspoons cornstarch mixed with ½ cup cold water

1. Mix the minced pork with half the dark soy sauce, 1 tablespoon of the thin soy sauce, 1 teaspoon of the sesame oil, 1 tablespoon of the cornstarch, and the egg whites. Add the chopped water chestnuts and minced ginger, and stir well.

2. Divide the meat mixture into four portions. Shape each portion into a ball, and then coat their entire surface with the remaining cornstarch. Set aside for 15 minutes to allow the cornstarch to become wet.

3. Heat the vegetable oil and deep-fry the meatballs until golden brown, about 3 minutes, then remove them from the pot and drain on paper towels, reserving 1 tablespoon of the oil and setting aside the rest for other purposes.

4. Mix together the remaining dark and thin soy sauces, and the remaining sesame oil, and stir in the oyster sauce and sugar.

5. Heat the reserved tablespoon of vegetable oil and stir-fry the bamboo shoots, ginger, and mushrooms for 1 minute. Add the Shanghai cabbage, meatballs, and the sauce mixture. Cover and simmer for 10 minutes, then add the cornstarch mixture. Stir gently until the sauce thickens. Transfer the meatballs to a deep platter, cut each in half, top with the greens, and finally pour the thickened sauce over the entire platter.

BRAISED PORK RIBS

What makes these classic Chinese ribs Fujianese is the addition of the rice wine lees. The dish can be prepared in advance, prior to the addition of the sauce. When stopping the cooking at this earlier point, cover and refrigerate the ribs. Then continue when ready to finish the dish, and add ten minutes more to the cooking time. **SERVES 8 TO 10**

- 1 tablespoon vegetable oil
- 6 cloves garlic, peeled, each cut into 4 or 5 slices
- 2 pounds spareribs, cut into 1-inch-long sections, and separated into individual pieces
- 3 tablespoons Chinese barbecue sauce (*sacha* sauce)
- 2 tablespoons dark soy sauce
- 2 tablespoons white rice wine lees
- ½ tablespoon sugar
- 1 teaspoon salt
- 1 teaspoon ground white pepper

1. Heat a wok or a large heavy skillet, heat the oil, and then add the garlic. Stir-fry for 30 seconds, and then add the spareribs. Stir-fry for 15 minutes, then remove and drain the ribs and set them on paper towels leaving ½ tablespoon of oil in the pan.

2. Reheat the pan and return the ribs to the pan with the barbecue and soy sauces, wine lees, sugar, salt, and pepper. Add 2 tablespoons of water, lower the heat, and simmer for 30 minutes, or until the meat almost falls from the bones. Serve on a deep platter.

BUDDHA JUMPS OVER THE WALL II

This popular recipe has many variations, and is most often capitalized due to its importance in the cuisine. It is made in layers and gets its name because of its heady aroma, once said to convince many a monk to leap the wall of his monastery, locate its source, and seriously consider breaking his vow not to eat any living creature. (See pages 81 and 147 for other versions of this recipe.)
SERVES 10 OR MORE

1 large soaked sea cucumber, cut into 1-inch pieces
½ pound pork tripe, cut into 2-inch pieces
2 tablespoons Chinese white rice vinegar
½ pound pork tendon, cut into 1-inch pieces
½ pound pork shoulder, cut into 2-inch cubes
2 chicken thighs, chopped into 2-inch pieces
6 fresh scallops
1 conpoy (dried scallop), soaked for 2 hours, then shredded
1 teaspoon small shrimp
10 dried Chinese black mushrooms (shiitake), soaked for 20 minutes, stems removed
½ pound taro root, peeled and cut into 2-inch cubes
1 large bamboo shoot, peeled and cut into 2-inch cubes
20 canned whole water chestnuts
20 dried Chinese red dates, pits removed
1 pound fish tail, scales removed, cut into 4 pieces
2 scallions, cleaned, rinsed, and knotted together
6 slices peeled fresh ginger
1 cup Chinese white rice wine
3 tablespoons white rice wine lees
1 teaspoon coarse salt
1 quart superior chicken stock (see page 234)

1. Blanch the sea cucumber in 4 cups boiling water, drain, cut into smaller pieces, then put into a large stockpot or heatproof casserole.

2. Mix together the pork tripe and vinegar, set aside for 15 minutes, then drain the tripe and add it as the next layer in the stockpot, on top of the sea cucumber.

3. Blanch the pork tendon and pork shoulder for 5 minutes each, then drain and add to the stockpot.

CONTINUED

4. Pour 6 cups water over the meat in the stockpot, bring to a boil, lower the heat, and simmer, uncovered, for 1 hour. The liquid should be reduced by half.

5. Add one at a time, layer by layer, the chicken thighs, scallops, conpoy, small shrimp, and mushrooms, and continue to simmer for another hour. Add the taro root, bamboo shoot pieces, water chestnuts, and dates in the same manner and simmer for another hour. Add the rest of the ingredients, and simmer the mixture for 30 more minutes. Serve in the casserole or transfer to a preheated bowl.

BUDDHA JUMPS OVER THE WALL, SHIH YEH-STYLE

Fu Pei Mei Fu said this dish was first sold during the Qing Dynasty (1644–1911) at Fuzhou's Qi-Chun restaurant. The Shih Yeh restaurant version, favored by her daughter Angela Cheng, is adapted below. Shin Yeh serves it in a blue-and-white wine-jar casserole, from which wafts those aromas said to make any Buddha leap his monastery wall. (See pages 81 and 145 for other versions of this recipe.) SERVES 10 OR MORE

- 1 pound fresh taro root, peeled and cut into large pieces
- 1 pound potatoes, peeled and cut into large pieces
- 1 tablespoon mushroom soy sauce
- ¼ cup plus 2 tablespoons vegetable oil
- 1 pig's foot, cut into 6 to 8 pieces
- ½ chicken, with skin and bones, cut into 1- to 2-inch pieces
- ¼ pound Smithfield-type ham, cut into 1- to 2-inch pieces
- ¼ pound pork stomach, well washed, cut into 1- to 2-inch pieces
- ¼ pound dried pork tendon, soaked for an hour, then cut into ½-inch pieces
- 10 dried chestnuts, soaked for an hour
- 10 dried Chinese red dates, soaked for 30 minutes, then pitted
- 4 chicken stomachs, cleaned, rinsed, each cut into 4 pieces
- 5 dried Chinese black mushrooms (shiitake), soaked for 10 minutes, stems discarded, each cut in half
- 10 dried mussels, soaked for 30 minutes, rinsed, each cut in half
- 2 dried scallops, soaked for 30 minutes, then shredded by hand
- 5 slices canned abalone, each cut in half
- 3 ounces dried shark's fin, soaked for 30 minutes, then shredded by hand
- 2 scallions, cut into ½-inch pieces
- 3 pieces peeled fresh ginger, each cut into 4 pieces
- ¼ cup all-purpose flour
- 6 to 10 cups superior stock (see page 234)
- ¼ cup Chinese rice wine
- 2 tablespoons thin soy sauce
- 2 tablespoons black soy sauce

1. Mix together the taro root, potatoes, and mushroom soy sauce, then heat ¼ cup of the oil in a wok or skillet, and fry the mixture until golden brown. Discard the used oil, and put the vegetables into a heatproof casserole that will fit in a deep canning pot.

CONTINUED

2. Scald the pig's foot pieces in 4 cups of boiling water, drain, and place in the casserole. Scald the chicken pieces, and then put them on top of the pig's foot pieces. Top with the ham, pork stomach, pork tendon, dried chestnuts, red dates, chicken stomachs, mushrooms, mussels, scallops, abalone, and shark's fin, one by one, and in that order.

3. Heat the 2 tablespoons of oil, fry the scallions and ginger for 1 minute, add the flour, and brown. Add the stock, rice wine, and both soy sauces, stir, and pour into the casserole. Poke with a chopstick to ensure there are no air bubbles, then cover with baking parchment and set the casserole on crumpled aluminum foil in a deep canning pot. Pour boiling water halfway up the outside of the casserole, cover and steam for 4 hours. Check every 30 minutes that enough water is in the outside pot. When done, remove the casserole and place on a trivet to serve.

CRISPY SWEET AND SOUR BEEF

This recipe, popularized by the Amoy Food Company, is now used throughout Fujian. They were kind enough to share it for use in this book. It has been adapted with their permission; brand names have been eliminated. SERVES 4 TO 6

7 ounces filet of beef
2 teaspoons thin soy sauce
½ teaspoon sesame oil
⅓ teaspoon five spice powder
½ teaspoon sugar
1 teaspoon cornstarch
3 eggs
⅔ cup all-purpose flour
Pinch of salt
Pinch of pepper
1 tablespoon vegetable oil
½ onion, shredded
½ green bell pepper, seeded and shredded
½ red bell pepper, seeded and shredded
6 ounces prepared sweet and sour sauce
1 teaspoon sugar
3 tablespoons water

1. Slice the beef thinly and marinate in a mixture of thin soy sauce, sesame oil, five-spice powder, sugar, and cornstarch. Set aside for 20 minutes.

2. Beat the eggs and flour with the salt and pepper.

3. Coat the beef with the egg batter. Heat a wok, add the vegetable oil, once the oil is hot fry half the beef until golden brown. Remove the beef from the oil and drain on paper towels. Repeat with the rest of the beef.

4. Combine both batches of beef and refry until crisp, then transfer the beef to a serving platter.

5. Reheat the oil, and stir-fry the onion and green and red peppers. Add the sweet and sour sauce, sugar, and 3 tablespoons of water. Bring to a boil and pour this over the beef. Serve.

FLAVORED RICE

This favorite and famous dish is served early in the morning, at a light lunch, an early dinner, or very late in the evening. Locals like theirs using fatty pork. Excess fat can be drained away late in the cooking process. **SERVES 4 TO 6**

- 4 large pork leg bones
- 6 slices peeled fresh ginger
- 2 tablespoons peanut oil
- 2 cloves fresh garlic, peeled and diced
- 1 tablespoon plus 1 teaspoon curry powder
- 4 dried Chinese black mushrooms (shiitake), soaked, stems removed, finely diced
- 1 pound very fatty ground pork, or ½ pound pork meat and ½ pound pork fat, ground
- 2 tablespoons dried red onions
- 1 teaspoon salt
- 1 teaspoon sugar
- ½ teaspoon ground white pepper
- 1 teaspoon ground cinnamon
- 1 teaspoon five-spice powder
- 4 cups or more cooked, hot rice

1. Simmer the pork bones and ginger in 8 cups of water for 4 hours. Remove the bones and ginger, and strain the liquid. Reserve 2 cups of this pork broth in the refrigerator, and use the rest for other purposes.

2. Heat a wok or skillet, heat the oil and add the garlic and stir-fry for 1 minute, then add the 1 tablespoon of curry powder and the diced mushrooms. Stir-fry for 1 minute.

3. Add the pork and continue to stir-fry for 3 minutes, and then add the red onions, salt, sugar, white pepper, cinnamon, five-spice powder, and the remaining teaspoon of curry powder. Mix well, transfer to a bowl, cover, and refrigerate for two days.

4. Break off any solid pieces of fat and discard them before returning the pork mixture to a preheated wok. Stir and add the 2 cups of reserved pork stock, bring to a boil, lower the heat, and simmer for 10 minutes. Skim any fat or surface solids before returning it to a boil. Again lower the heat and simmer for 5 more minutes, again skimming off any floating fat.

5. Put the rice in individual rice bowls and top each with a ladle of pork mixture.

NOTE: Any remaining pork can be refrigerated for later or another use.

LITCHI PORK

This dish originated in Fujian; it is also known as it was originally spelled, *lychee*, but *litchi* is the more acceptable spelling now. Popular with local seamen who tasted similar sweet meat and fruit dishes on neighboring islands, they probably brought it back to Fujian with them. Some modern versions make it with red dragon fruit in place of the litchi or with some of both fruits. **SERVES 6 TO 8**

- 1 pound pork loin, cut into thin 2-inch by ½-inch slices
- 1 egg yolk
- 1 tablespoon thin soy sauce
- 2 tablespoons Chinese rice wine
- ¼ cup sugar
- 3 tablespoons cornstarch
- 1 teaspoon sweet-potato flour
- 2 tablespoons vegetable oil
- ½ teaspoon sesame oil
- 1 red bell pepper, seeded with pith removed, cut into 1-inch diamonds
- 1 green bell pepper, seeded with pith removed, cut into 1-inch diamonds
- 3 scallions, white parts only, slivered
- 16 canned or peeled fresh litchi fruits

1. Mix the pork with the egg yolk, soy sauce, rice wine, and sugar, and marinate for 30 minutes, then add the cornstarch and sweet-potato flour.

2. Heat a wok or skillet and pour in both the vegetable and sesame oils. Drain the pork, if necessary, and stir-fry the meat in two batches, 1 minute each. Drain each batch with a slotted spoon. After both batches are fried and drained, set all but 2 tablespoons of the liquid aside for another use.

3. Reheat the pan and stir-fry the red and green peppers for 1 minute. Return the pork to the pan and stir-fry everything for 1 more minute. Add the fruits and stir-fry everything for 1 minute before transferring to a deep serving platter.

MANY LAYERS CASSEROLE

The beauty and creativity of this dish are the meat and vegetable layers. Those needing long cooking are lower; those higher need less cooking time. Flattened fish balls filled with meat can be near the bottom; they are always appreciated. The leafy vegetables near the top are both a textural and a visual contrast.
SERVES 8 OR MORE

- ½ cup vegetable oil
- 1 pound pork belly, chicken gizzards, or another meat requiring long cooking, cut into 1-inch pieces
- 10 to 20 Fujianese fish balls, whole or cut in half (frozen or homemade, see page 89)
- 1 or 2 sections lotus root, peeled and sliced
- ½ pound firm vegetables, cut into 2-inch slices
- 1 pound napa cabbage, cut into 2-inch slices
- 1 pound Chinese spinach, washed, stems removed
- 1 tablespoon dried shrimp or small fish
- 4 scallions, cut in 2-inch lengths
- 5 thin slices peeled fresh ginger
- 2 cups cold chicken, fish, or meat stock
- ½ cup Chinese black rice wine
- 3 tablespoons thin or mushroom soy sauce
- 1 teaspoon sugar
- ½ cup sweet-potato flour
- 1 teaspoon ground white pepper
- 1 teaspoon sesame oil
- 2 tablespoons Chinese black rice vinegar

1. Heat the vegetable oil in a wok or skillet, and fry the pork belly or other meat until golden and crisp on the outside. Drain, and save the oil for other purposes.

2. Put the drained meat into a large heatproof casserole that can be used on a stovetop. Put the fish balls in a single layer on top of the meat, then the lotus root and other firm vegetable slices. Top with napa cabbage and spinach. Try to keep the layers even.

3. Mix together the dried shrimp, scallions, ginger, stock, wine, soy sauce, sugar, sweet-potato flour, white pepper, sesame oil, and vinegar. Pour this mixture over the meat and vegetable layers. Cover and simmer for 2 hours. Serve in the casserole.

MEATBALLS WITH CRABMEAT

Sometimes called *Sunflower Pork*, this recipe dates back to Emperor Yang in the Sui Dynasty (581–618 CE). He visited Yangzhou and Sunflower Hill, and was served this combination of ingredients. When the dish became an important part of the cuisine is not known. SERVES 5 TO 10

- 1½ pounds minced pork
- 1 tablespoon Chinese rice wine
- 1 tablespoon soy sauce
- ½ teaspoon salt
- 1 teaspoon sugar
- 2 tablespoons minced scallion, white part only
- 3 slices peeled fresh ginger, minced
- 1 egg white
- 1 cup crabmeat, cartilage removed, minced
- 3 tablespoons water-chestnut flour or cornstarch
- 1 tablespoon vegetable oil
- 1 cup chicken broth
- 6 Chinese cabbage leaves, each cut in half widthwise

1. Mix together the pork, rice wine, soy sauce, salt, sugar, scallion whites, ginger, and egg white. Divide this mixture into ten parts. Likewise, divide the crabmeat into ten parts.

2. Flatten one portion of the pork mixture, put one portion of the minced crab in the center, and make a ball with meat on the outside and crabmeat in the middle. Be sure the crabmeat is totally enclosed by the meat mixture. Repeat until all ten are made. Roll each meatball in the flour or cornstarch. Set them aside for 30 minutes, until most of the flour or cornstarch has absorbed some liquid from the meat. Lightly flatten the balls into patties but do not break them open.

3. Heat the vegetable oil in a wok or skillet and fry the patties until browned. Add the chicken broth and cover. Simmer for 30 minutes, uncover, and remove the meat patties. Reserve the liquid.

4. Line a casserole that can be used on a stovetop with half the Chinese cabbage leaves. Place the meat on the leaves. Pour the reserved cooking liquid over the meat, and place the remaining leaves on top, completely covering all the patties. Cover the casserole, simmer for 15 minutes, uncover and then cook them five more minutes. To serve, place the casserole on a trivet.

PORK BELLY WITH MUSHROOMS

This recipe takes time to make but freezes well. Consider adding firm bean curd, potatoes, radish, pieces of Chinese pumpkin, and other foods that lend themselves to slow-cooking. **SERVES 10**

½ cup vegetable oil
2 to 3 pounds pork belly (raw unsmoked bacon), cut into 1-inch pieces
1 pound ground pork
12 to 15 dried Chinese black mushrooms (shiitake), soaked until soft, stems removed
6 scallions, each tied in a knot
12 large cloves garlic, peeled and cut in half
2 knobs (about 1 inch each) fresh ginger, peeled and cut in half
4 whole star anise
1 cup fried shallots or fried red onions
¼ cup red rice wine lees
1 cup dark soy sauce
1 cup Chinese dark rice wine, Fujianese preferred
½ cup brown rock sugar

1. Heat the oil in a wok or large pot, and fry about one-third of the pork belly until crisp on the outside. Drain and transfer to a large, heavy-bottomed pot from which you can serve, leaving the oil in the wok. Repeat until all of the pork belly is crispy brown and drained of oil. Reserve 2 tablespoons of the oil.

2. Reheat the 2 tablespoons of oil in the pan and fry the ground pork until it is no longer pink. Add the mushrooms, scallions, garlic, and ginger, and stir-fry for 1 minute. Drain and discard all the drippings.

3. Add the fried ingredients to the pot, along with the star anise, fried shallots, wine lees, soy sauce, rice wine, sugar, and 1 cup of cold water. Bring to a boil, lower the heat, and simmer, covered, for 1 hour. Uncover, and simmer for another 2 hours. If adding bean curd, potatoes, radish, or other vegetables, peel and cut them into 2-inch pieces and place in the casserole one hour after removing the cover from the pot. To serve, remove the star anise and scallion knots, and place the pot on a trivet.

PORK AND GARLIC VINEGAR

Most often made with pork, this recipe is also made with flank of beef. When using beef, reduce the marinating and cooking times by half. A common substitution these days is to replace the black rice vinegar with balsamic vinegar. **SERVES 6**

½ cup Chinese black rice vinegar
2 tablespoons thin soy sauce
1 tablespoon dark soy sauce
1 teaspoon sugar
¼ teaspoon ground white pepper
1 pound fatty pork, cut into 1-inch cubes
1 tablespoon vegetable oil
4 cloves garlic, peeled, then each sliced into 4 pieces
4 cups cooked hot rice or noodles

1. In a medium-size bowl, mix together the vinegar, both soy sauces, sugar, and pepper, then add the pork. Cover and refrigerate for 4 hours or overnight.

2. Drain the meat and discard the marinade. Heat a wok or heavy skillet, heat the oil, add the pork and the pieces of garlic. Stir-fry for 1 minute, then add 1 cup of water, lower the heat, and simmer for 30 minutes, or until the pork is very tender. Transfer to a serving bowl to be served alongside the rice or noodles, or pour over the hot rice or hot noodles previously divided among deep, individual bowls.

PORK WITH RED RICE WINE LEES

Although red and white rice wine lees are found in jars in the refrigerated sections of large Asian markets, people from Fujian often prepare their own. See page 214 to do so—the process will make your kitchens aromatic, indeed heavenly. SERVES 8 TO 10

- 1½ pounds lean pork, cut into ½-inch cubes
- 2 egg whites, beaten until frothy
- 3 tablespoons plus 2 teaspoons cornstarch
- 2 tablespoons red rice wine lees
- ½ cup cold chicken or pork broth
- 2 tablespoons Chinese rice wine, preferably Fujianese
- ½ teaspoon salt
- 1 teaspoon sugar
- ¼ cup vegetable oil
- 2 thin firm cucumbers, cut on an angle into ½-inch pieces

1. Combine the pork and egg whites, add the 3 tablespoons of cornstarch and mix well. Add the wine lees and continue to mix until thoroughly incorporated.

2. In a separate bowl, mix together the chicken broth, rice wine, salt, sugar, and 2 teaspoons of cornstarch, and set aside.

3. Heat a wok or a heavy skillet, heat the oil, and stir-fry the pork until the pieces separate. Add the cucumbers, stir-fry 1 minute, and then transfer with a slotted spoon to a bowl. Discard all liquid in the pan except for 1 tablespoon.

4. Reheat the oil, add the pork mixture, and stir-fry for 1 minute, then add the broth mixture. Stir-fry one minute or until the sauce thickens and clears somewhat. Pour into a serving bowl.

STEAMED CHINESE PUMPKIN

This popular Hakka dish is said to have originated in the mountainous regions of Fujian. Fujianese restaurants often have steamed pumpkins on reserve to fill with this stewed meat dish. Families get better results by steaming the pumpkin and the filling together. This melds the sweetness with additional flavors.
SERVES 8 TO 10

- 1 Chinese pumpkin (about 2 pounds)
- 1 tablespoon sesame oil
- 1 Chinese sausage, steamed for 20 minutes, then sliced into 3-inch pieces
- ½ cup cooked chestnuts (can be purchased precooked)
- 1 cup ½-inch carrots slices
- ½ cup small Chinese black mushrooms (shiitake), soaked, stems removed and discarded, quartered
- 1 cup cashews, toasted or dry-fried
- ½ cup chicken or beef broth
- 3 tablespoons red rice wine lees
- 1 tablespoon chili oil
- 1 egg
- 1 egg yolk
- 1 tablespoon cornstarch

1. Cut a slice off the pumpkin around the top, making a lid. Slice a little of the flesh from inside the top, just to make it flat and a bit thinner. Remove the seeds and stringy matter from the interior of the pumpkin base and rub it inside and out with the sesame oil. Make sure the bottom of the pumpkin is flat and that the inside is well-coated with sesame oil.

2. Mix together the sausage slices, chestnuts, carrot and mushroom pieces, and cashews, and put this mixture into the pumpkin.

3. Mix together the broth, wine lees, chili oil, egg, egg yolk, and cornstarch, and pour over the sausage mixture. Cover the pumpkin with its top and place it on a heatproof plate, then place in a steamer over rapidly boiling water. Cover the steamer, lower the heat, and simmer for 45 minutes. Carefully remove the pumpkin and its plate, and set on another large plate for ease of handling.

4. Pour off any liquid on the plate, and bring to the table. Remove the pumpkin cover, and cut slices about 2 inches apart and down to within 1 inch from the bottom, not cutting all the way down. Be sure to do this from center to the outside of the pumpkin. When you get to the last one, all the sections will fall outward like a flower.

STEWED PORK BELLY

Long-cooked, tender, and juicy, this dish can be made with large or small pieces of this fatty meat. Before serving, cut larger pieces into smaller ones for ease of consumption. **SERVES 10 OR MORE**

- 3 pounds pork belly (raw unsmoked bacon)
- 1 tablespoon vegetable oil
- 6 cloves garlic, peeled
- 1 tablespoon red rice wine lees
- 1 tablespoon Chinese rice wine
- ½ cup dark soy sauce
- ½ cup thin soy sauce
- 1 tablespoon thick soy sauce
- 2 tablespoons sugar
- 4 star anise
- 1 (2-inch) stick cinnamon
- 1 quart chicken or pork broth

1. Blanch the pork belly for 2 minutes in boiling water and then rinse with cold water.

2. In a large pot, heat the oil, and fry the garlic for 1 minute. Add the pork belly, wine lees, rice wine, all three soy sauces, sugar, star anise, and cinnamon. Stir-fry for 1 minute, then add the broth and bring to a boil. Lower the heat, cover, and simmer for 10 minutes, then remove the cover, and continue to simmer for 1 hour more.

3. Remove the meat from the sauce, cut into 1-inch cubes, and put into a serving bowl. Discard the star anise and cinnamon stick. Thicken the sauce by boiling it vigorously until ½ cup remains. Pour this over the pork belly pieces and serve.

STUFFED SLICED WINTER MELON

Winter melon sliced, stuffed, and then steamed is most popular in soup. This recipe is served without any sauce, with fish, shrimp, or crabmeat. Others place the rolls in a ring around a stir-fried shrimp or fish dish, and serve them as a main course. **SERVES 5 TO 10**

- 1 (1 pound) winter melon
- ½ pound pork or fresh bacon, minced
- 1 carrot, half minced, half sliced thinly
- ½ stalk Chinese celery, minced
- 3 Chinese black mushrooms (shiitake), minced
- 2 tablespoons fresh coriander (cilantro) leaves, minced
- 3 salted eggs, hard-boiled then yolks mashed (reserve egg whites for another use)
- 1 raw egg white
- 1 teaspoon vegetable oil
- 3 tablespoons cornstarch
- ½ cup vegetable broth

1. Peel the winter melon, and cut it in half crosswise. Then cut ten thin slices, five or fewer per inch. Make them all the same width, setting the ends aside. Blanch the slices in boiling water for 30 seconds; they will become somewhat clear and very pliable. Set them on paper towels. Be careful not to overcook the winter melon, just cook it enough so the slices are pliable and bend without breaking.

2. Finely dice 3 cups of the remaining uncooked winter melon. Use the rest for a soup or another purpose.

3. Mix together the diced winter melon, minced pork, minced carrots, celery, mushrooms, coriander, mashed egg yolks, and raw egg white. Divide this mixture into ten parts. Oil a plate that can go into a steamer.

4. Dust one side of the cooled winter melon slices with the cornstarch, reserving any leftover cornstarch. Take one slice and roll it around one portion of the meat mixture. Put the roll seam side down on the plate. Repeat until all ten are rolled and placed in a ring around the outside of the plate.

5. Place in steamer and steam over boiling water for 5 minutes. Then carefully slide the rolls, one by one, onto a clean serving platter. Pour any liquid on the plate into a small pot and add the remaining cornstarch mixed with the broth and sliced carrots, and bring to a boil. Stir for 1 to 2 minutes, until thickened and somewhat clear. Pour over the winter melon rolls and serve.

STUFFED BEAN CURD TRIANGLES

This recipe can be used as an appetizer, a soup, or a stew. Some folks deep-fry the leftovers in an egg-white/rice-flour batter, and serve them as a snack alone or with a red or black rice vinegar dipping sauce. Alternatively, they can be put into various soups or stews. SERVES 10 TO 12

- 6 firm bean curd squares, each about ¼ pound
- ¼ pound minced or ground pork
- 1 tablespoon dried shrimp, soaked until soft, then minced
- 1 scallion, minced
- 1 clove garlic, peeled and minced
- 1 teaspoon red rice wine lees
- 1 teaspoon cornstarch
- 6 tablespoons vegetable oil
- 1 tablespoon dark soy sauce
- 1 tablespoon Fujianese rice wine
- 1 teaspoon sugar
- Pinch of white pepper
- 2 cups chicken broth
- 2 tablespoons cornstarch mixed with 2 tablespoons cold water

1. Cut each bean curd square corner to corner into two triangles. Make a pocket in each triangle along the long side, but do not cut the piece of bean curd completely through into two pieces.

2. Mix together the pork, shrimp, scallion, garlic, wine lees, and cornstarch, and stuff 1 scant tablespoon of this mixture into each pocket.

3. In a wok or skillet, heat half the oil and fry half of the bean curd triangles, about 2 minutes per side, until crisp and golden brown. Drain them on paper towels and repeat with the rest of the oil and bean curd triangles.

4. Mix together the soy sauce, rice wine, sugar, pepper, and chicken broth, pour into the wok, and bring this mixture to a boil. Lower the heat, carefully add the bean curd triangles, and simmer for 5 minutes. Transfer triangles to a serving platter. Add the cornstarch mixture to the liquid in the wok, bring to a boil, and stir-fry until the liquid thickens. Pour over the triangles.

NOTE: If using as soup, add three or more cups of chicken broth. Some families prepare a batter of 2 egg whites and ½ cup of sweet-potato flour. They dip the triangles in it and deep-fry until lightly browned and crisp before putting them into the broth.

TRIPE WITH VEGETABLES

Tripe, the stomach lining of a pig or cow, is one of Fujian's favorite organ meats. It is eaten hot, warm, or cold, and enjoyed more by older people than by younger folk. SERVES 6 TO 8

1 pound beef tripe
3 tablespoons Chinese rice wine
1 tablespoon salt
2 tablespoons white rice wine lees
1 teaspoon sugar
1 tablespoon vegetable oil
3 slices peeled fresh ginger, slivered
¼ pound mung bean spouts, tails removed
1 red hot pepper, seeded and slivered
½ red bell pepper, seeded and cut in thin strips
2 sprigs fresh coriander (cilantro), stems removed, leaves cut in half

1. Blanch the tripe in boiling water for 1 minute, then soak it in ice water for an hour. Change the water, and soak it again in ice water for another hour. Drain, and discard the water.

2. Cut the tripe into 3-inch by 2- to 3-inch strips, and marinate in a mixture of the rice wine, salt, lees, and sugar for 1 hour. Drain the tripe, reserving the marinade.

3. When ready to serve, heat a wok or heavy skillet, heat the oil, and stir-fry the ginger for 30 seconds. Add the reserved marinade, tripe, bean sprouts, hot and bell peppers, and coriander leaves, and stir-fry for 1 minute more before putting on a small serving platter.

COVERED TEACUP AND CHOPSTICK REST

FISH AND FLOWER VEGETABLE CARVINGS

DISH OF BUDDHA JUMPS THE WALL IN A WINE JAR

DRIED BLACK FOREST MUSHROOMS (KNOWN AS SHIITAKE IN JAPANESE)

FRESH LITCHI FRUIT IN A WOK

SHANGHAI CABBAGE

RABBIT AND BALL–SHAPED VEGETABLE DUMPLINGS

DISH OF DIFFERENT JELLYFISH PREPARATIONS

TYPICAL BEAN SAUCES

OYSTER FLAVORED SAUCES

TWO DIFFERENT MOONCAKES CUT TO SHOW THEIR INTERIORS

FOUR DIFFERENT FILLED BUNS, SOMETIMES CALLED BREADS

SCALLION PANCAKE

STARCHES

THE MAIN STAPLE FOOD IN FUJIAN is steamed white rice. Another popular starch, perhaps second in importance, is sweet potatoes. Also used and cherished are boiled noodles, especially those made by pulling the dough exceptionally thin, into almost hair-like strands. These are made with wheat flour and used primarily in soups. Noodles can be of varying widths though. Only a few of them are made with eggs, most are just made with flour and water.

Northern Chinese prefer fresh noodles and steamed breads as their staple foods. Not so the Chinese from Fujian, which is a southern province. Here they sometimes make fresh noodles but eat more dried ones, perhaps because dried ones travel well and thus were embraced as an easily prepared seaman's meal.

Besides rice and noodles, dumplings and other dough-wrapped foods are popular, some used as an entire meal. They can be steamed, fried, baked, or cooked in many ways. Those made with sweet-potato or yam flour are favorites, as are those made with black, red, or white rice.

Meats with and without fish, and vice versa, can be mixed with rice, noodles, or sweet potatoes, and served at any meal. Usually, plain steamed white rice is also served, although sometimes it is the black or red rice that is included.

Years ago, almost everyone grew rice, raised a pig or two, and ground their own wheat, rice, and other flours. More common these days are commercially milled rice varieties and flours, and commercially prepared pastry products. Therefore, the variety and quantity of starches eaten by the Fujianese are greater than ever before.

BEEF, SHRIMP AND DUCK FRIED RICE

Throughout China, fried rice is a popular lunch or snack food. Each province, region, and family has a favorite preparation; almost all use cold or leftover rice. Fujian cooks prefer to use rice wine lees along with red rice. SERVES 6 TO 8

- 2 tablespoons vegetable oil
- ¼ cup chopped flank or chuck steak
- 2 eggs, well beaten
- 3 cups cooked rice (red preferred)
- 1 teaspoon soy sauce
- 1 conpoy (dried scallop), soaked for an hour, then shredded by hand
- 4 large shrimp, peeled, deveined, and cut in half head to tail
- 1 teaspoon oyster sauce
- 1 tablespoon red rice wine lees
- ½ teaspoon sugar
- ½ teaspoon salt
- ¼ teaspoon ground black or white pepper
- ¼ cup fresh or frozen peas
- ¼ cup roast duck meat, cut into thin strips
- 1 cup chicken stock
- 1 tablespoon cornstarch mixed with an equal amount of cold water

1. Heat a wok or skillet, heat the oil, and add the steak. Stir-fry for 1 minute, then using a slotted spoon, transfer the steak to a plate.

2. Add the eggs to the pan, and using a pair of chopsticks, scramble them until they start to set. Add the rice and stir-fry for 2 minutes. Transfer this to a separate bowl. Preheat a serving bowl.

3. Mix together the soy sauce, scallop, shrimp, oyster sauce, wine lees, sugar, salt, pepper, peas, steak, and duck. Reheat the pan, and pour in the stock and this sauce mixture, along with the cornstarch mixture. Stir-fry for 1 minute, then add the beef and the rice mixture, and stir-fry another 2 minutes. Transfer to the preheated serving bowl.

BLACK RICE WITH SWEET POTATOES

Black and red rice are popular in Fujian, as is white rice. The first two are most often glutinous rice, whereas most varieties of white rice are not, except for the rice used in sweet dishes. While all three colors of rice can be used to make wine lees, black rice rarely is. More commonly, it is used to make rice vinegars.
SERVES 8 TO 10

1½ cups black rice	2 tablespoons minced fresh ginger
1½ teaspoons salt	¼ teaspoon ground white pepper
1½ cups boiling water	2 sweet potatoes, peeled and diced into ½-inch pieces
¼ cup vegetable oil	
2 cups slivered scallions	

1. Rinse the rice three to five times, until the water is clear. Then put it into a 6-quart heavy Dutch oven and add 4 cups of cold water and the salt. Bring to a boil, lower the heat, and cover the pot, leaving a small opening for steam to escape. Simmer for an hour, or until all water is absorbed, whichever comes first. Remove from heat and set aside for 30 minutes. Repeat this cooking process using just 1 cup of boiling water, and cook the rice for another 30 minutes.

2. Heat a wok or skillet, heat the oil, stir-fry the scallions and ginger for 1 minute, then add the ground pepper and sweet potato pieces. Stir well, then add ½ cup of boiling water and continuing to stir on and off for 10 minutes, or until the sweet potatoes are tender.

3. Mix the black rice into the sweet potato mixture and serve.

HAW AND YAM DISKS

These disks can be used in various parts of a meal—breakfast, lunch, or dinner. They can also be a snack, put into soups or stews, served with cocktails, or eaten as a Western-style dessert, plain or in a hot, sweet syrup. Children also take them to school for lunch or snack. **SERVES 10 OR MORE**

6 cups high-gluten bread flour
⅛ cup sugar
1 whole egg
½ pound lard
⅛ cup all-purpose flour
½ pound Chinese yam flour
3 tablespoons light brown sugar
70 to 100 dried thin haw disks, broken into pieces
¼ cup pine nuts or walnuts, pounded or ground
2 tablespoons sesame seeds

1. Mix 3 cups of the high-gluten bread flour with the sugar, egg, and half the lard. Using two cleavers or knives, cut into small pieces. Then, with your hands, form the dough into a 1-inch-diameter roll and flatten it.

2. Mix together the other 3 cups of high-gluten flour and the remaining lard, and shape it as above. Place this on top of the first piece of dough. Roll them together to about twice their original length, then cut into thirty pieces. Gather each piece up, and roll each one into a ball. Flatten the balls. Sprinkle a flat surface with ⅛ cup all-purpose flour. On the floured surface roll each ball into a thin 4- to 5-inch circle.

3. Mix together the yam flour, brown sugar, haw, nuts, and 2 tablespoons of water.

4. Put a spoonful of the haw mixture in the center of each dough disk, wet the edges slightly with warm water, gather them together crimping the edges before flattening the dumpling gently with the palm of your hand. Put them, crimped side down, on an oiled baking sheet. Wet each top using a pastry brush, and sprinkle some sesame seeds on top. Tap the seeds lightly so they stick to the dough.

5. Bake in a preheated covered wok, or put the baking sheet into a preheated 400°F oven for 10 minutes.

NOTE: Serve warm or at room temperature. Leftovers can be reheated for 5 minutes in a hot oven, or cut in half or quarters and added to a soup or stew.

MEAT WITH NOODLES

Noodles served plain, in dishes, or in soups are popular. There are many creative mixtures based upon using leftovers and the fresh foods at hand. Do not be a slave to amounts and varieties of ingredients; use this dish's concept as a jumping-off point and be creative. Cut all ingredients the same size to assure they cook evenly. **SERVES 6**

- 1 tablespoon vegetable oil
- 1 tablespoon sesame oil
- 2 slices peeled fresh ginger, minced
- 2 cloves garlic, peeled and minced
- 1 small sweet or hot chili pepper, seeded, diced
- ¼ cup pound pork or other meat of your choice, diced
- 2 tablespoons Chinese red rice wine
- 1 teaspoon red rice vinegar
- ¼ cup diced fresh mushrooms of your choice
- 4 water chestnuts, coarsely diced
- ¼ cup coarsely diced bamboo shoots
- 1 to 4 cups chicken, meat, ham, or fish stock
- 2 scallions, sliced very thin
- ½ pound fresh noodles, cooked and cooled

1. Heat a wok or skillet, heat both oils, then add the ginger, garlic, and chili pepper and stir-fry 30 seconds. Add the pork, stir-fry for 1 minute, then with a slotted spoon transfer all solids to a bowl, leaving liquids in the pan.

2. Add the rice wine and vinegar to the cooking liquid, reheat, add the mushrooms, water chestnuts, and bamboo shoots, and simmer for 2 minutes. Add the stock, scallions, and noodles.

3. Bring to a boil, lower the heat, and return the pork mixture to the wok. Stir and simmer uncovered for 2 minutes.

4. Put the noodles into individual serving bowls or a tureen, and pour the pork mixture evenly divided into each bowl or into the tureen.

NOODLES AND VEGETABLES

Sometimes served at banquets as a final dish, this would have both heads and tails removed from the bean sprouts. At a wedding, the sesame seeds would be both white and black, and at a very fancy event, this dish would be made with red and black rice, serving each on half the platter or bowl.

SERVES 4 TO 6 AS A MAIN DISH; 10 AS A BANQUET'S FINAL COURSE

- ½ pound dried thin Fujianese noodles
- 2 teaspoons sesame oil
- ½ cup sesame paste
- ¼ cup cold tea
- 2 tablespoons thin soy sauce
- 3 tablespoons hoisin sauce
- 1 tablespoon vegetable oil
- 1 teaspoon chili oil
- 2 cloves garlic, peeled and minced
- ½ cup cucumber strips, cut into matchsticks
- ½ cup carrot strips, cut into matchsticks
- 1 cup fresh bean sprouts
- ½ cup slivered scallions
- Salt and pepper
- 2 tablespoons black sesame seeds

1. Cook the noodles according to the package directions, drain, and rinse with cold water until cool. Stir in half the sesame oil and set aside.

2. Mix together the sesame paste and tea, stir in the soy sauce and hoisin sauce, and set aside.

3. Heat a wok or skillet, pour in the vegetable and chili oils, then add the garlic, cucumber and carrot strips and stir-fry for 1 minute. Add the bean sprouts, scallions, some salt and pepper, the sauce, and the noodles.

4. Transfer to a large bowl and sprinkle with the sesame seeds.

PORK IN NOODLE NEST

There are many ways to make this dish, with or without the noodle nest. The noodle nests are fancy but not difficult. For a wedding, this dish could be made with a pair of intertwined nests as a final presentation, one egg put in each nest.
SERVES 6

- 2 cups vegetable oil
- 1 ounce bean thread noodles
- ¼ pound chopped or ground pork
- ¼ cup preserved or pickled vegetable, such as pickled cabbage, soaked for 10 minutes then rinsed
- ¼ cup pine nuts, minced
- 1 tablespoon dark soy sauce
- 1 tablespoon red rice wine lees
- 1 teaspoon black sesame oil
- 2 tablespoons sweet-potato flour
- ½ teaspoon salt
- ¼ teaspoon mixed ground white and black pepper (about half of each)
- 1 salted preserved duck egg, or raw chicken egg
- 1 teaspoon sesame oil
- ½ cup chicken stock
- 2 tablespoons cornstarch mixed with 2 tablespoons water

1. Put the vegetable oil in a wok or deep pot, and heat; to test if it is hot enough, put a tiny piece of the bean thread noodle in. If it expands upon contact, add half the noodles and turn them almost immediately when the bottom expands. After 30 seconds, remove the noodles and drain on paper towels. Repeat with the other half of noodles. Set them on a large platter, and using a little pressure, make a slight depression in the center.

2. Mix together the pork, preserved or pickled vegetable, pine nuts, soy sauce, wine lees, black sesame oil, sweet-potato flour, salt, and pepper. Shape into a single ball and flatten both the top and bottom a little. Make a well in the top, and put the egg in that indentation.

3. Oil a heatproof bowl that will fit in a steamer with the sesame oil, and put the pork ball into it. Steam over rapidly boiling water for 10 minutes. Place the meatball in the indentation that was made in the bean thread nest.

4. Put the chicken stock in a small pot, bring to a boil, and add the cornstarch mixture. Stir until thickened somewhat, then pour around the edge of the flattened meat, but not in its center.

POTATO CAKES

Made with white or sweet potatoes, or a mixture of both, these cakes, like many other dishes, are very versatile. At small meals such as breakfast or lunch, they can be cut in half. That is also a common technique when using them in stews or soups. **SERVES 5 TO 10**

- 1 pound white or sweet potatoes, peeled, diced
- ½ cup sweet-potato flour
- 1 teaspoon sugar
- ½ teaspoon salt
- ½ cup glutinous rice, soaked for 1 to 2 hours in 2 cups warm water
- 2 tablespoons regular rice
- 2 tablespoons black or white sesame seeds
- ½ cup vegetable oil

1. Cook the potatoes in a pot of water until soft. Drain, reserving ½ cup of the water. Mash the potatoes while hot, adding the sweet-potato flour, sugar, and salt.

2. Put the potatoes in a blender and add ¼ cup of the reserved cooking water. Blend until smooth. Remove the potatoes from the blender. Using another ¼ cup of the reserved water, blend both rices together. Mix the potato and rice mixtures well together by hand, and form into ten balls, flattening them into patties. Wet the tops with a little water and sprinkle sesame seeds on them, patting the seeds gently so they stick.

3. Heat the oil in a wok or a skillet, and fry half of the patties, unseeded side down, until golden brown, turn over, and then fry the other side. Drain on paper towels and keep warm in an oven. Do not cover them. Fry the second batch the same way. Serve warm.

SHREDDED YAM CAKES

Made with shredded yams, these cakes can have as much as a third of the yam replaced by white potatoes or turnips. These are popular snacks. Some people add slivers of fried pork belly or roast pork, even crispy fried fish slivers, or any combination of these or other ingredients. **SERVES 10**

- 1 pound yams, peeled and shredded
- ⅛ to ¼ pound white potatoes, shredded, steamed for only 10 minutes
- 3 to 6 tablespoons slivered fried pork belly or another cooked meat
- 2 tablespoons mashed raw or cooked fish
- 1 tablespoon sugar
- ½ teaspoon salt
- ⅛ teaspoon five-spice powder
- 3 tablespoons sweet-potato flour or cornstarch
- ⅛ teaspoon sesame oil
- 2 tablespoons dry-fried shallots
- 1 cup vegetable oil

1. Mix gently but thoroughly the yams, potatoes, meat, fish, sugar, salt, five-spice powder, sweet-potato flour, sesame oil, and fried shallots. Shape into ten patties, and set aside on racks to dry for 30 minutes.

2. Heat the vegetable oil, and fry the patties in small batches on one side, then the other, until lightly browned and crisp.

NOTE: The cakes can be kept warm in a warm oven for about an hour.

SWEET POTATO CAKE

These brown bread-like cakes can be made with any flour-based starter dough, but they cannot be made with a salt-raised bread starter. They can also be made with a cake of yeast or Chinese yeast ball. You will need 2 cups of a starter at room temperature. They are best when made at least a day in advance. SERVES 10 OR MORE

- 5⅛ cups high-gluten bread flour
- 1 teaspoon dry yeast
- 2 teaspoons white vinegar
- ½ pound sugar
- 3 eggs, beaten until light yellow
- ½ cup powdered milk or custard powder
- 1 teaspoon baking powder
- 6 tablespoons melted lard or margarine
- 1 pound sweet potatoes, peeled, grated, dropped into boiling water for 2 minutes, then drained well

1. Mix together ⅛ cup of the high-gluten bread flour, the dry yeast, and vinegar. Cover lightly and allow to rest for one day. It will foam and then the starter will settle down.

2. Mix the starter with the 5 cups of bread flour, sugar, eggs, and milk powder. Let rest for 8 hours or overnight.

3. Add the baking powder and melted lard to the dough and mix thoroughly, then add the sweet potatoes and mix well. Pour this batter into two cake pans lined with baking parchment. Cover lightly with another sheet of baking parchment. Let the paper overlap the edges of the pans. Place in a steamer and steam over rapidly boiling water for 30 minutes.

4. Remove the cakes from the pans and cool, then cut into individual pie-shaped pieces. If made earlier in the day or the day before, steam again, but only for 6 to 8 minutes, before serving.

BEAN CURD RICE ROLLS

This versatile dish is a popular snack and lunch item. It can be baked on the side of a wok or in an oven. Some people steam theirs, add sugar, and serve it as a sweet. SERVES 10 TO 12

- 2 bean curd sheets (about 10 x 20 inches each)
- 2 steamed rice sheets, about the same size as the bean curd sheets
- 1 cup bean curd noodles, cut into 2-inch lengths
- 1 ounce bean thread noodles, soaked for 30 minutes, then cut into 2-inch lengths
- 1 cup spinach, stems removed, leaves cut in half and blanched for 30 seconds in boiling water
- 1 cup cooked cold rice
- 1 teaspoon thin soy sauce
- 1 tablespoon sesame oil
- 1 tablespoon black sesame seeds
- 2 eggs, beaten well
- 2 tablespoons sugar (optional)
- 6 tablespoons vegetable oil

1. Cut the bean curd sheets into thirds, so each piece measures about 10 x 7 inches. Cut each rice sheet close to that size but a mite smaller, and put each on top of a bean curd sheet. Leave close to an inch along the short end of the bean curd sheet with no rice sheet on top of that edge.

2. Mix together the bean curd noodles, bean thread noodles, spinach, rice, soy sauce, sesame oil, sesame seeds, all but 1 tablespoon of the beaten eggs, and the sugar, if using. Divide this mixture into six parts, squeezing each one into a large cigar-shaped roll 1 inch shorter than the bean curd sheets. Place one of the rolls on a rice sheet at the covered short end of the bean curd sheet and roll up, turning in the sides. Brush some of the remaining egg on the plain bean curd edge and seal the roll. Repeat until all rolls are filled, sealed, and sitting on their sealed edges. Flatten each very slightly.

3. Heat a wok, heat 1 tablespoon of the vegetable oil, then put in one roll, seam side down. Fry for about 2 minutes on each side and transfer to a platter. Repeat until all six rolls are fried on both sides.

4. Add 1 cup of cold water to the wok and return the rolls to it, again putting them seam side down. Bring the water to a boil, lower the heat, cover the pan, and simmer for 10 minutes, or until all the water is absorbed. Transfer the rolls to a platter and cut each in half. They can be stood up on their ends, for a more decorative appearance.

VEGETABLES

FOR MANY FUJIANESE FAMILIES, after rice, vegetables are the main foods consumed. Vegetables are popular because many people grow their own, making them an economical food choice. Most are green and leafy, but some are starchy and tuberous. Most fresh vegetables are cooked before being eaten; others are pickled or preserved. They are central to Fujianese cuisine, as they are to all Chinese cuisine. They are so important that even banquets have special vegetable and/or vegetarian dishes.

Many different vegetables can appear in a main dish or appetizer, prepared in a variety of ways. Using any vegetable in one particular manner all the time is the antithesis of Fujianese thinking. Most are cooked with sauces ranging from the simple to the complex. A steamed vegetable, usually with a simple garlic or fermented bean sauce, is eaten at every main meal. The Fujianese also love to stuff their vegetables with many different kinds of foods. Vegetables are stuffed with bean curd, fish, meat, and even with other vegetables.

In Fujian, there is no limit to the variety and culinary techniques used with and for any and every vegetable, be it root, tuber, stem, bud, or leaf. The leaves of many types of plants not eaten in Western cookery are used by the Fujianese as vegetables. Two of the most beloved are the leaves of sweet potatoes and those of snow peas. These are the most expensive and the most savored of leafy greens.

Bean Sprouts and Bamboos Shoots

This vegetable combination can be enjoyed as a lunch dish; add meat and it is a main dish; change the meat and change its taste and character. It goes particularly well with kidney, sausage, and other strong meats, stir-fried separately then added a minute before serving. SERVES 4 TO 6

- 1 teaspoon vegetable oil
- 2 (1-inch) knobs of fresh young ginger, peeled and sliced
- 1 clove garlic, peeled and minced
- ¼ cup dried Chinese wolfberries (goji berries)
- ½ cup bamboo shoots
- 1 tablespoon thin soy sauce
- 2 cups bean sprouts, their heads and tails removed

1. Heat a wok or skillet, pour in the oil, and in 30 seconds add the ginger slices. Stir-fry for 30 seconds, add the garlic, and stir-fry for another 30 seconds.

2. Add the wolfberries and bamboo shoots, and stir-fry for 1 minute. Add the soy sauce and bean sprouts, and stir-fry for 1 more minute. Transfer to a serving bowl.

BRAISED EGGPLANT

This dish can be made without meat, or with crabmeat, shrimp, or any fish substituted for the ground pork. It can be served hot, warm, or at room temperature. Do not prepare it more than an hour before you are planning to eat it.
SERVES 8 TO 10

- 1 cup vegetable oil
- 6 thin purple eggplants, cut in half lengthwise and then each half cut widthwise into 4 pieces
- 6 tablespoons ground pork
- 2 cloves garlic, peeled and minced
- 3 slices peeled fresh ginger, minced
- 1 tablespoon thin soy sauce
- 2 tablespoons dark soy sauce
- 1 tablespoon Chinese rice wine or white rice wine lees
- 1 teaspoon sugar
- 1 cup chicken broth
- 1 tablespoon chili paste with garlic
- 1 tablespoon Chinese black rice vinegar
- 3 tablespoons minced water chestnuts
- 2 tablespoons minced bamboo shoots
- 1 tablespoon red rice wine lees
- 1 scallion, sliced thinly on an angle
- 1 teaspoon sesame oil

1. Heat a wok or heavy pot, pour in and heat the vegetable oil, add the eggplants and stir-fry for 2 minutes. Remove the eggplants and drain on paper towels. Pour out all but 1 tablespoon of the oil, reserving the rest for some other use.

2. Reheat the wok and stir-fry the pork for 1 minute, then add the garlic and ginger, and stir-fry for another minute. Add the eggplant and stir gently; then add both soy sauces and the rice wine, sugar, broth, chili paste, vinegar, water chestnuts, and bamboo shoots. Lower the heat and braise, stirring very gently, until the liquid is reduced to almost none, about 10 minutes. Add the wine lees, scallion, and sesame oil, and pour into a serving bowl.

BUDDHA'S BEAN NOODLES

This dish does not have eight vegetables, as does a classic vegetarian dish known as Buddha's Delight. It is served on top of, and not mixed with, the bean thread noodles and other vegetables. **SERVES 8 TO 10**

½ cup vegetable oil
4 (10- to 12-inch) *yaotai* (fried Chinese dough sticks), cut into 1-inch slices
1 pound Chinese cabbage, cut into ½-inch sections
3 tablespoons cloud ear fungus, soaked for 20 minutes in warm water, then chopped coarsely, any hard parts removed
30 daylily buds, soaked in warm water for 20 minutes, tough ends cut off, then individually knotted
2 (1-inch) squares fermented bean curd, mashed with ½ cup water
2 ounces dried bean thread noodles, soaked in warm water for 20 minutes, then cut into 3- or 4-inch pieces

1. Heat a wok, then pour in and heat the oil. When the oil is medium-hot, add the dough stick pieces, and stir-fry until lightly browned. Drain them on paper towels, and set the oil aside.

2. Mix the cabbage and cloud ear fungus together, and add the daylily buds.

3. Put 2 tablespoons of the oil back into the wok, add the cabbage mixture, and stir-fry for 1 minute, then add the mashed bean curd mixture and stir well.

4. Place the fried dough stick pieces on top, cover the wok, and lower the heat. Simmer for 2 minutes, remove the cover, stir, and add the bean thread noodles. Simmer uncovered for 5 minutes, stirring once or twice. Pour into a serving bowl.

CHINESE MUSHROOMS WITH SESAME SEEDS

This Fujianese recipe with Indonesian influences was probably brought back by seamen from forays to that part of Southeast Asia. It can be made on a Genghis Khan-type grill, an open fire, a metal plate atop any heat source, or in an oven. If fresh mushrooms are not available, soak dried ones until soft.
SERVES 10

30 fresh Chinese black mushrooms (shiitake), stems discarded
½ cup thin soy sauce
2 teaspoons sesame oil
2 teaspoons Chinese rice wine or white rice wine lees
1 teaspoon sugar
10 bamboo skewers, soaked in warm water for 30 minutes
2 tablespoons white sesame seeds

1. Score the caps of the mushrooms lightly in a cross-hatched pattern of four evenly spaced shallow cuts in each direction.

2. Mix together the soy sauce, sesame oil, rice wine or wine lees, and sugar, and brush it on both sides of each mushroom. Skewer three mushrooms on each bamboo skewer, weaving the skewers through the mushroom edges to prevent them from twisting or turning. Sprinkle the mushroom caps with sesame seeds.

3. Grill for 2 minutes per side, top side first.

COLD BEAN CURD

This dish is often eaten with Yam Congee (page 49) and/or Radishes and Eggs (page 187), or even eaten alone just as a snack. The Fujianese shave dried tuna or any other dried fish on top, and then call it "wood fish." Shredded dried fish is available prepackaged. SERVES 4 TO 6

1 (1-pound) cube soft bean curd
¼ teaspoon coarse salt
½ teaspoon sugar
1 tablespoon thin soy sauce
1 tablespoon coarsely chopped fresh coriander (cilantro) leaves
1 tablespoon shaved dried fish

1. Put the whole piece of bean curd on a deep serving plate or in a large Western-style soup bowl.

2. Mix together the salt, sugar, and soy sauce, and, if preferred, heat slightly. (Always do this if the bean curd is cold.) Pour this sauce over the bean curd.

3. Sprinkle the coriander and shaved dried fish on top. Just before eating, cut into pieces with a clean pair of chopsticks.

EGGPLANT WITH GARLIC

This easy-to-prepare dish, served hot, cold, or at room temperature, can be made a day in advance, but is best when made only two to three hours ahead of time. It is often served with the drained solids from Rice Noodles, Chicken, and Jellyfish Soup (page 64). **SERVES 4**

- 2 long, thin Asian-style eggplants, cut in half lengthwise
- 1 tablespoon oyster sauce
- 1 tablespoon sugar
- 1 teaspoon sesame oil
- 2 cloves garlic, peeled and diced
- 1 scallion, minced coarsely

1. Blanch the eggplants in boiling water for 2 minutes, then immediately put them in cold water for 2 minutes. Remove and weight them down under a plate or tray, with a glass of water or a book on top. Remove the weight after 5 minutes, and drain and discard the excess water. Cut into long slices and put on a serving plate.

2. In a small pot, combine ½ cup of water and the oyster sauce, sugar, and sesame oil. Bring to a boil, add the garlic, and remove from the heat. Let this sauce stand for 10 minutes before adding the minced scallions. Stir and pour over the eggplant and serve.

LONG BEANS AND BEAN SPROUTS

This vegetable dish can be made with a ¼ cup each of ground pork and minced preserved cabbage. Minced rabbit, oysters, clams, or shrimp are other possibilities. Add these common additions before the rice wine lees, cook them for 1 minute, then continue with the rest of the instructions. **SERVES 4 TO 6**

- 1 pound long beans, ends removed, cut into 2- to 2½-inch lengths
- 1 tablespoon vegetable oil
- ½ teaspoon red or white rice wine lees
- 2 cups bean sprouts, heads and tails removed
- ¼ teaspoon mixed salt and ground white pepper
- ½ teaspoon minced dried hot red pepper

1. Blanch the long beans in boiling water for 1 minute, then immerse in ice water and drain when very cold.

2. Heat a wok or skillet, pour in and heat the oil, then add the wine lees and long beans. Stir-fry for 2 minutes, add the bean sprouts and continue cooking for 1 more minute. Add the salt and pepper, and hot pepper pieces. Stir once or twice and then transfer to a serving platter.

MUSHROOM ROLLS

These rolls are popular at all meals and for snacks. Smaller ones are textural additions to thin soups and simple stews. Make a large supply, and do change the filling as desired. SERVES 10 OR MORE

- 30 large dried Chinese black mushrooms (shiitake), soaked in 1 cup warm water for 20 minutes, stems discarded
- ¼ cup bamboo shoots, cut into 1- to 2-inch-long slivers
- 1 carrot, cut into 1- to 2-inch-long slivers
- 1 tablespoon cornstarch
- ½ egg yolk, beaten until light yellow
- 1 teaspoon sesame oil
- 1 teaspoon soy jam (thick soy sauce)
- 1 slice peeled fresh ginger, minced
- 1 leek, cut into long thin strips to tie the rolls
- 2 teaspoons vegetable oil

1. Squeeze out and reserve the soaking water from the mushrooms. Pound each mushroom flat with the flat side of a cleaver.

2. Mix the bamboo shoot and carrot slivers with the cornstarch, egg yolk, sesame oil, soy jam, and minced ginger.

3. Put a small batch of this mixture on a mushroom, roll tightly, and tie and knot with one strip of leek. Repeat until all the mushrooms and filling are used.

4. Heat a wok or skillet, pour in and heat the vegetable oil, then stir-fry half the tied mushroom rolls until lightly browned. Remove with a slotted spoon and transfer to a platter. Stir-fry the second batch the same way and transfer to the platter.

5. Add the reserved mushroom liquid to any drippings in the pan and boil until reduced to 2 tablespoons. Pour over the mushrooms and serve.

PEA SHOOTS AND BEAN CURD

Pea shoots are also called "pea leaves." They are adored by the Chinese, and may be the most expensive of all Chinese fresh greens. Sweet potato leaves and spinach are successful substitutes. The special flavor in this dish is from the fermented bean curd, called *fuyu* in Chinese. These leaves are rarely served without this flavorful seasoning. **SERVES 4 TO 6**

2 tablespoons vegetable oil
2 slices peeled fresh ginger, slivered
2 cloves garlic, peeled and crushed
1 (1-cup) square firm white bean curd, cut into 1-inch cubes
1 (1- to 2-inch) piece firm brown bean curd, cut into slivers
1 (1-inch) cube fermented bean curd, mashed
1 tablespoon liquid from the bottle of fermented bean curd
½ pound pea shoots, stems trimmed, cut into 2- to 3-inch lengths
2 teaspoons dried Chinese wolfberries (goji berries), mixed with 2 teaspoons boiling water

1. Heat a wok or pan, put in half the oil, the ginger slivers and garlic, and stir-fry 30 seconds. Add the cubes of white bean curd, and stir-fry until the edges are crisp, about 2 minutes.

2. Add the brown and mashed fermented bean curd, and stir well. Then add the liquid from the fermented bean curd and stir until most of it has been absorbed. Set this aside.

3. Heat the rest of the oil and stir-fry the pea shoots until they begin to wilt. Put them on a preheated serving platter. Pour the bean curd mixture on top. Sprinkle the wolfberries over this and serve.

POTATOES WITH CHINESE CELERY

This recipe can also be made with just sweet potatoes or just white potatoes. Some people like theirs with pork, shrimp, and coriander added. If using pork, stir-fry it separately before adding it to the preparation of this dish. The shrimp is added raw 2 minutes before everything is cooked. The Chinese celery leaves can be replaced with coriander. SERVES 8 TO 10

2 sweet potatoes, peeled and cut into 2-inch chunks
2 white potatoes, peeled and cut into 1-inch chunks
¼ cup vegetable oil
1 scallion, coarsely minced
4 stalks Chinese celery, diced
½ teaspoon ground white pepper
1 teaspoon coarse salt
¼ cup coarsely minced Chinese celery leaves

1. Boil the sweet potatoes for 15 minutes, drain, and set aside, reserving their water.

2. Boil the white potatoes for 25 minutes, drain, and set aside.

3. Heat the oil in a wok or deep skillet, add the white potatoes, and stir-fry until they start to color, then add the sweet potatoes and continue to stir-fry until all are golden. Drain and remove from the oil. Set the oil aside for another use; do not wash or rinse the pan.

4. Reheat the pan, stir-fry the scallion for 30 seconds, then add the diced celery and stir-fry for another minute. Add the pepper, salt, the reserved potatoes, and ½ cup of the sweet potato water. Stir gently for 2 minutes, add the chopped celery leaves, toss well, and transfer to a serving bowl.

PUMPKIN WITH VEGETABLES

Stuffing larger vegetables with smaller ones is very popular in Fujian. Stuffings can also include but are not limited to seafood, meats, broth, and other animal products. This unusual one has the option of including or omitting an egg white, and so it can be free of any animal ingredient and totally acceptable to vegetarians. **SERVES 8 TO 10**

1 (1- to 2-pound) pumpkin, top and seeds removed, seeds discarded or used for another purpose
2 tablespoons Chinese celery, diced
2 tablespoons corn kernels
2 dried Chinese black mushrooms (shiitake), soaked, stems removed and discarded, caps diced
2 tablespoons fresh or frozen peas
2 tablespoons diced carrots
2 salted duck egg yolks, chopped (optional)
2 to 3 cups silken bean curd, mashed
½ teaspoon salt
½ teaspoon sugar
1 teaspoon cornstarch mixed with 1 teaspoon cold water
½ teaspoon sesame oil
Pinch of ground white pepper
2 teaspoons peeled, minced fresh ginger
2 egg whites, beaten until firm
2 cups vegetable broth

1. Place the pumpkin in a large, deep, heatproof bowl that will fit in a steamer.

2. Mix together the celery, corn, mushrooms, peas, carrots, egg yolks, and bean curd. Stir in the salt, sugar, cornstarch mixture, sesame oil, white pepper, ginger, and egg whites. Allow to stand for 10 to 15 minutes.

3. Put this vegetable mixture into the pumpkin, and fill the hollow with the broth, allowing any extra to overflow into the bowl.

4. Place the bowl in a steamer and steam for 30 minutes. Remove the cover of the pot, and allow the pumpkin to cool for 10 minutes before placing it on a trivet to serve.

RADISHES AND EGGS

A Taiwanese friend recalls this was often his only dish at dinnertime, sometimes served with the drained solids from Rice Noodles, Chicken, and Jellyfish Soup (page 64) or Yam Congee (page 49). His ancestors had moved from a small village in Fujian to Taiwan. Born in Taipei and now living on Long Island, he still often makes this comfort food. **SERVES 6 TO 10**

5 large eggs
½ teaspoon salt
1 teaspoon sugar
⅓ cup diced dried radish
½ to 1 cup leftover cooked noodles or rice
3 tablespoons vegetable oil
½ teaspoon sesame oil
1 scallion, minced

1. Break the eggs into a bowl and beat lightly. Add the salt and sugar, and beat a little more, then add the diced dried radish and the noodles or rice. Stir well.

2. In a wok or skillet, heat the vegetable oil until it is medium-hot. Add the egg mixture and stir continuously until lightly coagulated.

3. Stir in the sesame oil, top with the scallions, and transfer the eggs to a heated plate to serve.

STRAW MUSHROOMS WITH CHINESE CELERY

Use of any mushroom, fresh, dried, or canned, is commonplace in Fujian. Each is appreciated for its own texture and taste. Locals insist they are rarely mixed, though there is no reason not to combine them. Chinese black mushrooms take the longest to cook, abalone mushrooms less so. Therefore, adjust cooking times depending on the mushrooms being used. SERVES 4 TO 6

- 1 tablespoon vegetable oil
- 2 cloves garlic, peeled and minced
- ½ pound canned whole straw mushrooms, rinsed
- 1 tablespoon fermented black beans, rinsed and lightly crushed
- 1 teaspoon sugar
- 2 tablespoons mushroom soy sauce
- 4 stalks Chinese celery, cut into 1-inch pieces
- 2 teaspoons coarsely chopped Chinese celery leaves

1. Heat the oil in a heatproof clay pot on the top of the stove. Add the garlic and stir.

2. Add the mushrooms, black beans, sugar, and soy sauce, cover the pot, and simmer for 15 minutes.

3. Add the celery pieces and simmer for another 3 minutes; stir in the celery leaves, then simmer for another minute. Present in the claypot on a trivet.

STUFFED BITTER MELON

This vegetable will be less bitter and have less of a quinine taste if it is soaked for 30 minutes after the seeds and pith are removed. Adding ½ teaspoon of sugar when cooking helps, too. This particular steamed preparation aids in quinine reduction, as well. SERVES 6 TO 8

- 1 bitter melon, halved lengthwise, seeds and pith removed
- 1 tablespoon cornstarch
- ½ pound ground pork
- 1 Chinese sausage, steamed for 30 minutes then diced
- ¼ pound raw shrimp, peeled, deveined, and minced
- 1 clove garlic, minced
- 1 tablespoon Chinese white rice wine lees
- ⅛ teaspoon mixed salt and white pepper
- 1 egg white
- 2 tablespoons oyster sauce
- 1 teaspoon sesame oil
- ½ cup vegetable or chicken broth
- 4 teaspoons water chestnut flour or 1 tablespoon cornstarch, mixed with 1 tablespoon water

1. Steam the bitter melon over boiling water for 4 minutes.

2. Oil a plate with 2 teaspoons of vegetable oil, preparing it for the bitter melon.

3. Dust the cornstarch on the insides of the melon.

4. Gently mix together the ground pork, minced sausage, shrimp, and garlic; then add the rice wine lees, salt and pepper mixture, and egg white, and mix well. Stuff both halves of the bitter melon with this mixture and put on the prepared plate. Steam them over the boiling water for 20 minutes. Transfer from the steamer to a serving platter.

5. Mix the oyster sauce, sesame oil, broth, and flour mixture in a small pot. Bring to a boil, stir until thickened, then pour over the bitter melon.

TARO ROOT CASSEROLE

This dish is a Fujianese staple. One woman said she eats it daily. Sometimes it is the only dish served by her mom to accompany their several soups. Other times her mom makes it with more chicken stock, and it is yet one more soup at the table. **SERVES 10**

- 1 cup white rice
- 1 cup taro root, peeled and diced
- 1 tablespoon vegetable oil
- 2 cloves garlic, minced
- 1 cup 1-inch pieces boneless chicken thighs
- 8 shrimp, peeled and deveined
- ¼ pound ground pork
- 1 cup chicken broth
- 1 tablespoon sugar
- 2 tablespoons bottled fish sauce
- 2 tablespoons red rice wine lees mixed with 2 tablespoons cornstarch

1. Steam the rice with 2 cups of water for 20 minutes. Let it rest for 10 minutes before using it.

2. Steam the taro root for 12 minutes, then set aside, uncovered, until needed.

3. Heat a wok or skillet, pour in and heat the oil, then add the garlic. Stir-fry for 30 seconds, then add the chicken and stir-fry for 5 minutes.

4. Add the shrimp and pork, and stir-fry for another 2 minutes, then add the broth, sugar, fish sauce, and wine lees mixture. Bring to a boil.

5. Put the rice and taro root in a bowl, one on top of the other. Pour the chicken mixture over them and serve.

SWEET DISHES

CHINESE CUISINE, IN FUJIAN OR ANY PROVINCE, does not include Western-style desserts at ordinary meals, though fresh fruit is often served after them. There are sweet foods eaten as snacks, but the very sweet ones are not usually eaten every day or at meals. At banquets, sweet dishes are served interspersed with starch, meat, and vegetable dishes. However, even these are not heavily sugared, and rarely are they as sweet as any typical Western dessert.

At formal Fujianese meals, appetizers are often made a mite sweeter than the same dish might ordinarily be. The degree of difference might be a teaspoon or two of sugar per dish. This small amount of sweetener might also be added to a final main dish at such a meal.

Thus, there are some sweet dishes, but they are reserved for banquets, special meals, and snacks. Eight Treasure Stone Fruits is one of these. It would not be served at a regular family meal, nor would Ginseng and Bird's Nest Sweet Soup, Pear-shaped Sweet Dumplings, or any of the others in this chapter.

There are exceptions, sweet soups the most common among them. Others are candies and some foods for the New Year, special wedding foods, and several snack foods, including small fried and baked cakes. These can be served at any time during a banquet and at any time as a snack.

A common snack in China's southern regions is dim sum. While not as popular or as elaborate in Fujian as in the Guangdong province, there are some snack foods associated with Fujian. Deep-fried Chestnuts and Stuffed Sweet Potato Cakes are foods served as snacks and at meals. However, these snack foods are often served differently than Western-style desserts. One stuffed pastry will be cut in thin pieces to share with many other diners. As such, a sweet is considered a delicacy to the Chinese, to be savored in small portions.

CLOUD EAR AND FRUIT SOUP

Though called "soup," this dish is often served at the end of a meal, but before a fresh fruit finale. The "cloud ears" used in this dish are white tree ear fungus. Some refer to them as "jelly fungus." This type of gelatinous tree or cloud ear fungus appears most often in a sweet dish, and this soup is a very typical example. SERVES 10

- ½ cup glutinous rice, soaked overnight, then boiled for 2 hours until very soft
- 16 dried pitted longans, boiled for 20 minutes, then cut in half
- 1 cup mung beans, skins removed after soaking, and boiled for 1 hour
- 8 dried Chinese wolfberries (goji berries)
- 1 ounce white tree ear fungus, soaked in warm water for 1 hour, hard centers discarded
- ½ cup sugar
- ½ cup cooked Job's tears or barley

1. Drain the glutinous rice. Bring 6 cups of water to a boil, add the rice, and simmer for another hour.

2. Add the longans, mung beans, wolfberries, fungus, sugar, and Job's tears, and simmer for another hour.

3. Cool until warm, and then serve in individual bowls.

DEEP-FRIED CHESTNUTS

The chestnut is both a staple food and considered the king of nuts. They are used in main and dessert dishes, and as a snack. Preparation is easy as they now come peeled and cooked. In years past, children helped their parents boil and peel them. Now, as adults, they prefer them in this prepared fashion, but admit they are not as good as the fresh ones. SERVES 10 OR MORE

2 pounds chestnuts, cooked and peeled, and left whole
2 ounces rock sugar
2 ounces granulated sugar
2 tablespoons molasses
2 tablespoons vegetable oil

1. For those still using raw chestnuts, use a knife to make an X on the flat side and boil them for 30 minutes. While still warm, peel away both the exterior shell and the skinlike inner membrane. Discard any moldy or black-streaked chestnuts. If using precooked packaged ones, soak them in hot water for 30 minutes, drain, and set aside for ten minutes to dry.

2. Bring both sugars, the molasses, and 4 cups of water to a boil. Add the chestnuts, lower the heat, and simmer for 20 minutes, until almost all the liquid has boiled away. Remove the chestnuts from the pot and place in a strainer basket to cool.

3. Heat the vegetable oil in a wok or skillet, add the chestnuts, lower the heat, and stir-fry them until they are golden brown. Drain and cool.

EIGHT TREASURE STONE FRUITS

Symbols of good fortune, pears are used more often than apples in this dessert, though both of these so-called "stone fruits" are popular. Eight is a lucky number, and when using apples said to bring double luck. **SERVES 8**

Juice and zest of 1 lemon or orange, zest chopped
8 nicely-shaped apples that stand straight on a flat surface
1½ cups cooked and cooled glutinous rice
2 tablespoons sugar
10 roasted peanuts, chopped
¼ cup mashed sweetened red beans
1 teaspoon sesame seeds

1. Mix the citrus juice with 2 cups of cold water. Immerse the apples, stems not removed, in the liquid.

2. Cut ½-inch off the top of each apple, below the stem. Put these into the juice. Remove the core of each apple, being careful not to cut through the skin. Cut away some of the area around the core, leaving ½-inch-thick circular wall of apple. Put the apples back in the juice.

3. Mix together the rice, sugar, peanuts, red beans, and zest, and divide this filling into eight parts. Use one portion to stuff each apple. Sprinkle a few sesame seeds on the stuffing. Set the apples on a square of foil in a large bamboo basket on a steamer rack.

4. Steam the apples for 15 minutes, then remove carefully, setting each one in a Chinese soup bowl to serve.

GINSENG AND BIRD'S NEST SWEET SOUP

This special-occasion soup for weddings, sixtieth birthday dinners, and other equally honorific meals can be doubled, tripled, or made even larger to meet the needs of any number of guests in attendance at such an event. **SERVES 8**

1 cup cleaned and soaked bird's nests
½ cup fresh or dried ginseng
2 cups cold chicken broth
½ cup white rock sugar
8 cups boiling water
½ cup dried Chinese wolfberries (goji berries)

1. Soak the bird's nests in 1 quart of tepid water for 1 hour. Check over to be sure any extraneous materials are removed, and then tear into ½-inch pieces.

2. If using dried ginseng, soak it in the 2 cups of cold chicken broth. Remove from the broth and peel or trim, if necessary. Fresh or dried, slice the ginseng thin, and cut each slice into 3- x ½-inch pieces.

3. Put the bird's nests, ginseng, chicken broth, rock sugar, and 2 cups of boiling water into a heatproof bowl that will fit in a steamer. Place in the steamer, cover and steam over boiling water for 15 minutes. Lower the heat and steam for an additional hour, checking often to see if there is enough water in the steamer.

4. Add 6 more cups of boiling water and the wolfberries to the bowl, and steam for another 30 minutes. Pour into individual soup bowls to serve.

PAPAYA AND SHARK'S FIN SWEET SOUP

This wedding or birthday soup is also served at other times by the affluent. For special occasions, they would cut the edges of the fruit in a decorative fashion. A more ordinary presentation would see it peeled and simply cut into cubes. SERVES 6 OR MORE

6 small or 1 large almost-ripe papaya
¼ cup precooked shark's fin
6 cups chicken broth
1 teaspoon minced, fully cooked Yunnan or Smithfield ham

1. Slice the top(s) off the papaya, about 3 inches from the top, and reserve. Remove and discard the seeds. Cut a decorative edge around the top of the bottom section(s), if desired. Use a spoon to remove the papaya flesh from the center(s) of the papaya. Cut the removed fruit into ½-inch dice and set aside.

2. Put the shark's fin and chicken broth into the papaya(s) dividing equally and replace the top(s). Place in a steamer and steam over simmering water for 1 hour. Carefully remove the papaya(s) from the steamer, sliding onto a large, shallow platter. Remove the top(s) and add the minced ham and diced papaya.

PEAR-SHAPED SWEET DUMPLINGS

Often used in fall and winter, these dumplings look like, but do not taste like, pears. Many families use them at the end of a meal, others use them as an appetizer. Some serve them with tea, especially during the New Year holiday.
SERVES 8

- 1 large preboiled white potato, peeled, cut in large cubes
- 1 large preboiled sweet potato, peeled, cut in large cubes
- 3 tablespoons sweet-potato flour
- 1 egg, separated
- 1 teaspoon salt
- ½ teaspoon brown sugar
- 2 cups plus 1 tablespoon vegetable oil
- 2 tablespoons ground pork
- 1 large Chinese black mushroom (shiitake), soaked, stem removed, and cut into 3-inch cubes
- 2 large shrimp, peeled, deveined, and finely diced
- 3 longans, pitted, peeled, and diced
- 1 (1-inch) ham cube, cut into 8 thin strips
- 1½ cups steamed bread, sliced, dried, then finely diced

1. Mash both kinds of potatoes together, adding the sweet-potato flour, egg white, salt, and brown sugar.

2. Heat a pan, add and heat 1 tablespoon of the vegetable oil, and add the pork. Stir-fry for 1 minute then add the mushroom, shrimp, longans, and egg yolk, and stir well. Stir-fry for 2 minutes, then remove from the heat and cool.

3. Divide the potato mixture into eight parts. Roll each into a ball. Elongate one part to emulate the shape of a pear. Make an indentation into the opposite end with a spoon, and insert 1 tablespoon of the pork mixture. Press the potato mixture around the base of the "pear," enclosing this filling. Shape this filled end so it looks like the bottom of a pear, the other end narrowing like the top of one. Insert one thin piece of ham at the top to represent the stem.

4. Roll the dumplings in the diced bread and allow them to dry for 1 hour.

5. Heat the remaining 2 cups of vegetable oil, and using a large cooking spoon, gently immerse half the dumplings in the oil. Deep-fry them, stirring often, until evenly browned on the outside. Remove them from the pan and drain on paper towels while deep-frying the rest of the dumplings. After all are fried, stand three in the center of a flat platter. Put the others around them and serve.

"PEAR" SURPRISE

A meat and sweet combination is almost as common as meat and fish. The name of this recipe may be misleading, as there are no pears in this dish. However, it does look like a platter of them. The eye tricks the mind into believing they are very sweet. **SERVES 8**

¼ pound ground pork, cooked and cooled
4 dried Chinese black mushrooms (shiitake), soaked until soft, stems discarded, caps minced
8 shrimp, peeled, deveined, and minced
2 whole canned water chestnuts, minced
2 tablespoons minced Yunnan or Smithfield ham
4 teaspoons sugar
3 pounds potatoes, boiled, peeled, mashed, and cooled
8 whole cloves
1 to 2 cups dried bread crumbs
6 cups vegetable oil

1. Mix together the pork, mushrooms, shrimp, water chestnuts, ham, and sugar. Divide into eight parts.

2. Divide the mashed potatoes into eight parts and mold each portion into a ball.

3. Stuff one batch of pork mixture into one mashed potato ball, seal, and elongate top of ball so that it looks like a pear. Put a clove at that end to resemble the stem, and roll the mock pear into the bread crumbs. Set aside. Repeat until all potato balls are filled, shaped like pears, and coated with bread crumbs. Set aside, covered, in the refrigerator or a cool place for 1 to 2 hours.

4. Heat the oil to 300°F and fry half the potato-pears until crisp; do not stir them but do use a ladle to pour hot fat over them continuously. Then remove and gently put them on paper towels to drain. Repeat with the other potato-pears. Serve on a platter.

RICE WINE, EGGS, AND FRUIT

One friend's family makes this dessert without fruit, another says her family likes it with fruit. The former makes hers with white glutinous rice, the latter with red glutinous rice. As with many dishes originating in Fujian, there are ever so many variations. **SERVES 8**

1 whole egg	2 tablespoons sugar
2 egg whites	3½ cups cooked glutinous rice
2 cups red rice wine lees	1 or 2 ripe mangoes, or any other ripe fruits, diced
3½ cups boiling water	

1. Gently beat the whole egg and egg whites until frothy but not firm.

2. Mix the wine lees with the boiling water, add the sugar, and bring this mixture back to a boil. Turn off the heat and add the glutinous rice and then the egg mixture, stirring slowly until well mixed.

3. Divide the mango evenly among eight individual bowls and pour the egg mixture into each. Place the bowls in a steamer and steam over rapidly boiling water for 5 minutes. Remove from the steamer; they will not be completely coagulated. Serve.

Steamed Eggs, Asparagus, and Milk

This recipe can be served at breakfast with other leftovers, or eaten as part of a dim sum lunch. The Chinese like their eggs soft. These are pretty, with the vegetable slices looking like flower petals, and their centers topped with tiny eggs.
SERVES 5 OR 6

- 1 large spear asparagus, blanched for 1 minute, then put into cold water
- 4 eggs, beaten well
- ½ cup condensed milk mixed with ½ cup cold water
- 1 teaspoon cornstarch
- ½ teaspoon vegetable oil
- 1 teaspoon crab roe or another red roe

1. Thinly slice the asparagus spear into twenty or twenty-five slices.

2. Slowly stir together the eggs, condensed milk mixture, and cornstarch, being sure to keep bubbles to a minimum.

3. Use the oil to wipe the bottom and sides of a somewhat shallow heatproof dish, and put it in a steamer. Slowly pour in the egg mixture and steam over simmering water for 5 minutes.

4. Arrange the asparagus pieces like flower petals with four or five per blossom in several locations around the outside of the steamed egg mixture. Put a scant amount of roe in the center and steam for another minute before serving.

STUFFED SWEET POTATO CAKES

These popular sweets are used at either the beginning or end of a regular meal. They can be found in the middle of a banquet, as well. There are even times when these exceptionally popular cakes are served as a snack or a breakfast food. SERVES 10

3 pounds deep red sweet potatoes
½ cup sugar
1 cup wheat starch
1 cup glutinous rice flour
½ cup rice flour
¼ cup sesame seeds, ground
1 cup melted lard
3 tablespoons whole sesame seeds
2 cups vegetable oil

1. Peel the sweet potatoes, then cut into quarters and boil in 6 cups of water until soft. Mash them with the sugar. When cool, divide into five parts.

2. Heat a wok, and fry the wheat starch, rice flours, and ground sesame seeds until aromatic and barely colored. Stir in the lard, set aside to cool, and then divide this mixture into five parts. Flatten each of them.

3. Take one part of the sweet-potato mixture and cut it into two parts. Pat one into a ½-inch thick pancake, put the flattened flour pancake on it, and cover it with the other sweet-potato mixture half. Be sure to cover the flour mixture, pressing the sweet potato edges together to seal. Put about 1 teaspoon of the whole sesame seeds on top and bottom of the stuffed cake, pressing them in. Repeat until all five cakes are assembled. Cover and chill for 2 or more hours.

4. Heat the oil and fry half the stuffed cakes until crisp on one side, then turn and fry on the other side. Set the cakes aside to drain on paper towels. Repeat until all are done. Cut each in half and serve on a platter.

Sweet Potato Sweet Soup

Many dishes in Fujianese cuisine appear to be soups, this being no exception. Made with granulated sugar in the United States but with large pieces of brown sugar-cakes in Fujianese homes, it can be served anytime during a meal, at a banquet, or as a snack food. **SERVES 10**

1 pound sweet potatoes, peeled and cut into 2-inch pieces
6 slices peeled fresh ginger, slivered
½ cup brown rock sugar, or to taste
16 dried Chinese wolfberries (goji berries)

1. Bring 2 quarts of water to a boil, lower the heat, and gently put in the sweet potato pieces. Simmer for 10 minutes, and then add the ginger, sugar, and wolfberries.

2. Simmer for 15 more minutes. Cool and serve in individual bowls.

BEVERAGES

TEA IS NOT THE MOST COMMON BEVERAGE in China—soup has that honor. Tea is also not the most common beverage at a banquet meal. At those and many special meal occasions, wine and harder spirits such as *maotai* are served. They are presented with a specific protocol, not simply consumed, but used for toasts. One never picks up one's own glass for a drink, but rather one lifts it up, toasts another person at the table, then this person lifts a glass in return, and both individuals drink together.

Aside from soups, teas and alcoholic beverages, health drinks, water from cooking vegetables, and more recently, sodas and juices have made their way to dining tables.

When someone comes to the house or office, tea is the preeminent drink on those occasions and it is served almost immediately upon their arrival. In the Fujian province, pu-er tea is the most common tea variety. Made from larger leaves than most teas, even though it is oxidized twice, pu-er tea can be green, oolong, or black.

ALMOND TEA

This beverage is usually served hot. It can also be made into a gelatin and eaten with a spoon. Cubed fruit can be added to the gelatin during the setting period, if desired. SERVES 8 TO 10

1 cup ground almonds
3 tablespoons ground glutinous rice powder
1 (10 to 15 ounce) can evaporated skim milk
1 cup sugar
¼ cup cornstarch mixed with ¼ cup cold water

1. In the top of a large double boiler, mix together the ground almonds, glutinous rice powder, evaporated milk, and sugar. Add 8 cups of cold water and the cornstarch mixture.

2. Put boiling water in the bottom of the double boiler, bring back to a boil, and set the top of the double boiler on it. Simmer, stirring continuously, until the mixture is thick. Serve hot, to drink or eat with Chinese ceramic soup spoons. This beverage can also be served chilled in hot weather.

ALMOND MANGOSTEEN TEA

This "queen of fruits" beverage is a popular drink in Taiwan, Guangdong, and the Fujian province. For those unable to locate mangosteens, the litchi or the fire dragon fruit is an appropriate substitute—the textures are similar but the flavors are not the same. **SERVES 4 TO 6**

¼ pound almonds, shelled, paper skins removed by blanching for 1 minute
2 tablespoons glutinous rice, soaked in water for 2 hours
2 candied dates, soaked in water for 2 hours
¼ cup evaporated milk
1 teaspoon sugar
3 fresh mangosteens, segments separated and pits removed

1. Mix together the almonds, rice, and dates, and put them in a blender with 2 cups of cold water. Blend for 2 minutes in 1-minute or shorter time increments, turning the motor off for 1 minute between each blending.

2. Line a 2-quart pot with a double layer of cheesecloth, and pour the blender contents into it. Twist the cloth tightly by its ends and squeeze out all liquid into the pot. Discard the solids. Heat the liquid to just below the boiling point, lower the heat, and simmer for 10 minutes.

3. Add the evaporated milk and sugar, and stir until all the sugar is dissolved. Then add 4 cups of cold water and the mangosteen segments. Heat this to just below the boiling point, then remove the pot from the heat source. This beverage can be served hot, warm, or cold in glasses, or eaten from soup bowls.

CHINESE OLIVE DRINK

Chinese green olives are bittersweet. They are appreciated for healing sore throats, aiding digestion, and quenching thirst. Some herbalists also credit them with detoxifying poisons. However, rarely do they specify exact ones. They advise drinking but a tenth of this recipe at any one time, and storing the rest on ice. SERVES 10

20 pitted Chinese green olives	20 dried Chinese wolfberries (goji berries)
1 cup rock sugar crystals	

1. Mash the olives with the end of a cleaver handle or in a blender, and process with ½ cup of water.

2. Bring 2 quarts of water to a boil, then add the olive mixture, sugar, and wolfberries. Lower the heat and simmer, uncovered, until the liquid is reduced to 2 cups. Do not consume more than one Chinese teacupful every few hours. This can be served hot, warm, or cooled.

GINGER BEEF TEA

This beverage is loved hot in winter before a main meal. If used as a soup, add bean sprouts, shredded cabbage, or any other shredded greens just before serving. Some families remove the beef before serving; however, the less affluent leave the meat in or remove it and add it to a fried rice or stew. **SERVES 8**

½ pound boneless beef such as chuck, cut into ½-inch cubes
1 tablespoon Chinese rice wine or any dry sherry
6 slices peeled fresh ginger
Pinch of ground white pepper
⅛ teaspoon salt

1. Put the beef cubes and wine into a wok or a deep nonstick pan, and stir-fry until browned.

2. Add the ginger, pepper, and salt, and stir well. Add 2 quarts of water and simmer, covered, for 2 hours. Strain before drinking.

GINGER TEA

The Chinese believe crabs are philosophically "cold" in the yin/yang dichotomy, and should be neutralized by drinking a "hot" beverage. Therefore, they drink this tea with or immediately following consuming crabs. **SERVES 6 TO 12**

4 tablespoons minced peeled fresh ginger
1 large cube (about a teaspoon) brown rock sugar
4 to 6 cups boiling water

1. Macerate the ginger by mashing with the side of a cleaver or the end of its handle. Put the macerated ginger into a teapot, along with the brown sugar.

2. Pour 4 to 6 cups of boiling water into the pot and cover it. Let the tea steep for about 4 minutes, or until flavorful. Some strain out the ginger pieces, others consume them.

NOTE: A second batch of boiling water can be poured after the first is consumed, if the pieces of ginger remain. It needs to steep 6 minutes the second time around.

MUNG BEAN TEA

Tea masters keep many teapots, each for brewing a different type of tea. Fujianese families keep a teapot just for bean and beef teas, and they advise it is best not to use regular teapots for this tea, because it could flavor their daily teas. **SERVES 6**

- 2 tablespoons *longjing* or any other green tea leaves
- 2 teaspoons mung-bean flour
- 2 teaspoons sugar

1. Put the tea leaves in a teapot along with the mung-bean flour and sugar.

2. Pour in 6 cups of boiling water and brew for 3 minutes; it is then ready to drink.

NOTE: If mung-bean flour is unavailable, remove the green outer skins of 2 tablespoons whole dry mung beans and discard, then put unshelled beans into a coffee grinder. Pulse until the beans are ground into flour. They can also be ground into flour with a mortar and pestle.

Soy Milk

Soy milk is popular cold or hot as a beverage, or as a dip for crullers and dumplings. Vegetarians and others have used this milk since Prince Liu An, said to be the first to make this nondairy beverage, drank it during the Han Dynasty (202 BCE–220 CE). **SERVES 8**

2 cups soybeans

1. Discard any broken or moldy beans and any other matter mixed with them.

2. Put the soybeans in a large pot, add 2 cups of water, and soak them overnight or for at least 6 hours before discarding the water.

3. Put 1 cup of the beans in a blender with 2 cups of cool water. Blend for 30 seconds on medium, then for another 30 seconds on high. Strain this mixture through a cheesecloth placed over a large bowl. Squeeze out as much additional liquid into the bowl as possible, twisting the cheesecloth tightly. Put the residue in a separate bowl. Repeat until all the beans have been blended and strained.

4. Add 2 cups of water to the bean mash, and pour the liquid and solids through the cheesecloth over the bowl one more time, extracting as much liquid from the mash as possible. Discard the bean mash.

5. Pour the resulting soy milk into a 10- or 12-quart pot, and slowly bring to a boil. Watch it carefully so that it does not foam or boil over—stirring helps. When almost boiling, lower the heat, and simmer for 15 minutes. Refrigerate any soy milk not consumed immediately. It can be kept for about five days.

RICE WINE AND RICE WINE LEES

A friend's father makes this wine using both unpolished and polished glutinous rice, red or white. There are minor differences in taste, and major ones in color. Making rice wine results in a residue after pouring out the wine. The residue is called rice wine lees, sometimes known simply as wine lees. The wine lees, as has been seen throughout this volume, is used for desserts, main dishes, and ever so many other preparations. Fujianese people prefer theirs made from red rice wine residue, but they do use both red and white.

Those allergic to rice can replace the rice wine lees with another beverage made from barley, potatoes, even grapes. MAKES 4 QUARTS

4 cups glutinous rice
1 (1-inch) commercially made Chinese yeast ball
1 teaspoon all-purpose flour

1. Soak the rice in hot but not boiling water for 1 hour, then drain, and discard the water.

2. Steam the rice over boiling water for 25 minutes. Rinse the rice with warm water until it has cooled to 95°F.

3. Crush the yeast until it is totally powdered, then mix it with the flour.

4. Put the rice in a preheated 3-quart pan and using your hand, mix in the yeast until thoroughly incorporated. Gently pat the rice, making it even and flat across the top. Make a well in the center and push the rice up the sides of the pan. Cover tightly with plastic wrap and put the pan in a warm place. Add additional coverings, using several heavy towels or blankets.

5. After four or five days, uncover and put the rice and its liquid, equally divided, into one or more clean jars with lids. Cover and refrigerate. The clear liquid is the rice wine, the solids are the wine lees. They can stay refrigerated for a year or two.

Miscellaneous Recipes

HOMEMADE MOCK WINE LEES

This chapter begins with another mystery. No one could explain this recipe's name or its origin. We know it serves well as a substitute for rice wine lees, particularly for red rice wine lees. MAKES ABOUT 1 PINT

- 2 tablespoons corn oil
- 1 tablespoon peeled fresh ginger, minced
- 3 cloves garlic, peeled and minced
- 3 scallions, minced
- ½ red bell pepper, minced
- 3 tablespoons tomato paste
- 2 tablespoons hoisin sauce
- 1 tablespoon granulated sugar
- ½ cup unsweetened rice wine
- 3 tablespoons *maotai* or any flavorless brandy

1. Heat a wok or small pot, add the oil, ginger, garlic, scallions, and red bell pepper, and stir-fry for 3 minutes. Add the tomato paste, hoisin sauce, sugar, and rice wine, cover the pot, and lower the heat. Simmer for 30 minutes.

2. Remove the cover, add the *maotai*, bring to a boil, and stir until thick. Then remove from the heat and cool. Store in a glass jar in the refrigerator. This can keep for a month or two.

PICKLED FRUIT

At weddings, the fruit used in this recipe would be peaches because they are emblematic of marriage and wishes for longevity. Any stone fruit works well though, and all should be peeled. Timing varies, based upon the fruit's texture and ripeness. MAKES 6 QUARTS

40 small to medium unripe stone fruits, such as peaches or plums	1 cup coarse brown sugar crystals
1 cups coarse white sugar crystals	2 cups Chinese white rice vinegar
	3 or more whole fresh chili peppers

1. Wash and dry the fruits. Bring 4 cups of water to a boil, put five fruits into it for 1 minute, remove, and slip off their skins. Repeat until all are peeled. Discard the water.

2. Sterilize three quart-size jars and their covers, boiling them for 20 minutes.

3. Bring the sugars, vinegar, peppers, and 6 cups of cold water to a boil. Remove from the heat.

4. Put 1 or 2 chili peppers and some fruit into each jar, filling to ½ inch from the top. Pour the hot sugar-water over them, and cover loosely. Let cool. Tighten the lids when cool and store the jars in the refrigerator for two weeks before using.

RED WINE PASTE

A variation of this recipe appeared in *Flavor and Fortune* and is on its Web site. The accompanying article was about the Fujian province and its foods. This paste is thicker than purchased red rice wine lees, and it has a slightly different taste. The restauranteur who provided it says his patrons adore it.
MAKES ABOUT 12 OUNCES

- 2 (1-inch) cubes fermented red bean paste
- ¼ cup cooked glutinous rice
- 3 tablespoons *maotai* or other hard liquor
- ½ cup Fujianese rice wine
- ½ cup Chinese rice wine
- 3 ounces brown sugar or brown brick sugar, broken into small pieces
- 2 teaspoons minced garlic
- 2 teaspoons minced, peeled fresh ginger
- 2 teaspoons rice or sweet-potato flour
- 1 teaspoon dark soy sauce
- 2 or 3 drops red food coloring
- 1 (2-inch) piece dried tangerine peel, soaked for 10 minutes in warm water, then minced finely

1. Put all the ingredients in a blender and let stand for 15 minutes until the sugar is wet and dissolved; then blend for 2 minutes in 30-second increments, letting the blender rest for 1 minute between them.

2. Put the blended mixture into an enamel or other nonreactive metal pot, and simmer over very low heat for 30 minutes. Cool and store in the refrigerator. This paste will keep for about a month in the refrigerator, or for six months in the freezer.

PORK FLOSS

This common topping is made from very lean meat, usually pork, though beef floss is made as well. It can be purchased commercially, and though many do so, others cannot locate it or prefer to make their own. MAKES ALMOST 2 CUPS

2 pounds lean pork, sliced thinly and across the grain
3 tablespoons thin soy sauce
1 tablespoon coarse salt
2 tablespoons sugar
3 tablespoons lard or solid shortening

1. Put the meat and 4 cups of cold water into a Dutch oven or heavy, ovenproof, lidded casserole. Add the soy sauce, salt, and sugar and mix well. Bring to a boil.

2. Preheat the oven to 275°F. Cover the pot, put in the oven, and bake for 2 hours, stirring every 15 minutes. (Add additional water ¼ cup at a time, if the liquid boils away.) Raise the oven temperature to 325°F and cook another hour, stirring every 10 minutes. Then remove the pot from the oven. Remove the cover and let the mixture cool to room temperature. Transfer the meat to a plate and let it sit for 30 minutes. Cut the meat into thin strips.

3. Heat a wok and heat half the lard. Put in half the strips of meat and fry, turning frequently. Cook until the pork is dry and falls apart. Repeat with the rest of the lard and meat. Cool.

4. With your fingers and a fork, separate the pork into the finest strips possible—hairlike is the goal. Place the pork on a heatproof plate. Return the meat to the oven for 1 hour more, then cool. Refrigerate in a closed glass jar, taking out amounts as needed.

WARM MANGO AND PAPAYA

Westerners might call this a relish. Fujianese use it hot or cold to flavor their dumplings, many of their meats, some of their fish, and also some of their starch dishes. There are even some who eat it as a side dish or an entire meal when warm or at room temperature. MAKES 2 CUPS

- 1 ripe mango, peeled, pitted, and minced
- 1 ripe papaya, peeled, seeded, and minced
- 1 red chili pepper, seeded and minced
- ¼ cup finely minced coriander (cilantro) stems
- 4 scallions, minced
- 1 tablespoon sesame oil
- ½ teaspoon sugar
- ¼ cup lemon or other citrus juice

1. Mix together in a bowl the mango, papaya, chili pepper, cilantro stems, and scallions. Add the sesame oil and sugar, and let rest 10 minutes.

2. Bring 2 tablespoons of water and the lemon juice to a boil, and pour it over the fruit mixture. Let cool slightly or until room temperature.

ASSORTED DIPS

The Fujianese enjoy many dips, most involving soy sauce with some other ingredient, or just soy sauce by itself. These dips are common for dipping pieces of meat, fish, vegetables (or foods including all of these items) to increase or intensify their flavor. They use no recipes, per se; the following ingredients are often used, but do not reflect the complete range of possible ingredients or combinations:

Chicken fat

Chili sauce

Fresh ginger

Garlic

Hoisin sauce

Honey

Hot pepper flakes

Hot sauce

Mustard

Salt

Sesame oil

Sesame paste

Soy sauce

Sugar

White pepper

Wine

Wine vinegar

Wine lees

GLOSSARY

This glossary is arranged in categories as follows:

EQUIPMENT 223

FATS AND OILS 223

FISH AND SEAFOOD 224

FRUITS AND NUTS 225

MEATS 228

MILK AND NONDAIRY MILK PRODUCTS . . . 229

POULTRY, GAME, AND EGGS 230

SAUCES, SEASONINGS, AND SPICES 231

STARCHES AND OTHER STAPLE FOODS 235

VEGETABLES 235

EQUIPMENT

Listed below are main items of culinary equipment used by this culture. Most Chinese home kitchens commonly have a wok or two, several steamer and strainer baskets, a cleaver or two, a large pot, and some small spoons, etc.

CHOPSTICKS: Bamboo chopsticks, 10 inches in length, are most common, with square-shaped tops and rounded bottoms. They come in pairs and can also be made of metal, plastic, or different woods.

CLEAVER: Large rectangular-bladed knife, usually with a blade 3 to 4 inches wide and 8 inches long and with a wooden handle, the small round end of which is used to mash garlic and other small ingredients.

HOTPOT: Also called Mongolian hotpot, chrysanthemum pot, or firepot, this brass or aluminum tabletop stove is traditionally heated with charcoal, though modern ones, for safety, use electricity. Foods are cooked in a covered or open metal basket that rings the central chimney.

STEAMER BASKETS: Commonly made of bamboo, though restaurants do use metal and plastic ones, these are stacked in a steamer or over a wok or a large pot. Food is usually placed on an oiled plate or bowl, or on a small square of parchment paper. They do work best in a steamer, and can be stacked rather high, that is six to ten baskets tall, topped with a basket cover.

STRAINER: Long-handled and basket-shaped, an 8- to 10-inch diameter strainer basket is most common. These are more shallow than Western strainers, and are commonly made of wire. Some flatter varieties are made of sheet metal with holes punched for drainage.

WOK: A thin, round-bottomed iron pan, best used on a ring to avoid spilling its contents. Fourteen inches in diameter is the most common household size; commercial woks can be two to three times larger. Those with one long wooden or metal handle or two small metal ones directly across from each other are the preferred styles.

FATS AND OILS

In the past, the most commonly used fat in Fujian was lard. There are many other animal and vegetable fats and oils now used; soy and peanut are the most common ones in use now among the vegetable oils.

CAUL FAT: The lacelike fatty membrane surrounding the stomach of a pig. This can be purchased at a butcher or Chinese market.

CHILI OIL: This oil is made by heating hot chili peppers in peanut or a vegetable oil until they start to darken. The pot is then removed from the heat source, and the peppers left in the oil to cool overnight. The peppers are strained out the next day and discarded before the oil is used or stored.

HOT OIL: A term sometimes used both for chili oil or oil previously heated for another purpose and being used a second time.

LARD: Melted and clarified fat from pigs or hogs.

PEANUT OIL: Also known as groundnut oil, this commonly used oil made from peanuts is often the preferred oil in southern China and the Fujian province because it can be heated to very high temperatures without burning.

SESAME OIL: Made from white sesame seeds toasted to an amber color, this oil has an aromatic, nutty taste, and is often used to flavor-finish a dish. The Chinese, when using this term, do not mean the clear pressed sesame oil, but the darker-colored one made from toasted sesame seeds.

FISH AND SEAFOOD

The Chinese use almost every kind of creature living in the sea or in fresh waters, as well as many of the vegetables that live in or near both fresh and sea waters. They prefer their fish as fresh as possible, though some are used dried, and a few are fermented into sauces.

AIR BLADDER: Also known as **FISH MAW**, this expanding and contracting organ allows fish to adjust to different water pressures at different water depths. Maw was a favorite of at least one emperor, Qi Ming Ti, who liked his with honey, and ate pints of it at one meal. Though not used in any recipes in this book, it's often added to soups and stews. Soak in water, then cut into one- or two-inch squares. It comes dried and fried, and is often found hanging from ceiling hooks in Asian supermarkets. A fish maw can be a foot or more in length.

CLAMS: All kinds of clams are used in Fujian cuisine. Razor clams are especially adored in towns and villages near the sea. What is unusual is that they are often sliced lengthwise. Most often, though not always, dried clams are razor clams.

CONPOY: This is the common term for dried scallops. Conpoy are always soaked until soft, then shredded by hand into very thin strips before use.

FISH MAW: See air bladder.

JELLYFISH: These are marine animals with no bones. They provide a crisp texture, primarily to cold dishes, and also to a few other items. They can be found dried or already soaked; these need washing to remove their salt.

SEA CUCUMBER: Adored for its gelatinous and somewhat slippery texture, these sea slugs are known to the French as *bêche de mer*, to others as *trepang*. They are considered a tonic food to the Chinese who also call them "sea ginseng." There are two common types, one smooth, the other spiny. They can be white to somewhat clear or more black, depending upon their habitat, diet, and genetics. Available dry or presoaked, the latter is a process that takes three to six days, with frequent multiple changes of water daily.

SHARK'S FIN: Usually sold with skin removed, this luxury food is as it's name implies, the fin of a shark. It needs simmering in a fine chicken broth before use. One of the most comprehensive details of the process is to be found in F. T. Cheng's *Musing of a Chinese Gourmet*; another Chinese cookbook that includes great detail on how to soak them is G. B. Miller's *The Thousand Recipe Chinese Cookbook*.

SHRIMP PASTE: Sometimes referred to as shrimp sauce, this grayish to brown concentrate of brined, ground, dried shrimp is very pungent and used in small amounts. It is akin to anchovy paste. Sold in jars it must be stored in the refrigerator after opening.

SQUID: Available fresh or dried, these tentacled mollusks are loved for their texture and their taste. The dried ones are best soaked in warm water for one to two days, changing the water every six hours or so. After soaking, their center bones are discarded, and for ones larger than a few inches, their tentacles are separated from their bodies for cooking. The bodies are scored and cut into smaller pieces before cooking.

FRUITS AND NUTS

Lesser-known Chinese fruits and nuts are listed below. Apples and pears, for example, are not listed, but Chinese apples and Chinese pears do appear in this glossary.

ALMONDS: There are sweet almonds—known as regular almonds, and there are bitter almonds. Both are relatives of the peach family. Both nuts are blanched, then used whole, halved, or crushed. Bitter almonds are often smaller and flatter, and must be cooked to remove some of their toxicity. The so-called sweet almonds, not the bitter varieties, are used chopped and as a paste primarily in sweet dishes. Bitter almonds have more herbal usage than do sweet almonds.

CASHEWS: Blanched and/or toasted, these are primarily used for garnishing, and sometimes for textural contrast, particularly in chicken dishes.

CHESTNUTS: These tree nuts can be boiled, roasted, stir-fried, or preserved in sugar. Any of these preparations are popular. Chinese chestnuts are related to the European chestnut, but not identical to them. In Chinese and other Asian markets, it is common these days to purchase chestnuts already prepared. They come peeled and precooked in vacuum-sealed envelopes; these should be added near the end of the cooking process.

CHINESE APPLES: Larger, rounder, and most often with more yellowish and firmer skin than Western apples, these are used as a fresh fruit and believed to improve one's *qi*, or vital energy. They are also dried and powdered, and used in herbal medications and decoctions, and in some Chinese sweet bakery products.

CHINESE PEARS: Chinese pears, also known as autumn pears or mountain pears, are ball-shaped, with yellow-green skin. The fruit is sour-sweet, crisp, and considered cool (in the hot-cold dichotomy).

CHINESE OLIVES: These fruits can be white, bluish, or yellow. Their pits come to sharp points at either end, and the flavor of these fruits is astringent. Mostly used medicinally or for so-called crack seed, a common salty-sweet snack candy, they are said to relieve fever and help soothe a sore throat.

DATES: Also known as the **CHINESE JUJUBE**, these fruits are available red, brown, or black. All three can be found fresh, dried, or candied. Used in soups, stews, and desserts, the Chinese believe they are valuable after childbirth, promote vital *qi*, and are good for weight-loss reversal and relief of insomnia.

DAYLILY BUDS: See lily buds.

GINGKO NUTS: Also called **WHITE FRUIT** or **SILVER APRICOT**, gingko nuts grow only on female trees. When they ripen, their aroma is less than pleasant. That is probably why they are sold dried, shelled and blanched. They require very long cooking, which removes any toxins. That is why canned ones are used more frequently. Gingko nuts are used primarily in soups and poultry, and in bakery and vegetarian dishes.

GOJI BERRIES: See Wolfberries.

GOOSEBERRIES: See Kiwi fruit.

HAW FRUIT: Also known as **HAWTHORN** or **HAW APPLES**, these small fruits are used in many poultry and meat dishes. They ripen to dark red, and at first taste astringent, then have a sweet aftertaste. This fruit is used fresh, dried, powdered, and as wafers. The Chinese believe haw reduces stomach acid and is good for skin rashes. They recommend not consuming any if constipated.

JOB'S TEARS: Erroneously called "pearl barley" in many Asian markets, this grain is used in Chinese bakery-type products, in soups, and in herbal decoctions.

KIWI FRUIT: Also called **CHINESE GOOSEBERRY**, yellow-fleshed kiwis have been hybridized recently from the common green-fleshed ones. These have a lighter exterior skin. They also can be found with red and pink flesh. They are primarily eaten raw, and have a taste somewhat reminiscent of a mix of strawberries and pineapples.

LILY BUDS: Also known as **TIGER-LILY VEGETABLES**, these long, thin flower parts are from this plant's immature yet-to-open flower bud. Sold most commonly dried, they are available fresh, and as vegetables, can be stir-fried or simmered after soaking. They are commonly paired with cloud ear fungus, and best known for their use in *mu shu* meat dishes.

LILY BULBS: The bases or bulbs of the lily flower are used whole, or their leaflike bulb components separated and used that way. When used dried, they need long soaking, and twenty or more minutes of simmering before use.

LITCHI: Before hybridizing, these fruits were loved for their juicy sweetness and their red color. Eaten fresh or dried, they are now somewhat larger than the original litchis, juicier, and can be greenish-red yet ripe. They are said to improve the blood; and the elderly adore them as they have a reputation for dispersing evils and easing pain. The peel and pits are used in Chinese traditional medicine.

LONGAN: Also known as **DRAGON-EYE FRUIT**, these cherry-size fruits of an evergreen tree have a large pit and a tan seed-coat. They are available for only a short season, which is why they are more common dried or canned than fresh. Looking somewhat similar to the litchi, they are smaller, not as sweet, nor as juicy. Healthwise, the Chinese like them for reducing blurred vision and delaying senility.

MANGO: Many varieties of this large-stoned fruit are used both ripe and less than ripe. If ripe, they are very sweet. The Chinese believe, among other things, that they are good for bleeding gums, skin irritations, and indigestion. They recommend moderation and not consuming many at one time; and they tell those with nephritis to avoid them altogether.

MANGOSTEEN: This is a hard, dark-skinned fruit with a many-sectioned white interior, usually with a stone within. Some mistake the fruit for the litchi or the longan, however, its sections give it away. It is not as sweet as either of those other fruits, also it is a mite less juicy. Most often, mangosteens are eaten raw or used in beverages.

PAPAYA: This large fruit, sometimes incorrectly but commonly referred to as a "pawpaw," has many, many seeds. It has been called "tree melon," and can weigh many pounds. Ripe ones are eaten raw, green ones are used in cooking. This fruit is said to heal the pains of poor digestion; and the Chinese believe it kills parasites.

RED DRAGON FRUIT: Also known as **FIRE DRAGON FRUIT,** this Malaysian fruit is now common throughout south China. It has a spiky, firm exterior and is usually red on the outside and soft and white inside with black seeds. Some varieties though have yellow exteriors, and any of them can have yellow or red interiors.

TANGERINE: The dried peel of this citrus fruit is used for meat dishes and in sweets. Tangerine fruit is recommended to reduce fevers, improve appetite, and aid those with hangovers.

WOLFBERRIES (GOJI BERRIES): Also known as **MEDLAR,** these *Lycium barbarum* berries have recently been renamed *goji berries.* Almost always sold dried or semidried, they grow in many countries, and have been used in China and in and around Tibet and Manchuria for hundreds if not thousands of years. Like the Chinese gooseberry, their renaming has provided an increase in appreciation and sales.

MEATS

The Chinese eat most animals on two or four legs, albeit in small quantities—and every part of each of them.

PORK BELLY: Common name for raw fresh bacon; it is not smoked fatback or bacon, just the fresh cut of this meat. It is often boiled or fried before stir-frying.

PORK FLOSS: Dried finely shredded pork most often used as a topping or a garnish, but also used in baked and fried dim sum-type dishes. (See recipe, page 217.)

ROAST PORK: Most Chinese do not have ovens, so this popular commercially prepared meat, often rubbed with maltose (barley-sugar) during the cooking, is purchased by the ounce and used more to flavor their foods. Larger pieces of roast pork usually only appear at banquets and other formal meals.

SAUSAGES: Chinese sausages are cured, and most commonly made from pork. Those from duck or liver are next in popularity. They are best if steamed or simmered until almost translucent (about 20 minutes) before stir-frying. Usually sold in pairs, they hang from strings in their marketplaces. Newer varieties are sold in pound packages and do need refrigeration, the dried hanging ones do not.

TENDON: Some call tendon "sinew." It's a connective tissue that holds muscle (meat) to bone. Beef and pork tendon are used in appetizers and long-cooked meat dishes.

TRIPE: This stomach organ meat is usually from a cow or a pig; it can be smooth or honeycombed. Virtually all tripe purchased commercially is cleaned, washed, and blanched.

YUNNAN HAM: A beloved cured ham, the best is from the Yunnan province; it is used in small quantities in many dishes. Smithfield ham is a very close approximation and a common substitution.

MILK AND NONDAIRY MILK PRODUCTS

Animal milks are used in small quantities in some parts of China, and obtained from cows, yaks, or sheep. Soy milk is the most common nondairy milk used; and is made into ever so many bean-curd products, as *doufu/tofu* items are called. Nut milks are also popular, and used for cooking and for beverages. Some canned evaporated and condensed milks are used in Fujianese and other Chinese cookery.

BEAN CURD AND PASTES: Also known in English as DOUFU or TOFU, these soy products are used in many sauces, pastes, and other food items. Some are used as foods, others more as seasonings. A few varieties are:

BROWN BEAN CURD: Soft white bean curd is pressed, then cooked in soy sauce and spices. It is most often used as or with vegetables, meats, and poultry.

BEAN CURD CHEESE: A misnomer for fermented bean curd squares correctly called *fuyu* (see below).

DOUFU: The Chinese word for "bean curd"; in Japanese it is called *tofu*.

FERMENTED BEAN CURD: *See* FUYU *below.*

FUYU: Common Chinese name for fermented bean curd squares. They are most often used to season foods, and can be, though rarely, made using red or white rice wine lees, hence their color differences. Some *fuyu* is seasoned with leeks or chili peppers, or both.

BEAN CURD SKIN: Also called BEAN CURD SHEET. Bean curd milk, when cooking, develops a skin, as does cows milk. It is removed from the cooked milk, usually with a stick, then dried. To use, bean curd skin must be soaked and cut. It is commonly used with vegetables, meat, or poultry; and vegetarians use it as the meat substitute in many of their dishes.

COCONUT MILK: Coconut milk is made from the flesh of the coconut found inside the huge husk, after breaking open the coconut and discarding the liquid found therein. The flesh is grated and mixed with hot water, then squeezed to extract the milk. Do not confuse this with coconut water, which is the liquid naturally found inside a fresh coconut.

DOUFU: See Bean curd and pastes.

TOFU: See Bean curd and pastes.

POULTRY, GAME, AND EGGS

As with meats, the Chinese use all parts of every poultry, be they small or big, wild or raised. Only those unusual to Western cookery are listed below. Rabbit is often used instead of poultry, and vice versa.

BIRD'S NESTS: Not actually poultry but a product of it, these are swallow nests, most of which are imported from Thailand. They are rare, expensive, gelatinous, and beige or white nests that need extensive cleaning and soaking, and then more of both. They are served at banquets, and are a mark of great respect and much expense from a host to an honored diner. They are most commonly used in soups. A single bowl of Bird's Nest Soup at a restaurant banquet or formal meal can cost one hundred dollars or more per person.

DUCK TONGUES: Bought raw and whole, when partially cooked, the bones and cartilage of the tongues may be removed before completing a dish. These are a popular food throughout southern China.

EGGS: In addition to ordinary hen's eggs, the Chinese eat the following:

IRON EGGS: Chicken or smaller eggs cooked many times with seasonings, now also prepared under pressure, so firm they are referred to as "iron eggs." They are most popular as snacks, and are also used cut up in some dishes.

PIGEON AND QUAIL EGGS: More commonly used for garnishes and

small dishes, these speckled eggs are also made into "Iron Eggs," a Taiwanese snack specialty now found in the Fujian province.

SALTED EGGS: These dark-orange-yolk eggs, usually from ducks, are kept in a concentrated salt solution for about a month. They should be cooked before consuming; and often are added to the preparation of other dishes, or boiled and eaten as hard-cooked eggs.

THOUSAND-YEAR EGGS: Almost all thousand-year eggs are made by preserving eggs in a mixture of ash, lime, and salt for up to a hundred days. The whites turn black, the yolks more greenish. They are most often a snack or appetizer, almost always served with pickled young ginger.

SAUCES, SEASONINGS, AND SPICES

Common commodities such as cloves, coarse salt, curry pastes, fennel, white and black sesame seeds, etc. are used; however, only those with differences to common Western items are included below.

BARBECUE SAUCE, CHINESE: Commonly known as SACHA SAUCE. There are many sauces so-named and used on roasted or barbecued meats; a few are even used on fish. Common ingredients include fermented shrimp and baby fish (krill and brill), rice wine, vinegar, hoisin sauce, ginger, garlic, and honey.

BEAN PASTES: Red, yellow, or brown, sometimes called BROAD BEAN PASTES, these sauces are made from a soybean base, some sweeter than others. Most are fermented somewhere during their processing. They can be sweet, salty, or pungent; and almost all are made commercially, as their temperature and processing needs considerable control.

BOUILLON POWDER: Similar to bouillon cubes, these are powders flavored with beef, chicken, ham, shrimp, or other protein source, or are completely vegetarian. They are used to make stocks or flavor dishes.

BROAD BEAN PASTES: See Bean pastes.

CHILI PASTES: Either liquid or thick pastes, these bottled seasonings are often made with lemon, garlic, and sometimes fruits. Their sole purpose is to make foods piquant.

CHILI PEPPERS: Hot green or red peppers are most often used fresh; the hot red ones are most often made into chili pastes (see above).

CILANTRO: See Coriander.

CINNAMON: There are two types of cinnamon, one called "cassia." Most often they are not labeled, and differences between them are small, though real. The Chinese use the bark of either, rarely the powder.

CORIANDER: Also known as CILANTRO and CHINESE PARSLEY, the Chinese use this seasoning as fresh leaves (with or without their stems). They rarely use the seeds or leaves in dried form.

FAGARA: See Sichuan pepper.

FERMENTED BEAN PASTES: These can be made from red, yellow, brown, or black beans, with any number of flavorings added. Or they can be made with bean curd (see page 223). All are commercially prepared, because their temperature and other conditions need lots of control. Red bean pastes are primarily sweet and used in pastries. Also see bean pastes, above.

FERMENTED BLACK BEANS: Also sold as BLACK BEAN SAUCE, this southern Chinese seasoning made of dried small fermented round or oval-shaped salted black beans needs soaking, and the beans are most often chopped or mashed before use.

FIVE-SPICE POWDER: A light brown seasoning powder traditionally made of star anise, anise pepper, fennel, cloves, and cinnamon. Some manufacturers use other spices, and some even use more then five, including fenugreek.

GINGER: Mistakenly called "gingerroot," the Chinese use this rhizome fresh, and rarely, if ever, dried or as a powder. Sometimes they squeeze liquid from the ginger or soak a few slices in warm water; this they call "ginger juice." Some recipes call for young ginger. That is when the rhizome is less mature and its skin tinged with purple. Fresh ginger's peel is very light tan, the older rhizome is a little less sharp and darker tan. Both can be peeled or not, as desired, but if not peeled, wash the ginger well.

GINSENG: This herb that looks like a human form can be used in soups and stews. Most often, due to price considerations, it is used as a drink for health reasons. Ancient Chinese writings claimed it is a cure-all and that it has the ability to prolong life, thus its popularity, particularly among those along in life.

HOISIN SAUCE: This thick, sweet, brownish-red sauce is usually made from fermented soybeans plus garlic, chili peppers, vinegar, and other seasonings. It is popular for making spare-ribs, other meats and seafoods, poultry, and vegetable dishes.

LICORICE: Genuine licorice (not the Western candy) is used as a dried root primarily to season long-cooked meat dishes. It is also a popular herbal used to somewhat sweeten decoctions and other medicinal preparations.

MALTOSE: A common thick liquid sugar primarily used in bakery products. Maltose is derived from barley.

OYSTER SAUCE: A thick liquid made using oyster extracts, water, starch, caramel coloring, and other ingredients. In the United States, no whole oysters are used, and the label specifically says the preparation is "oyster-flavored" sauce. In some countries, the brine used to preserve the oysters is an added ingredient, in others, only the liquid drained off the bottom of the vats when preserving them is used.

PLUM SAUCE: This chutney-type sauce has one or more varieties of fruit in it, plus chilis, vinegar, sugar, and sometimes other ingredients. Some call it "duck sauce" as restaurants do serve it with roast or Peking duck and spareribs.

RICE WINE LEES: See Wine, Wine Lees.

SACHA: See Barbecue sauce, Chinese.

SHALLOTS, DRY-FRIED: Dry-fried shallots are sold in jars or plastic bags in some food markets. Some manufacturers fry them in very little oil and then dry them; some have a process that does both simultaneously.

SICHUAN PEPPER: Also known as **FAGARA** and Sichuan flower pepper, this small berry seasons many piquant dishes. It is very popular in the Sichuan province, and in foods made Sichuan-style.

SOY SAUCES AND JAMS: Soy sauce is a salty brown condiment made from fermenting soybeans with wheat (though wheatless varieties are available), yeast, and salt. Very thick soy sauce is known as "soy jam" or simply as "soybean paste." Darker and thicker soy sauce with caramel color, with or without additional sugar or molasses, is called "dark soy sauce"; some made even darker and sweeter is called "black soy sauce." Standard bottled soy sauce, which is a bit saltier and thinner, used to be called "light soy sauce," but now that term means it has at least 25 percent less sodium, so the term "thin" has surfaced to distinguish it from "thick soy sauce" and "dark/black soy sauce." (In most cookbooks, "soy sauce," without any further description, refers to this kind. One can substitute one variety for another, but the end taste will be different.) There is a soy sauce with mushroom extract added, called "mushroom soy sauce"; and there are shrimp soy sauce, abalone soy sauce, scallop soy sauce, etc., each variety made with that specific extract added to basic soy sauce.

STAR ANISE: No relation to aniseed, this eight-pointed, star-shaped seasoning is used in meat dishes, and when ground is an ingredient in five-spice powder.

SUGARS: White and brown rock sugars, and granulated white sugar are the most common sweeteners, as is maltose; occasionally a slab of sugar, known as brown bar sugar (a solid block of brown sugar), is called for.

SUPERIOR STOCK: A long-cooked rich stock made with pork, chicken, and other bones, this needs to be cooked for hours and reduced considerably. Frequently some fresh ginger, garlic, and a scallion or two are added along with the bones. Before use, the stock is strained, its bones and seasonings discarded.

THAI BASIL: Related to European or sweet basil, this Asian variety is less pungent and almost always used fresh.

VINEGARS: Chinese use and prefer rice vinegars—white, red, and black. Red rice vinegar is preferred for dips; black and white ones are used for braised dishes and dips. Chinese rice vinegars are used in sweet-and-pungent (a.k.a. sweet and sour) dishes, and other cooked foods.

WHITE PEPPER: This is the dried exterior of black peppercorns, and is almost always used ground.

WINE AND OTHER ALCOHOLIC BEVERAGES: In China, the term wine means all alcoholic beverages, no matter what their proof or alcohol content is. They are usually made from one or another type of rice: long- or short-grain, regular or glutinous rice, and/or white, red, or black rice. Wines are also made from other grains, such as barley and sorghum, and from legumes. A few are made from grapes, plums, and other fruits. In the Fujian province, white, yellow, or black rice wines are most popular; as are the dregs made from them (see wine lees, below). Common wines in this province are called Fujian rice wines; Shaoxing wine is also very popular. Fermented substances include:

CHINESE YEAST BALL: This item looks like a moth ball but with no aroma. It is used as a starter to make rice wines and wine lees, and used in some bakery products and in other fermented food manufacture.

MAOTAI: A high-alcohol beverage, some reach 100 proof. Most are made from sorghum, a few from other grains or mixed grains.

WINE LEES, ALSO KNOWN AS RICE WINE LEES: These are the dregs or solids remaining when making rice wines, found at the bottom of the wine barrels. Commercially prepared wine lees are sold in jars and found in the refrigerator sections of Asian markets. See the recipe on page 211 also.

STARCHES AND OTHER STAPLE FOODS

BARLEY: Sometimes referred to as Job's tears, though that is another grass, barley is used to make bakery products. It is also fermented and used to make wines and higher-proof alcoholic beverages.

BEAN THREAD NOODLES: Primarily made from mung-bean flour, though they can be made from sweet-potato flour. Those made from the former are translucent and almost clear when cooked.

FLOURS: See vegetable flours.

MUNG BEAN NOODLES: See Bean thread noodles.

POTATO FLAKES: Usually made from white potatoes, potato flakes are used as a thickener and when making pastry products.

RICE: There are many types of rice, polished (bran removed) or not. Primarily, the Chinese use white long- or short-grain, or regular or glutinous types of rice. Glutinous rice is also called "sticky rice." There is white, red, and black glutinous rice. Any of these may be dried and ground to make rice flours, or used to make wines. Rice flours are also used to make noodles and assorted types of dough wrappers.

RICE SHEETS: Made with rice flour and a small amount of wheat flour steamed, these can be found round in or near the refrigerated section of Asian markets.

VEGETABLE FLOURS: Arrowroot, water chestnuts, lotus seeds, mung beans, sweet and regular potatoes and yams, tapioca, and many other plants are dried and made into flour.

WHEAT STARCH: A wheat flour with the protein, also called gluten, removed.

WRAPPERS: Used to enclose dumplings and other foods, these are usually made of wheat flour, though some are made with sweet-potato or other vegetable flours. Other items are used to wrap foods. Lotus and other leaves are used, and in Fujianese cooking ground or chopped meats or fish also enclose foods.

YAOTAI: A fried cruller or dough stick made with wheat flour; a popular breakfast food.

VEGETABLES

BAMBOO PITH: *See* Mushrooms.

BAMBOO SHOOTS: Both winter and spring shoots are used as a vegetable.

BEAN SPROUTS: These are sprouted mung beans; though larger ones are sprouted from soy beans. They are used in many dishes; in fancy ones their heads and tails are removed.

CABBAGES: The Chinese cook many *Brassica* vegetables, from bok choy (now spelled *bokcai*) to kale, kohlrabi, Shanghai cabbage, mustard greens, and so on.

CHINESE CHIVES: Somewhat similar to Western chives, these leaf-shoots are flat, not rounded.

CHINESE MUSHROOMS: *See* Mushrooms.

CHESTNUTS: *See* Fruits and Nuts section.

CHINESE OLIVES: *See* Fruits and Nuts section.

CLOUD EAR FUNGUS: *See* Mushrooms.

CORIANDER: *See* Sauce, Seasonings, and Spices section.

EGGPLANT: Chinese primarily use the thin purple eggplants sometimes called "Japanese eggplants." They also use those of any shape, white or green, and tiny ones of any color. They rarely use the large purple Italian-type eggplants.

FUNGI: *See* Mushrooms.

GINGER: *See* Sauce, Seasonings, and Spices section.

GINSENG: *See* Sauce, Seasonings, and Spices section.

HAIR VEGETABLES: This seaweedlike vegetable grows at the edge of many seas; it is sometimes called "hair seaweed." It is sold dried, and especially enjoyed around Chinese New Year. It is always soaked before use.

LAVER: Another name for seaweed sheets, known by their Japanese name of *nori*. They can be green, purple, or black, depending upon type of seaweed, and whether the seaweed was ground or flaked to make them.

LONG BEAN: This is a 12- to 18-inch bean related to the cow pea family. The seeds within are also used as a vegetable and ground as a flour.

LOTUS: The root, its seeds, and the leaves are used as vegetables. When dried they are also ground into flour and used as thickeners, and made into wrappers, noodles, etc.

MUSHROOMS: The Chinese use many kinds of mushrooms. Those commonly known by their Japanese name of "shiitake" are called "Chinese black mushrooms," "black forest mushrooms," and/or "black mushrooms." The Fujianese and other southern Chinese people also use bamboo pith mushrooms, a fungus that grows on dead bamboo shoots. And they use wood ear or cloud ear fungus; white tree ear fungus; and many more varieties of gelatinous or non-gelatinous fungi.

MUSTARD GREENS: A common green vegetable, often preserved.

PEA SHOOT LEAVES: Adored young leaves of snow peas. These and sweet potato leaves are used similarly to spinach and other tender green leaves; they are best loved prepared with lots of garlic.

PUMPKIN: In China, what is called pumpkin is a member of the squash family that is green on the outside and orange within. It is used cut up, also stuffed and steamed when whole.

SEAWEED: See Laver; Hair Vegetables.

SNOW PEAS: Thin flat pea-less pods used as a vegetable.

SOYBEANS: Soybeans, also known in Japan and the West as EDAMAME, are cooked as a vegetable, and made into a myriad of fermented soybean sauces, flours, milks, and so on. Healthwise, they should always be cooked, never eaten raw.

SWEET POTATOES: See Yams.

TARO ROOT: Taro root is a large, brown, starchy tuber used in all types of dishes, after peeling and cooking. When purchasing these roots, a slice is almost always removed to show tan strands inside; this insures that one is not a toxic variety.

TEA: Many varieties are used in cooking and as a beverage. In Fujian, *longjing* leaves are preferred for cooking; any types of tea can be used in their place.

THAI BASIL: See Sauce, Seasonings, and Spices section.

WATER CHESTNUTS: These are used as a crunchy white vegetable, and dried and used as a flour.

WHITE FUNGUS: These are gelatinous fungi commonly called white tree ear fungus (*see* Mushrooms).

WHITE RADISH: Known more commonly by its Japanese name of DAIKON, this white vegetable root is used in many long-cooked dishes and in several baked ones.

YAMS: In the Fujianese province, sweet potatoes and yams are used interchangeably (as the terms are in this volume). They use them fresh, sliced or diced, and dried and made into flours.

RESOURCES

BOOKS

Anderson, E. N. *The Food of China*. New Haven, CT: Yale University Press, 1988.
Chang, K. C., ed. *Food in Chinese Culture*. New Haven, CT: Yale University Press, 1977.
Chang, W. W. and I. B., and W. and A. K. Kutscher. *An Encyclopedia of Chinese Food and Cooking*. New York: Crown Publishers, 1977.
Cheng, F. T. *Musings of a Chinese Gourmet*. London: Hutchison, 1954.
Fu, P. M. *Pei Mei's Best Selections Chinese Cuisine I*. Tapei, Taiwan: Ju Zi Wn Hua Chu Ban, 2004.
Hom, K. *Fragrant Harbor Taste*. New York: Simon and Schuster, 1989.
Hu, S. Y. *Food Plants of China*. Hong Kong: Chinese University Press, 2005.
Huang, H. T. *Joseph Needham Science and Civilization in China, Vol. VI:5*. Cambridge, UK: Cambridge University Press, 2000.
Kwong, P. and D. Miščevič. *Chinese America*. New York: The New Press, 2005.
Liang, C. P., ed. *The Heavenly Gift of Chinese Culinary Art–Fukien Cuisine*. Taipei, Taiwan: Gourmand Press, 2001.
Liang, C. P. *The Taste of China*. Taipei, Taiwan: Culture and Life Publishing, 2000.
Lin, H. J. and T. F. Lin *Chinese Gastronomy*. New York: Pyramid Publications, 1972.
Miller, G. B. *The Thousand Recipe Chinese Cookbook*. New York: Grosset and Dunlap, 1970.
Newman, J. M. *Food Culture in China*. Westport, CT: Greenwood Press, 2004.
___, ed. *Flavor and Fortune*. A quarterly magazine available from PO Box 91, Kings Park, NY 11754. Issues 1994 to date.
Simmons, F. J. *Food in China*. Boca Raton, FL: CRC Press, 1991.

INTERNET

Begin by using such search engines as www.google.com, www.altavista.com, www.askjeeves.com, www.scholar.google.com, and others for specific questions about the Fujianese cuisine and its foods.

Also, query *Flavor and Fortune*, the only English-language food magazine about the science and art of Chinese cuisine, at www.flavorandfortune.com. This Web site features several articles by Gary Allen that draw attention to other sites that provide information about the foods and food cultures of China.

Query tourism and travel resources, consular and ambassadorial offices, Fujianese benevolent and religious organizations, and so on. Ask Fujianese restauranteurs, some have their own Web sites, about their foods and how to prepare them.

For information about English-language Chinese cookbooks, go to www.stonybrook.edu/libspecial/collections/rarebooks. This author has donated thousands of English-language Chinese cookbooks there.

INDEX

A

ABALONE
Buddha Jumps Over the Wall, Shih Yeh-Style, 147–148
air bladder (fish maw), 223
ALMONDS, 225
Almond Mangosteen Tea, 205
Almond Tea, 204
Eight Treasure Soup, 51
Quail Egg Sweet Soup, 63
Shrimp Wrapped in Almonds, 102
ALMONDS, BITTER, 225
Eight Treasure Soup, 51
Quail Egg Sweet Soup, 63
APPETIZERS, 7–44
Bean Curd Dumplings, 8
Bean Curd-Wrapped Beef, 9
Beef Rolls, 10
Bobin Scallion Pancakes, 11–12
Boneless Spareribs, 13
Chicken, Bean Curd, and Jellyfish in Sesame Sauce, 14
Chicken Wings with Bean Curd, 15
Clam Omelet Triangles, 16
Crab and Noodle Cakes, 82
Deep-Fried Hard-Cooked Eggs, 17
Double-Cooked Eggs, 18
Duck Tongues, 19
Eel and Mustard Cabbage Dumplings, 22
Egg White Spring Rolls, 20
Egg Whites and Sweet Potatoes, 21
Fish-Stuffed Bean Curd, 23
Fluffy Eggs with Pork Floss, 24
Hair Seaweed Rolls, 25
Long Bean Cups, 26
Lotus Balls, 27
Mixed Seafood Pancakes, 28
New Year Money Bags, 29
Papaya and Peppers, 30
Pickled Papaya Slices, 31
Pig's Ears with Chili Sauce, 32
Piquant Peanuts, 33
Pork and Spinach Dumplings, 34
Shrimp Chips, 35
Soy Sauce Eggs, 36
Steamed Chicken and Egg Whites, 132
Steamed Sea Cucumber Pockets, 37
Steamed Seafood Rolls, 38
Stuffed Lotus Disks, 39
Stuffed Meat and Radish Buns, 40
Stuffed Taro Cakes, 41
Sweet Potato-Sesame Seed Eggs, 42
Two-Colored Sesame Rice Rolls, 43
Vegetable and Fish Dumplings, 44
APPLES
Chinese, 226
Eight Treasure Stone Fruits, 194
Sliced Chicken with Fruit, 131
APRICOTS
Pickled Fruit, 215
ASPARAGUS
Steamed Eggs, Asparagus, and Milk, 200

B

BACON, FRESH. See PORK BELLY
BAMBOO PITH MUSHROOMS. See MUSHROOMS, BAMBOO PITH
BAMBOO SHOOTS, 235
Bean Sprouts and Bamboo Shoots, 176
Bobin Scallion Pancakes, 11–12
Braised Eggplant, 177
Braised Meatballs with Vegetables, 143
Braised Sea Cucumber, 80
Buddha Jumps Over the Wall II, 145–146

Chicken Wings with Bean Curd, 15
Meat with Noodles, 167
Mushroom Rolls, 183
Pork and Sea Cucumber Soup, 59
Sea Cucumber Soup, 65
Shark's Fin and Eggs, 100
Squid Soup with Vegetables, 68
Thin Noodles and Pork Soup, 74
BANQUETS
first-course items. *See* appetizers
soups, 203
sweet dishes, 191
whole fish, 77
BARBECUE SAUCE, CHINESE (SACHA SAUCE), 231
Braised Pork Ribs, 144
Grilled Chicken Wings, 127
BARLEY, 235
Cloud Ear and Fruit Soup, 192
BASIL. *See also* THAI BASIL
Chicken with Basil, 118
BEAN CURD AND PASTES, 229–230. *See also* BEAN CURD SHEETS/SKINS
Bean Curd, Pork, and Shrimp Paste Casserole, 78
Bean Curd-Wrapped Beef, 9
bean pastes, 231, 232
Bobin Scallion Pancakes, 11–12
broad bean pastes, 231
Buddha's Bean Noodles, 178
Chicken, Bean Curd, and Jellyfish in Sesame Sauce, 14
Chicken Wings with Bean Curd, 15
Cold Bean Curd, 180
fermented bean curd. *See fuyu*
Fish-Stuffed Bean Curd, 23
Fish-Stuffed Bean Curd in Casserole, 92
Pea Shoots and Bean Curd, 184
Pumpkin with Vegetables, 186
Red Rice Rabbit on Cabbage Shreds, 129
Red Wine Paste, 216
Stuffed Bean Curd Triangles, 160
Taro Root, Pork Belly, and Red Bean Curd Soup, 71
BEAN CURD NOODLES. *See* NOODLES
BEAN CURD SHEETS/SKINS, 22, 230
Bean Curd Dumplings, 8
Bean Curd Rice Rolls, 173
Bean Curd-Wrapped Beef, 9
Bean Sheets with Rabbit Sauce, 112
Braised Chicken Rolls, 113
Two-Colored Sesame Rice Rolls, 43
BEAN PASTES. *See* BEAN CURD AND PASTES
BEAN SPROUTS, 236
Bean Sprouts and Bamboo Shoots, 176
Egg White Spring Rolls, 20
Long Beans and Bean Sprouts, 182
Noodles and Vegetables, 168
Thin Noodles and Pork Soup, 74
Tripe with Vegetables, 161
BEAN THREAD NOODLES. *See* NOODLES, BEAN THREAD
BEEF, 139. *See also* TRIPE
Bean Curd-Wrapped Beef, 9
Beef, Shrimp and Duck Fried Rice, 164
Beef Cakes with Watercress, 140
Beef Rolls, 10
Beef Short Ribs, 141
Beef with Mushrooms in Soup, 46
Crispy Sweet and Sour Beef, 149
Ginger Beef Tea, 207
Mixed-Meat Dumpling Soup, 54
Shrimp Wrapped in Almonds, 102
Spicy Beef Noodle Soup, 67
BELL PEPPERS
Crispy Sweet and Sour Beef, 149
Litchi Pork, 151
Spicy Clams with Basil, 103
Tripe with Vegetables, 161
BEVERAGES, 203–211. *See also* SOUPS
Almond Mangosteen Tea, 205
Almond Tea, 204
Chinese Olive Drink, 206
Ginger Beef Tea, 207
Ginger Tea, 208
Mung Bean Tea, 209
Rice Wine and Rice Wine Lees, 211
Soy Milk, 210

BIRD'S NESTS, 230
Crabmeat, Bird's Nest, and Egg Whites, 84
Ginseng and Bird's Nest Sweet Soup, 195
BITTER ALMONDS. *See* ALMONDS, BITTER
BITTER MELONS
Duck, Bitter Melon, and Salted Duck Eggs, 123
Stuffed Bitter Melon, 189
BLACK BEAN SAUCE/FERMENTED BLACK BEANS, 232
Razor Clams with Black Bean Sauce, 97
Straw Mushrooms with Chinese Celery, 188
Black Rice with Sweet Potatoes, 165
Bobin Scallion Pancakes, 11–12
Boiled Crabs, 79
Boneless Spareribs, 13
Braised Chicken Rolls, 113
Braised Eggplant, 177
Braised Leg of Pork, 142
Braised Meatballs with Vegetables, 143
Braised Pork Ribs, 144
Braised Sea Cucumber, 80
broad bean pastes, 231
BROCCOLI, CHINESE
Braised Leg of Pork, 142
Buddha Jumps Over the Wall, Shih Yeh-Style, 147–148
Buddha Jumps Over the Wall I, 81
Buddha Jumps Over the Wall II, 145–146
Buddha's Bean Noodles, 178

C

CABBAGE, 236. *See also* CABBAGE, CHINESE; CABBAGE, SHANGHAI
Boiled Crabs, 79
Buddha Jumps Over the Wall I, 81
Chicken with Red Fermented Bean Curd, 119
Chinese celery, Five for Five Oyster Cakes, 93
Eel and Mustard Cabbage Dumplings, 22
Many Layers Casserole, 152
Seafood Casserole, 110
CABBAGE, CHINESE
Buddha's Bean Noodles, 178
Fish Ball Casserole, 89
Fish-Stuffed Bean Curd in Casserole, 92
Meatballs with Crabmeat, 153
Pigeon and Tangerine in Casserole, 128
Red Rice Rabbit on Cabbage Shreds, 129
Stuffed Chicken, 135
CABBAGE, SHANGHAI
Braised Meatballs with Vegetables, 143
Fish Ball Casserole, 89
CARP
Pumpkin, Corn, and Fish Soup, 62
CARROTS
Bobin Scallion Pancakes, 11–12
Eight Treasure Soup, 51
Five for Five Oyster Cakes, 93
Noodles and Vegetables, 168
Pork, Vegetable, and Fish Soup, 61
Steamed Chinese Pumpkin, 157
CASHEWS, 226
Eight Treasure Soup, 51
Steamed Chinese Pumpkin, 157
CASSEROLES
Bean Curd, Pork, and Shrimp Paste Casserole, 78
Buddha Jumps Over the Wall, Shih Yeh-Style, 147–148
Buddha Jumps Over the Wall I, 81
Buddha Jumps Over the Wall II, 145–146
Chestnut, Chicken, and Fruit Casserole, 114
Crabmeat and Shrimp Ball Casserole, 83
Fish Ball Casserole, 89
Grilled Chicken Wings, 127
Many Layers Casserole, 152
Pigeon and Tangerine in Casserole, 128
Seafood Casserole, 110
Steamed Chicken and Egg Whites, 132

Taro Root Casserole, 190
Thin Noodles and Pork Soup, 74
Three-Cup Chicken Casserole, 137
CAUL FAT, 223
Crab Rolls, 85
CELERY, CHINESE
Potatoes with Chinese Celery, 185
Pumpkin with Vegetables, 186
Straw Mushrooms with Chinese Celery, 188
CHAYOTE
Beef with Mushrooms in Soup, 46
CHESTNUTS, 226
Buddha Jumps Over the Wall, Shih Yeh-Style, 147–148
Buddha Jumps Over the Wall I, 81
Chestnut, Chicken, and Fruit Casserole, 114
Chicken and Chestnuts, 115
Deep-Fried Chestnuts, 193
Eight Treasure Soup, 51
Pumpkin, Corn, and Fish Soup, 62
Steamed Chinese Pumpkin, 157
CHICKEN, 111. *See also* CHICKEN GIZZARDS; CHICKEN LIVERS; CHICKEN STOMACH; CHICKEN WINGS
Braised Chicken Rolls, 113
Braised Sea Cucumber, 80
Buddha Jumps Over the Wall I, 81
Buddha Jumps Over the Wall II, 145–146
Chestnut, Chicken, and Fruit Casserole, 114
Chicken, Bean Curd, and Jellyfish in Sesame Sauce, 14
Chicken and Chestnuts, 115
Chicken Cubes in Three Sauces, 116
Chicken Soup in Coconut, 47
Chicken Soup with Pear, 48
Chicken with Basil, 118
Chicken with Red Fermented Bean Curd, 119
Chicken with Red Rice, 120
Crispy-Coated Chicken, 121
Red Wine and Chicken Legs, 130
Rice Noodles, Chicken, and Jellyfish Soup, 64
Sleep-Well Soup, 66
Sliced Chicken with Fruit, 131
Steamed Chicken and Egg Whites, 132
Steamed Chicken with Ginger and Scallions, 133
Stuffed Chicken, 135
Stuffed Taro Cakes, 41
Taro Root Casserole, 190
Tea, Chicken, and Date Soup, 73
Three-Cup Chicken Casserole, 137
CHICKEN GIZZARDS
Many Layers Casserole, 152
CHICKEN LIVERS
Chicken Livers with Scallops, 117
CHICKEN STOMACH
Buddha Jumps Over the Wall, Shih Yeh-Style, 147–148
CHICKEN WINGS
Chicken Wings with Bean Curd, 15
Grilled Chicken Wings, 127
Stewed Chicken Wings, 134
chili oil, 223
chili pastes, 231
CHILI PEPPERS, 231
Chicken with Basil, 118
Double-Cooked Eggs, 18
Mung Bean Soup, 55
Papaya and Peppers, 30
Pickled Fruit, 215
Pickled Papaya Slices, 31
Piquant Peanuts, 33
Spicy Beef Noodle Soup, 67
Sweet-Potato Leaves with Rabbit, 136
Tripe with Vegetables, 161
Warm Mango and Papaya, 218
CHINESE APPLES. *See* APPLES
CHINESE BLACK MUSHROOMS. *See* MUSHROOMS, CHINESE BLACK
CHINESE BROCCOLI. *See* BROCCOLI, CHINESE
CHINESE CABBAGE. *See* CABBAGE, CHINESE
CHINESE CELERY. *See* CELERY, CHINESE
CHINESE CHIVES. *See* CHIVES, CHINESE
CHINESE DATES. *See* DATES
Chinese gooseberry (kiwi fruit), 227
CHINESE GREEN VEGETABLES, 108. *See also* GREENS

CHINESE JUJUBE. See DATES
Chinese Mushrooms with Sesame Seeds, 179
Chinese Olive Drink, 206
CHINESE OLIVES. See OLIVES, CHINESE
CHINESE PARSLEY. See CORIANDER
CHINESE PEARS. See PEARS, CHINESE
CHINESE PUMPKIN. See PUMPKIN, CHINESE
CHINESE SAUSAGE. See SAUSAGE, CHINESE
CHINESE WOLFBERRIES. See WOLFBERRIES (GOJI BERRIES)
Chips, Shrimp, 35
CHIVES, CHINESE, 236
  Egg White Spring Rolls, 20
chopsticks, 223
CILANTRO LEAVES. See CORIANDER LEAVES
cinnamon, 232
CLAMS, 223
  Clam Omelet Triangles, 16
  Mixed Seafood Pancakes, 28
  Razor Clams with Black Bean Sauce, 97
  Seafood Casserole, 110
  Spicy Clams with Basil, 103
cleavers, 223
Cloud Ear and Fruit Soup, 192
CLOUD EAR FUNGUS. See MUSHROOMS, CLOUD EAR FUNGUS
COCONUT
  Chicken Soup in Coconut, 47
  Taro Soup, 72
coconut milk, 230
Cold Bean Curd, 180
CONGEES, 45
  Vegetable Congee, 75
  Yam Congee, 49
CONPOY (DRIED SCALLOPS), 224
  Beef, Shrimp and Duck Fried Rice, 164
  Buddha Jumps Over the Wall, Shih Yeh-Style, 147–148
  Buddha Jumps Over the Wall II, 145–146
CORIANDER (CILANTRO) LEAVES, 232
  Beef with Mushrooms in Soup, 46
  Bobin Scallion Pancakes, 11–12
  Chicken Livers with Scallops, 117
  Crab and Noodle Cakes, 82
  Fried Squid in Shrimp Paste, 94
  Mixed-Meat Dumpling Soup, 54
  New Year Money Bags, 29
  Papaya and Peppers, 30
  Sea Cucumber, Spareribs, and Sweet Potato, 98–99
  Seafood Casserole, 110
  Shrimp with Seaweed, 101
  Shrimp Wrapped in Almonds, 102
  Spicy Beef Noodle Soup, 67
  Steamed Seafood Rolls, 38
  Tea, Chicken, and Date Soup, 73
  Thin Noodles and Pork Soup, 74
  Warm Mango and Papaya, 218
CORN
  Corn Soup with Shrimp, 50
  Pumpkin, Corn, and Fish Soup, 62
CORNISH GAME HENS
  Game Hen with Rice Wine Lees, 126
CRABS/CRABMEAT
  Boiled Crabs, 79
  Crab and Noodle Cakes, 82
  Crabmeat, Bird's Nest, and Egg Whites, 84
  Crabmeat and Shrimp Ball Casserole, 83
  Crab Rolls, 85
  Meatballs with Crabmeat, 153
  Mixed-Meat Dumpling Soup, 54
Crispy-Coated Chicken, 121
Crispy Sweet and Sour Beef, 149
CUCUMBERS
  Noodles and Vegetables, 168
  Pork with Red Rice Wine Lees, 156
CURRY POWDER
  Flavored Rice, 150
  Mung Bean Soup, 55

D

DAIKON. See RADISHES, WHITE (DAIKON)
DATES, 226. See *individual varieties*
DATES, BLACK, 226
  Tea, Chicken, and Date Soup, 73
  Up and Down Shrimp, 109

DATES, BROWN, 226
  Almond Mangosteen Tea, 205
  Beef with Mushrooms in Soup, 46
  Eight Treasure Soup, 51
  Sleep-Well Soup, 66
  Up and Down Shrimp, 109
DATES, RED, 226
  Beef with Mushrooms in Soup, 46
  Buddha Jumps Over the Wall, Shih Yeh-Style, 147–148
  Buddha Jumps Over the Wall II, 145–146
  Papaya Soup, 56
  Tangerine and Double Lotus Soup, 70
  Tea, Chicken, and Date Soup, 73
  Up and Down Shrimp, 109
DAYLILY BUDS. *See* LILY BUDS
Deep-Fried Chestnuts, 193
Deep-Fried Hard-Cooked Eggs, 17
DESSERTS. *See* SWEET DISHES
dim sum, 191
DIPPING SAUCES
  assorted, 219
  Bobin Scallion Pancakes, 11–12
  Boiled Crabs, 79
  Boneless Spareribs, 13
  Crab Rolls, 85
  Red Rice Rabbit on Cabbage Shreds, 129
Double-Cooked Eggs, 18
DOUFU. *See* BEAN CURD AND PASTES
DUCK, 111. *See also* DUCK TONGUES
  Beef, Shrimp and Duck Fried Rice, 164
  Duck, Bitter Melon, and Salted Duck Eggs, 123
  Duck and Taro in Oyster Sauce, 122
  Duck in Red Rice Wine Lees, 124
  Flavored Duck, 125
DUCK EGGS. *See* EGGS, DUCK
DUCK TONGUES, 230
  Duck Tongues, 19
DUMPLING WRAPPERS
  Mixed-Meat Dumpling Soup, 54
  New Year Money Bags, 29
  Steamed Seafood Rolls, 38
  Vegetable and Fish Dumplings, 44
DUMPLINGS, 163
  Bean Curd Dumplings, 8
  Eel and Mustard Cabbage Dumplings, 22
  Mixed-Meat Dumpling Soup, 54
  Pear-Shaped Sweet Dumplings, 197
  Pork and Spinach Dumplings, 34
  Vegetable and Fish Dumplings, 44

E

EEL
  Eel and Mustard Cabbage Dumplings, 22
  Eel with Hoisin and Oyster Sauces, 86
  Eel with Red Rice Wine Lees, 87
  Stewed Eel with Mushrooms and Pork, 106
EGG NOODLES. *See* NOODLES
EGG WHITES
  Corn Soup with Shrimp, 50
  Egg Whites and Sweet Potatoes, 21
  Egg White Spring Rolls, 20
  Pork with Red Rice Wine Lees, 156
  Quail Egg Sweet Soup, 63
  Steamed Chicken and Egg Whites, 132
EGGPLANT
  Braised Eggplant, 177
  Eggplant with Garlic, 181
  Vegetable and Fish Dumplings, 44
EGGS, CHICKEN, 111. *See also* EGG WHITES; EGGS, DUCK; EGGS, PIGEON; EGGS, QUAIL
  Clam Omelet Triangles, 16
  Crab and Noodle Cakes, 82
  Crabmeat, Bird's Nest, and Egg Whites, 84
  Deep-Fried Hard-Cooked Eggs, 17
  Double-Cooked Eggs, 18
  Fluffy Eggs with Pork Floss, 24
  iron eggs, 230
  Lotus Root with Oysters, 95
  Mixed Seafood Pancakes, 28
  Oyster Omelet, 96
  Radishes and Eggs, 187
  Rice Wine, Eggs, and Fruit, 199

salted, 231
Sea Cucumber Soup, 65
separating, 21
Shark's Fin and Eggs, 100
Soy Sauce Eggs, 36
Steamed Eggs, Asparagus, and Milk, 200
Stuffed Sliced Winter Melon, 159
Sweet Potato Cake, 172
thousand-year eggs, 231

EGGS, DUCK
Duck, Bitter Melon, and Salted Duck Eggs, 123
Pumpkin with Vegetables, 186
Winter Melon Soup, 76

EGGS, PIGEON, 230–231
Sea Cucumber Soup, 65
Soy Sauce Eggs, 36

EGGS, QUAIL, 230–231
Beef Rolls, 10
Long Bean Cups, 26
Quail Egg Sweet Soup, 63

Eight Treasure Soup, 51
Eight Treasure Stone Fruits, 194

F

FACAI (HAIR VEGETABLES), 236
Hair Seaweed Rolls, 25

fermented bean pastes, 232
fermented rice ball, 234

FIGS
Papaya Soup, 56

Firecracker Shrimp with Litchi, 88
fire dragon fruit, 228
FIRST COURSES. *See* APPETIZERS

FISH. *See also* FISH, DRIED; FISH PASTE; FISH TAIL
Bobin Scallion Pancakes, 11–12
Braised Chicken Rolls, 113
Buddha Jumps Over the Wall I, 81
Fish Ball Casserole, 89
Fish Ball Soup, 52
Fish Cakes, 90
Fish Slices with Sweet and Sour Wine Sauce, 91
Fish-Stuffed Bean Curd, 23
Fish-Stuffed Bean Curd in Casserole, 92
Many Layers Casserole, 152
Mixed Seafood Pancakes, 28
Pork, Vegetable, and Fish Soup, 61
Pumpkin, Corn, and Fish Soup, 62
Shredded Yam Cakes, 171
Steamed Fish in Sweet-Potato Flour, 104
Steamed Fish with Litchi, 105
Steamed Seafood Rolls, 38
Stuffed Fish, 107

FISH, DRIED
Cold Bean Curd, 180
Piquant Peanuts, 33

fish maw (air bladder), 223

FISH PASTE
Steamed Sea Cucumber Pockets, 37

fish sauces, 6

FISH TAIL
Buddha Jumps Over the Wall II, 145–146

Five for Five Oyster Cakes, 93
five-spice powder, 232
Flavored Duck, 125
Flavored Rice, 150
FLOUR, 235. *See individual varieties*

FLOUR, HIGH-GLUTEN BREAD
Haw and Yam Disks, 166
Sweet Potato Cake, 172

FLOUR, MUNG-BEAN
Mung Bean Tea, 209
Shrimp Chips, 35

FLOUR, RICE
Lotus Balls, 27
Stuffed Meat and Radish Buns, 40
Stuffed Sweet Potato Cakes, 201
Sweet Potato-Sesame Seed Eggs, 42

FLOUR, SWEET-POTATO
Crispy-Coated Chicken, 121
Haw and Yam Disks, 166
Many Layers Casserole, 152
Potato Cakes, 170
Steamed Fish in Sweet-Potato Flour, 104

Fluffy Eggs with Pork Floss, 24
Fried Rice, Beef, Shrimp and Duck Fried Rice, 164
Fried Squid in Shrimp Paste, 94

FUJIANESE NOODLES. *See* NOODLES
FUJIAN PROVINCE
culinary resources of, 5
described, 4, 5
foods of, 4
home-grown specialties of, 6
Min tribes, 3–4
municipalities of, 4
people of, 3–4
subregions of, 5–6
FUNGUS. *See individual varieties of mushrooms*
FUYU (FERMENTED BEAN CURD), 229–230
Buddha's Bean Noodles, 178
Chicken with Red Fermented Bean Curd, 119
Pea Shoots and Bean Curd, 184
Fuzhou-style cuisine, 5

G

Game Hen with Rice Wine Lees, 126
GINGER, 232
Bean Sprouts and Bamboo Shoots, 176
Black Rice with Sweet Potatoes, 165
Braised Leg of Pork, 142
Buddha Jumps Over the Wall, Shih Yeh-Style, 147–148
Chestnut, Chicken, and Fruit Casserole, 114
Chicken, Bean Curd, and Jellyfish in Sesame Sauce, 14
Eel and Mustard Cabbage Dumplings, 22
Flavored Rice, 150
Ginger Beef Tea, 207
Ginger Tea, 208
Pickled Pig's Feet Soup, 58
Pork Belly with Mushrooms, 154
Seafood Casserole, 110
Spicy Beef Noodle Soup, 67
Steamed Chicken with Ginger and Scallions, 133
Stewed Chicken Wings, 134
Three-Cup Chicken Casserole, 137
GINGKO NUTS, 226
Chicken Soup in Coconut, 47
Tea, Chicken, and Date Soup, 73
GINSENG, 232
Ginseng and Bird's Nest Sweet Soup, 195
Sleep-Well Soup, 66
GOJI BERRIES. *See* WOLFBERRIES
GREENS. *See also* CABBAGE; MUSTARD GREENS; PEA SHOOTS/LEAVES; SWEET-POTATO LEAVES
Many Layers Casserole, 152
Squid with Greens, 108
Sweet-Potato Leaves with Rabbit, 136
Vegetable Congee, 75
Grilled Chicken Wings, 127

H

HAIR VEGETABLES (*FACAI*), 236
Hair Seaweed Rolls, 25
HAM. *See also* YUNNAN HAM
Pear-Shaped Sweet Dumplings, 197
HAW APPLES. *See* HAW FRUIT
HAW FRUIT, 226–227
Haw and Yam Disks, 166
HAWTHORN. *See* HAW FRUIT
HOISIN SAUCE, 232
Eel with Hoisin and Oyster Sauces, 86
Homemade Mock Wine Lees, 214
hot oil, 223
hotpots, 223

J

JELLYFISH, 225
Chicken, Bean Curd, and Jellyfish in Sesame Sauce, 14
Jellyfish Soup, 53
Rice Noodles, Chicken, and Jellyfish Soup, 64
JOB'S TEARS, 227
Cloud Ear and Fruit Soup, 192
JUK, 45. *See also* CONGEES

K

kiwi fruit (Chinese gooseberry), 227

L

LAMB. See MUTTON
LARD, 223
  Haw and Yam Disks, 166
  Pork Floss, 217
  Stuffed Sweet Potato Cakes, 201
LAVER/NORI, 236
  Beef Rolls, 10
  Shrimp with Seaweed, 101
LEEKS
  Mushroom Rolls, 183
LEMONS
  Eight Treasure Stone Fruits, 194
LICORICE, 232–233
  Up and Down Shrimp, 109
LILY BUDS, 227
  Buddha's Bean Noodles, 178
LILY BULBS, 227
  Papaya Soup, 56
LITCHI, 6, 227
  Firecracker Shrimp with Litchi, 88
  Litchi Pork, 151
  Steamed Fish with Litchi, 105
LONGANS, 227
  Cloud Ear and Fruit Soup, 192
  Pear-Shaped Sweet Dumplings, 197
LONG BEANS, 236
  Long Bean Cups, 26
  Long Beans and Bean Sprouts, 182
LOTUS ROOT, 236
  Lotus Root with Oysters, 95
  Many Layers Casserole, 152
  Stuffed Lotus Disks, 39
  Tangerine and Double Lotus Soup, 70
LOTUS SEEDS, 236
  Lotus Balls, 27
  Pork Soup with Lotus Seeds, 60
  Tangerine and Double Lotus Soup, 70
LYCHEE. See LITCHI

M

maltose, 233
MANGOES, 227
  Rice Wine, Eggs, and Fruit, 199
  Warm Mango and Papaya, 218
MANGOSTEENS, 228
  Almond Mangosteen Tea, 205
Many Layers Casserole, 152
maotai, 234
MEATBALLS
  Braised Meatballs with Vegetables, 143
  Meatballs with Crabmeat, 153
Meat with Noodles, 167
MELON. See BITTER MELONS; WINTER MELON
MELTING MOUTH PEAS
  Game Hen with Rice Wine Lees, 126
MILK, 229
  Almond Mangosteen Tea, 205
  Almond Tea, 204
  coconut milk, 230
  Soy Milk, 210
Minnan-style cuisine, 5–6
Minxi-style cuisine, 6
Mixed-Meat Dumpling Soup, 54
Mixed Seafood Pancakes, 28
MOLASSES
  Deep-Fried Chestnuts, 193
MUNG BEAN NOODLES. See NOODLES, BEAN THREAD
MUNG BEANS. See *also* BEAN CURD SHEETS/SKINS; BEAN SPROUTS
  Cloud Ear and Fruit Soup, 192
  Mung Bean Soup, 55
  Spicy Beef Noodle Soup, 67
Mushroom Rolls, 183
MUSHROOMS, 237. *See also individual varieties below*
  Meat with Noodles, 167
MUSHROOMS, BAMBOO PITH
  Eight Treasure Soup, 51
MUSHROOMS, CHINESE BLACK (SHIITAKE MUSHROOMS)
  Beef with Mushrooms in Soup, 46
  Braised Leg of Pork, 142

Braised Meatballs with Vegetables, 143
Braised Sea Cucumber, 80
Buddha Jumps Over the Wall, Shih Yeh-Style, 147–148
Buddha Jumps Over the Wall I, 81
Buddha Jumps Over the Wall II, 145–146
Chestnut, Chicken, and Fruit Casserole, 114
Chicken Wings with Bean Curd, 15
Chicken with Red Rice, 120
Chinese Mushrooms with Sesame Seeds, 179
Egg White Spring Rolls, 20
Eight Treasure Soup, 51
Fish-Stuffed Bean Curd in Casserole, 92
Flavored Rice, 150
Hair Seaweed Rolls, 25
Jellyfish Soup, 53
Lotus Root with Oysters, 95
Mung Bean Soup, 55
Mushroom Rolls, 183
New Year Money Bags, 29
Pear-Shaped Sweet Dumplings, 197
"Pear" Surprise, 198
Pork and Sea Cucumber Soup, 59
Pork Belly with Mushrooms, 154
Pumpkin with Vegetables, 186
Sea Cucumber Soup, 65
Shark's Fin and Eggs, 100
Steamed Chinese Pumpkin, 157
Stewed Eel with Mushrooms and Pork, 106
Stuffed Chicken, 135
Stuffed Sliced Winter Melon, 159
Stuffed Taro Cakes, 41
Thin Noodles and Pork Soup, 74

MUSHROOMS, CLOUD EAR FUNGUS
Buddha's Bean Noodles, 178

MUSHROOMS, SHIITAKE. *See* MUSHROOMS, CHINESE BLACK

MUSHROOMS, STRAW
Straw Mushrooms with Chinese Celery, 188

MUSHROOMS, WHITE TREE EAR FUNGUS
Cloud Ear and Fruit Soup, 192
Eight Treasure Soup, 51
Pumpkin, Corn, and Fish Soup, 62

MUSSELS
Buddha Jumps Over the Wall, Shih Yeh-Style, 147–148
Seafood Casserole, 110

MUSTARD CABBAGE. *See* CABBAGE

MUSTARD GREENS, 237
Steamed Fish in Sweet-Potato Flour, 104
Stuffed Fish, 107

MUTTON
Stewed Mutton Soup, 69

N

New Year Money Bags, 29

NOODLES, 163. *See individual varieties below*

NOODLES, BEAN CURD
Bean Curd Rice Rolls, 173

NOODLES, BEAN THREAD, 235
Bean Curd Rice Rolls, 173
Buddha's Bean Noodles, 178
Fish Slices with Sweet and Sour Wine Sauce, 91
Pork in Noodle Nest, 169
Red Wine and Chicken Legs, 130
Seafood Casserole, 110
Thin Noodles and Pork Soup, 74

NOODLES, EGG
Crab and Noodle Cakes, 82

NOODLES, FUJIANESE, 4
Meat with Noodles, 167
Mixed Meat Dumpling Soup, 54
Noodles and Vegetables, 168
Pork and Garlic Vinegar, 155
Radishes and Eggs, 187
Spicy Beef Noodle Soup, 67
Taro Soup, 72
Thin Noodles and Pork Soup, 74

NOODLES, RICE
Rice Noodles, Chicken, and Jellyfish Soup, 64

NORI. *See* LAVER/NORI

O

OLIVES, CHINESE, 226
Chinese Olive Drink, 206
OMELETS
Clam Omelet Triangles, 16
Oyster Omelet, 96
ORANGES
Eight Treasure Stone Fruits, 194
OYSTERS
Five for Five Oyster Cakes, 93
Lotus Root with Oysters, 95
Mixed Seafood Pancakes, 28
Oyster Omelet, 96
OYSTER SAUCE, 233
Beef Cakes with Watercress, 140
Chicken Livers with Scallops, 117
Duck and Taro in Oyster Sauce, 122
Eel with Hoisin and Oyster Sauces, 86
Razor Clams with Black Bean Sauce, 97

P

PANCAKES
Bobin Scallion Pancakes, 11–12
Egg White Spring Rolls, 20
Mixed Seafood Pancakes, 28
PAPAYAS, 228
Papaya and Peppers, 30
Papaya and Shark's Fin Sweet Soup, 196
Papaya Soup, 56
Pickled Papaya Slices, 31
Warm Mango and Papaya, 218
PEACHES
Chestnut, Chicken, and Fruit Casserole, 114
Pickled Fruit, 215
Taro Soup, 72
peanut oil, 223
PEANUTS
Eight Treasure Stone Fruits, 194
Peanut and Sesame Seed Soup, 57
Pickled Pig's Feet Soup, 58
Piquant Peanuts, 33
PEARS
Chicken Soup with Pear, 48
Chinese, 226
Pear-Shaped Sweet Dumplings, 197
"Pear" Surprise, 198
PEAS. *See also* MELTING MOUTH PEAS; SNOW PEAS
Beef, Shrimp and Duck Fried Rice, 164
Pumpkin with Vegetables, 186
PEA SHOOTS/LEAVES, 237
Pea Shoots and Bean Curd, 184
Steamed Chicken and Egg Whites, 132
PEPPERS. *See* BELL PEPPERS; CHILI PEPPERS
PICKLED DISHES
Pickled Fruit, 215
Pickled Papaya Slices, 31
Pickled Pig's Feet Soup, 58
Pork in Noodle Nest, 169
PIGEON
Pigeon and Tangerine in Casserole, 128
PIGEON EGGS. *See* EGGS, PIGEON
PIG'S EARS
Pig's Ears with Chili Sauce, 32
PIG'S FEET
Buddha Jumps Over the Wall, Shih Yeh-Style, 147–148
Pickled Pig's Feet Soup, 58
PINEAPPLE
Steamed Fish with Litchi, 105
PINE NUTS
Haw and Yam Disks, 166
Papaya Soup, 56
Pork in Noodle Nest, 169
Shrimp Wrapped in Almonds, 102
PLUMS
Pickled Fruit, 215
plum sauce, 233
PORK, 139, 228–229. *See also* HAM; PIG'S EARS; PIG'S FEET; PORK, DRIED; PORK BELLY; PORK FLOSS; YUNNAN HAM
Bean Curd, Pork, and Shrimp Paste Casserole, 78
Bean Curd Dumplings, 8
Beef Rolls, 10
Boneless Spareribs, 13
Braised Eggplant, 177
Braised Leg of Pork, 142

PORK *(continued)*
Braised Meatballs with Vegetables, 143
Braised Pork Ribs, 144
Buddha Jumps Over the Wall I, 81
Buddha Jumps Over the Wall II, 145–146
Buddha Jumps Over the Wall, Shih Yeh-Style, 147–148
Chicken Soup in Coconut, 47
Crabmeat and Shrimp Ball Casserole, 83
Crab Rolls, 85
Duck, Bitter Melon, and Salted Duck Eggs, 123
Eel and Mustard Cabbage Dumplings, 22
Egg White Spring Rolls, 20
Fish Cakes, 90
Fish-Stuffed Bean Curd, 23
Flavored Rice, 150
Jellyfish Soup, 53
Litchi Pork, 151
Long Bean Cups, 26
Meatballs with Crabmeat, 153
Meat with Noodles, 167
Mixed-Meat Dumpling Soup, 54
New Year Money Bags, 29
Oyster Omelet, 96
"Pear" Surprise, 198
Pork, Vegetable, and Fish Soup, 61
Pork and Garlic Vinegar, 155
Pork and Sea Cucumber Soup, 59
Pork and Spinach Dumplings, 34
Pork Belly with Mushrooms, 154
Pork Floss, 217
Pork in Noodle Nest, 169
Pork Soup with Lotus Seeds, 60
Pork with Red Rice Wine Lees, 156
Sea Cucumber, Spareribs, and Sweet Potato, 98–99
Sea Cucumber Soup, 65
Shrimp Wrapped in Almonds, 102
Steamed Sea Cucumber Pockets, 37
Stuffed Bean Curd Triangles, 160
Stuffed Fish, 107
Stuffed Lotus Disks, 39
Stuffed Meat and Radish Buns, 40
Stuffed Sliced Winter Melon, 159
Taro Root Casserole, 190
Thin Noodles and Pork Soup, 74
Vegetable and Fish Dumplings, 44
Winter Melon Soup, 76

PORK, DRIED
Buddha Jumps Over the Wall, Shih Yeh-Style, 147–148

PORK BELLY, 228
Bobin Scallion Pancakes, 11–12
Firecracker Shrimp with Litchi, 88
Many Layers Casserole, 152
Pork Belly with Mushrooms, 154
Shredded Yam Cakes, 171
Stewed Eel with Mushrooms and Pork, 106
Stewed Pork Belly, 158
Stuffed Sliced Winter Melon, 159
Taro Root, Pork Belly, and Red Bean Curd Soup, 71

PORK FLOSS, 228
Egg Whites and Sweet Potatoes, 21
Fluffy Eggs with Pork Floss, 24

POTATO FLAKES, 235
Eel with Hoisin and Oyster Sauces, 86

POTATOES
Buddha Jumps Over the Wall, Shih Yeh-Style, 147–148
Pear-Shaped Sweet Dumplings, 197
"Pear" Surprise, 198
Potato Cakes, 170
Potatoes with Chinese Celery, 185
Shredded Yam Cakes, 171

PUMPKIN, CHINESE, 237
Beef with Mushrooms in Soup, 46
Pumpkin, Corn, and Fish Soup, 62
Pumpkin with Vegetables, 186
Steamed Chinese Pumpkin, 157

QUAIL EGGS. *See* EGGS, QUAIL

R

RABBIT, 111
Bean Sheets with Rabbit Sauce, 112
Red Rice Rabbit on Cabbage Shreds, 129
Sweet-Potato Leaves with Rabbit, 136
RADISHES, DRIED
Radishes and Eggs, 187
RADISHES, WHITE (DAIKON), 238
Chicken Wings with Bean Curd, 15
Pork, Vegetable, and Fish Soup, 61
Stuffed Meat and Radish Buns, 40
Razor Clams with Black Bean Sauce, 97
RED BEAN CURD
Red Rice Rabbit on Cabbage Shreds, 129
RED BEAN PASTE
Red Wine Paste, 216
RED BEANS
Eight Treasure Stone Fruits, 194
red dragon fruit, 228
Red Rice Rabbit on Cabbage Shreds, 129
Red Wine and Chicken Legs, 130
RICE, 6, 163, 235. *See also* STEAMED RICE SHEETS; *individual varieties below*
Bean Curd Rice Rolls, 173
Flavored Rice, 150
Pork and Garlic Vinegar, 155
Radishes and Eggs, 187
Yam Congee, 49
Vegetable Congee, 75
RICE, BLACK
Black Rice with Sweet Potatoes, 165
RICE, GLUTINOUS
Almond Mangosteen Tea, 205
Cloud Ear and Fruit Soup, 192
Eight Treasure Stone Fruits, 194
Potato Cakes, 170
Red Wine Paste, 216
Rice Wine, Eggs, and Fruit, 199
Rice Wine and Rice Wine Lees, 211
Two-Colored Sesame Rice Rolls, 43
Vegetable Congee, 75
RICE, RED
Beef, Shrimp and Duck Fried Rice, 164
Chicken with Red Rice, 120
Vegetable Congee, 75
RICE NOODLES. *See* NOODLES, RICE
RICE WINE. *See also* RICE WINE LEES
Buddha Jumps Over the Wall, Shih Yeh-Style, 147–148
Buddha Jumps Over the Wall II, 145–146
Duck in Red Rice Wine Lees, 124
Homemade Mock Wine Lees, 214
Many Layers Casserole, 152
Red Rice Rabbit on Cabbage Shreds, 129
Red Wine Paste, 216
Three-Cup Chicken Casserole, 137
Rice Wine, Eggs, and Fruit, 199
RICE WINE LEES, 234
Duck in Red Rice Wine Lees, 124
Eel with Red Rice Wine Lees, 87
Flavored Duck, 125
Game Hen with Rice Wine Lees, 126
Homemade Mock Wine Lees, 214
Pork Belly with Mushrooms, 154
Pork with Red Rice Wine Lees, 156
Red Rice Rabbit on Cabbage Shreds, 129
Red Wine and Chicken Legs, 130
Rice Wine and Rice Wine Lees, 211
Rice Wine, Eggs, and Fruit, 199
Sea Cucumber, Spareribs, and Sweet Potato, 98–99
Spicy Beef Noodle Soup, 67
Three-Cup Chicken Casserole, 137
ROE
Steamed Eggs, Asparagus, and Milk, 200

S

SACHA. *See* BARBECUE SAUCE, CHINESE
salted eggs, 231
SAUSAGE, CHINESE 229
Steamed Chinese Pumpkin, 157
Stuffed Bitter Melon, 189

SCALLIONS
Black Rice with Sweet Potatoes, 165
Bobin Scallion Pancakes, 11–12
Boneless Spareribs, 13
Braised Leg of Pork, 142
Noodles and Vegetables, 168
Steamed Chicken with Ginger and Scallions, 133
SCALLOPS. *See also* CONPOY (DRIED SCALLOPS)
Braised Sea Cucumber, 80
Buddha Jumps Over the Wall, Shih Yeh-Style, 147–148
Buddha Jumps Over the Wall II, 145–146
Chicken Livers with Scallops, 117
Fish Cakes, 90
Seafood Casserole, 110
Shark's Fin and Eggs, 100
Stuffed Chicken, 135
SEA CUCUMBERS, 225
Braised Sea Cucumber, 80
Buddha Jumps Over the Wall I, 81
Buddha Jumps Over the Wall II, 145–146
Pork and Sea Cucumber Soup, 59
Sea Cucumber, Spareribs, and Sweet Potato, 98–99
Sea Cucumber Soup, 65
Steamed Sea Cucumber Pockets, 37
SEAFOOD. *See specific types*
Seafood Casserole, 110
SEAWEED, 236. *See also* HAIR VEGETABLES (*FACAI*); LAVER/NORI
sesame oil, 223
SESAME PASTE
Noodles and Vegetables, 168
SESAME SEEDS, BLACK
Mixed Seafood Pancakes, 28
Noodles and Vegetables, 168
Two-Colored Sesame Rice Rolls, 43
SESAME SEEDS, WHITE
Haw and Yam Disks, 166
Lotus Balls, 27
Peanut and Sesame Seed Soup, 57
Stuffed Sweet Potato Cakes, 201
Sweet Potato-Sesame Seed Eggs, 42
Two-Colored Sesame Rice Rolls, 43
SHALLOTS
Deep-Fried Hard-Cooked Eggs, 17
dry-fried, 233
Pigeon and Tangerine in Casserole, 128
SHANGHAI CABBAGE. *See* CABBAGE, SHANGHAI
SHARK'S FIN, 225
Buddha Jumps Over the Wall, Shih Yeh-Style, 147–148
Buddha Jumps Over the Wall I, 81
Papaya and Shark's Fin Sweet Soup, 196
Shark's Fin and Eggs, 100
SHIITAKE MUSHROOMS. *See* MUSHROOMS, CHINESE BLACK
Shredded Yam Cakes, 171
SHRIMP. *See also* SHRIMP, DRIED; SHRIMP PASTE
Bean Curd Dumplings, 8
Beef, Shrimp and Duck Fried Rice, 164
Braised Sea Cucumber, 80
Corn Soup with Shrimp, 50
Crabmeat and Shrimp Ball Casserole, 83
Eel and Mustard Cabbage Dumplings, 22
Egg White Spring Rolls, 20
Firecracker Shrimp with Litchi, 88
Fish Ball Soup, 52
Fish Cakes, 90
Long Bean Cups, 26
Mixed Seafood Pancakes, 28
New Year Money Bags, 29
Pear-Shaped Sweet Dumplings, 197
"Pear" Surprise, 198
Seafood Casserole, 110
Shrimp Chips, 35
Shrimp with Seaweed, 101
Shrimp Wrapped in Almonds, 102
Steamed Chicken and Egg Whites, 132
Steamed Seafood Rolls, 38
Stuffed Bitter Melon, 189
Stuffed Chicken, 135
Stuffed Taro Cakes, 41
Taro Root Casserole, 190
Up and Down Shrimp, 109
SHRIMP, DRIED
Fish Slices with Sweet and Sour Wine Sauce, 91

Fish-Stuffed Bean Curd, 23
Stuffed Bean Curd Triangles, 160
Stuffed Chicken, 135
Up and Down Shrimp, 109
SHRIMP PASTE, 225
Bean Curd, Pork, and Shrimp Paste Casserole, 78
Fried Squid in Shrimp Paste, 94
Sichuan pepper, 233
Sleep-Well Soup, 66
Sliced Chicken with Fruit, 131
SNACKS, 191. *See also* APPETIZERS; SWEET DISHES
SNOW PEAS, 237
Game Hen with Rice Wine Lees, 126
Squid Soup with Vegetables, 68
SOUPS, 45–76. *See also* BEVERAGES; CONGEES
Beef with Mushrooms in Soup, 46
Chicken Soup in Coconut, 47
Chicken Soup with Pear, 48
Cloud Ear and Fruit Soup, 192
Corn Soup with Shrimp, 50
Eight Treasure Soup, 51
Fish Ball Soup, 52
Ginseng and Bird's Nest Sweet Soup, 195
Jellyfish Soup, 53
Mixed-Meat Dumpling Soup, 54
Mung Bean Soup, 55
Papaya and Shark's Fin Sweet Soup, 196
Papaya Soup, 56
Peanut and Sesame Seed Soup, 57
Pickled Pig's Feet Soup, 58
Pork, Vegetable, and Fish Soup, 61
Pork and Sea Cucumber Soup, 59
Pork Soup with Lotus Seeds, 60
Pumpkin, Corn, and Fish Soup, 62
Quail Egg Sweet Soup, 63
Rice Noodles, Chicken, and Jellyfish Soup, 64
Sea Cucumber Soup, 65
Sleep-Well Soup, 66
Spicy Beef Noodle Soup, 67
Squid Soup with Vegetables, 68
Steamed Chicken and Egg Whites, 132
Stewed Mutton Soup, 69
Sweet Potato Sweet Soup, 202
Tangerine and Double Lotus Soup, 70
Taro Root, Pork Belly, and Red Bean Curd Soup, 71
Taro Soup, 72
Tea, Chicken, and Date Soup, 73
Thin Noodles and Pork Soup, 74
Winter Melon Soup, 76
SOYBEANS, 237
Chicken with Red Rice, 120
Soy Milk, 210
SOY SAUCE, 6, 233
Braised Eggplant, 177
Chicken with Basil, 118
Chinese Mushrooms with Sesame Seeds, 179
Many Layers Casserole, 152
Pork and Garlic Vinegar, 155
Sea Cucumber, Spareribs, and Sweet Potato, 98–99
Soy Sauce Eggs, 36
Stewed Pork Belly, 158
SPARERIBS
Boneless Spareribs, 13
Braised Pork Ribs, 144
Sea Cucumber, Spareribs, and Sweet Potato, 98–99
Spicy Beef Noodle Soup, 67
Spicy Clams with Basil, 103
SPINACH
Bean Curd Rice Rolls, 173
Crab and Noodle Cakes, 82
Five for Five Oyster Cakes, 93
Many Layers Casserole, 152
Pigeon and Tangerine in Casserole, 128
Pork and Spinach Dumplings, 34
Steamed Chicken and Egg Whites, 132
Spring Rolls, Egg White, 20
SPRING ROLL WRAPPERS
Crab Rolls, 85
Hair Seaweed Rolls, 25
SPROUTS. *See* BAMBOO SHOOTS; BEAN SPROUTS; PEA SHOOTS/LEAVES

SQUID, 225
Fried Squid in Shrimp Paste, 94
Squid Soup with Vegetables, 68
Squid with Greens, 108
STAR ANISE, 234
Pork Belly with Mushrooms, 154
Soy Sauce Eggs, 36
Stewed Pork Belly, 158
Taro Root, Pork Belly, and Red Bean Curd Soup, 71
Steamed Chicken and Egg Whites, 132
Steamed Chicken with Ginger and Scallions, 133
Steamed Chinese Pumpkin, 157
Steamed Eggs, Asparagus, and Milk, 200
Steamed Fish in Sweet-Potato Flour, 104
Steamed Fish with Litchi, 105
STEAMED RICE SHEETS
Bean Curd Rice Rolls, 173
Two-Colored Sesame Rice Rolls, 43
Steamed Sea Cucumber Pockets, 37
Steamed Seafood Rolls, 38
steamer baskets, 223
Stewed Chicken Wings, 134
Stewed Eel with Mushrooms and Pork, 106
Stewed Pork Belly, 158
strainers, 223
STRAW MUSHROOMS. See MUSHROOMS, STRAW
Stuffed Bean Curd Triangles, 160
Stuffed Bitter Melon, 189
Stuffed Chicken, 135
Stuffed Fish, 107
Stuffed Lotus Disks, 39
Stuffed Meat and Radish Buns, 40
Stuffed Sliced Winter Melon, 159
Stuffed Sweet Potato Cakes, 201
Stuffed Taro Cakes, 41
sugars, 7, 234
superior stock, 234
SWEET AND SOUR SAUCE
Crispy Sweet and Sour Beef, 149
SWEET DISHES, 7, 191–202
Cloud Ear and Fruit Soup, 192
Deep-Fried Chestnuts, 193
Eight Treasure Stone Fruits, 194
Ginseng and Bird's Nest Sweet Soup, 195
Papaya and Shark's Fin Sweet Soup, 196
Pear-Shaped Sweet Dumplings, 197
"Pear" Surprise, 198
Rice Wine, Eggs, and Fruit, 199
Steamed Eggs, Asparagus, and Milk, 200
Stuffed Sweet Potato Cakes, 201
Sweet Potato Sweet Soup, 202
Tangerine and Double Lotus Soup, 70
Sweet Potato Cake, 172
SWEET POTATOES. See YAMS/SWEET POTATOES
SWEET-POTATO LEAVES, 237
Steamed Chicken and Egg Whites, 132
Sweet-Potato Leaves with Rabbit, 136
Sweet Potato-Sesame Seed Eggs, 42
Sweet Potato Sweet Soup, 202
Sweet Sauce, 105

T

Tangerine and Double Lotus Soup, 70
TANGERINE PEEL, 228
Beef Cakes with Watercress, 140
Eel and Mustard Cabbage Dumplings, 22
Fish Ball Soup, 52
Papaya Soup, 56
Pigeon and Tangerine in Casserole, 128
Pork, Vegetable, and Fish Soup, 61
Pork Soup with Lotus Seeds, 60
Pumpkin, Corn, and Fish Soup, 62
Red Wine Paste, 216
Shrimp Wrapped in Almonds, 102
Spicy Beef Noodle Soup, 67
Stewed Eel with Mushrooms and Pork, 106
Vegetable Congee, 75
TARO ROOT, 237
Buddha Jumps Over the Wall, Shih Yeh-Style, 147–148

Buddha Jumps Over the Wall II, 145–146
Duck and Taro in Oyster Sauce, 122
Five for Five Oyster Cakes, 93
Stuffed Chicken, 135
Stuffed Taro Cakes, 41
Sweet-Potato Leaves with Rabbit, 136
Taro Root, Pork Belly, and Red Bean Curd Soup, 71
Taro Root Casserole, 190
Taro Soup, 72
TEA, 6, 203, 237
Almond Mangosteen Tea, 205
Almond Tea, 204
Ginger Beef Tea, 207
Ginger Tea, 208
Mung Bean Tea, 209
Tea, Chicken, and Date Soup, 73
TENDON, 229
Buddha Jumps Over the Wall, Shih Yeh-Style, 147–148
Buddha Jumps Over the Wall II, 145–146
THAI BASIL, 234
Spicy Clams with Basil, 103
Three-Cup Chicken Casserole, 137
Thin Noodles and Pork Soup, 74
thousand-year eggs, 231
Three-Cup Chicken Casserole, 137
TIGER-LILY VEGETABLES. See LILY BUDS
TOFU. See BEAN CURD AND PASTES
TOMATOES
Beef with Mushrooms in Soup, 46
TREE EAR FUNGUS. See MUSHROOMS, WHITE TREE EAR FUNGUS
TRIPE, 139, 229
Braised Sea Cucumber, 80
Buddha Jumps Over the Wall, Shih Yeh-Style, 147–148
Buddha Jumps Over the Wall II, 145–146
Tripe with Vegetables, 161
Two-Colored Sesame Rice Rolls, 43

Up and Down Shrimp, 109

Vegetable and Fish Dumplings, 44
Vegetable Congee, 75
VINEGARS, 234

WALNUTS
Chestnut, Chicken, and Fruit Casserole, 114
Haw and Yam Disks, 166
Warm Mango and Papaya, 218
WATER CHESTNUTS, 237
Bean Curd-Wrapped Beef, 9
Braised Eggplant, 177
Braised Meatballs with Vegetables, 143
Buddha Jumps Over the Wall II, 145–146
Crab Rolls, 85
Eight Treasure Soup, 51
Firecracker Shrimp with Litchi, 88
Hair Seaweed Rolls, 25
Jellyfish Soup, 53
Long Bean Cups, 26
Meat with Noodles, 167
Oyster Omelet, 96
"Pear" Surprise, 198
Pork and Sea Cucumber Soup, 59
Squid Soup with Vegetables, 68
Steamed Seafood Rolls, 38
Thin Noodles and Pork Soup, 74
WATERCRESS
Beef Cakes with Watercress, 140
Chicken Wings with Bean Curd, 15
Eight Treasure Soup, 51
wheat, 6

WHITE FUNGUS; WHITE TREE EAR FUNGUS. *See* MUSHROOMS, WHITE TREE EAR FUNGUS
white pepper, 234
WHITE RADISH. *See* RADISHES, WHITE (DAIKON)
WINE. *See* RICE WINE
WINE LEES. *See* RICE WINE LEES
WINTER MELON
  Stuffed Sliced Winter Melon, 159
  Winter Melon Soup, 76
woks, 223
WOLFBERRIES (GOJI BERRIES), 228
  Bean Sprouts and Bamboo Shoots, 176
  Chicken Soup with Pear, 48
  Chinese Olive Drink, 206
  Cloud Ear and Fruit Soup, 192
  Ginseng and Bird's Nest Sweet Soup, 195
  Pea Shoots and Bean Curd, 184
  Pork Soup with Lotus Seeds, 60
  Sleep-Well Soup, 66
  Sweet Potato Sweet Soup, 202
  Up and Down Shrimp, 109
WRAPPERS, 235. *See also* BEAN CURD SHEETS/SKINS; DUMPLING WRAPPERS; LAVER/NORI; PANCAKES; SPRING ROLL WRAPPERS; STEAMED RICE SHEETS

YAMS/SWEET POTATOES, 6, 163, 238. *See also* SWEET-POTATO LEAVES
  Black Rice with Sweet Potatoes, 165
  Braised Chicken Rolls, 113
  Egg Whites and Sweet Potatoes, 21
  Mung Bean Soup, 55
  Pear-Shaped Sweet Dumplings, 197
  Potato Cakes, 170
  Potatoes with Chinese Celery, 185
  Sea Cucumber, Spareribs, and Sweet Potato, 98–99
  Shredded Yam Cakes, 171
  Stuffed Chicken, 135
  Stuffed Fish, 107
  Stuffed Sweet Potato Cakes, 201
  Sweet Potato Cake, 172
  Sweet Potato-Sesame Seed Eggs, 42
  Sweet Potato Sweet Soup, 202
  Yam Congee, 49
YAOTAI (FRIED DOUGH STICKS), 235
  Buddha's Bean Noodles, 178
  Stuffed Fish, 107
YUNNAN HAM, 229
  Buddha Jumps Over the Wall, Shih Yeh-Style, 147–148
  Corn Soup with Shrimp, 50
  Firecracker Shrimp with Litchi, 88
  Fish-Stuffed Bean Curd in Casserole, 92
  Papaya and Shark's Fin Sweet Soup, 196
  "Pear" Surprise, 198
  Pork, Vegetable, and Fish Soup, 61
  Steamed Chicken and Egg Whites, 132